Reasoning Models in Climate Science

Dr. Horen Kuecuekyan

Technics Publications
SEDONA, ARIZONA

⊂⊡ TECHNICS PUBLICATIONS

115 Linda Vista, Sedona, AZ 86336 USA
https://www.TechnicsPub.com

Edited by Steve Hoberman
Cover design by Lorena Molinari

First Printing 2025

Copyright © 2025 by Dr. Horen Kuecuekyan

ISBN, print ed.   9798898160463
ISBN, Kindle ed.   9798898160470
ISBN, PDF ed.   9798898160487

Contents

ONE

Climate Modeling and AI

The Earth's climate system represents one of the most complex dynamical systems known to science, characterized by intricate interactions across multiple scales of time and space.

Traditional climate modeling approaches, while foundational to our understanding of climate processes, face substantial computational and conceptual constraints in capturing the full spectrum of climate phenomena. The advent of artificial intelligence (AI) and machine learning techniques presents unprecedented opportunities to augment climate modeling capabilities, encompassing the refinement of parameterizations and the facilitation of novel reasoning paradigms. This chapter serves as an introduction to the convergence of climate science and AI, elucidating how reasoning models can address enduring challenges in climate prediction and comprehension. We delve into the inherent complexity of the climate system, review conventional modeling approaches, and introduce the transformative potential of AI-driven reasoning paradigms in advancing climate science.

The Climate System

The Earth's climate system is a coupled, nonlinear dynamical system comprising the atmosphere, hydrosphere, cryosphere, lithosphere, and biosphere. Each component operates across vastly different temporal and spatial scales, ranging from microscopic aerosol interactions that occur in milliseconds to ice sheet dynamics that evolve over millennia. This multi-scale nature creates what climate scientists refer to as the "scale separation problem," where phenomena at different scales influence each other in ways that are difficult to capture comprehensively in numerical models.

The atmosphere alone is complex enough to challenge our modeling capabilities. Atmospheric motions range from turbulent eddies with scales of meters and lifetimes of minutes to planetary waves spanning thousands of kilometers and persisting for weeks. The nonlinear interactions between these scales mean that small perturbations can grow exponentially, leading to the well-known phenomenon of sensitive dependence on initial conditions, or "chaos." This fundamental property of the climate system imposes theoretical limits on predictability, particularly for weather forecasting beyond approximately two weeks.

Ocean dynamics add another layer of complexity to the climate system. The oceans store vast amounts of heat and carbon, redistributing them globally through a complex network of currents driven by wind stress, density differences, and the Coriolis effect. The thermohaline circulation, often referred to as the "global conveyor belt," operates on timescales of hundreds to thousands of years. Yet, it can influence regional climate patterns on much shorter timescales. The interaction between oceanic and atmospheric processes creates coupled modes of variability, such as the El Niño-Southern Oscillation (ENSO), demonstrating how local oceanic changes in the tropical Pacific can have global climate implications.

One of the most challenging aspects of climate modeling is capturing the interactions between processes operating at different scales. Cloud formation, for example, depends on microphysical processes involving individual water droplets and aerosol particles, yet clouds collectively influence global energy balance and precipitation patterns. The formation of a single cloud droplet depends on supersaturation conditions, the presence of cloud condensation nuclei, and local turbulence—all processes occurring at scales much smaller than the typical grid spacing of global climate models.

Similarly, vegetation dynamics operate across multiple scales, from leaf-level photosynthesis and stomatal conductance to ecosystem-scale carbon and water fluxes, to continental-scale patterns of forest distribution. Plants respond to environmental conditions on timescales from minutes (stomatal closure during drought stress) to decades (forest succession), while simultaneously modifying their environment through processes such as evapotranspiration and albedo changes.

The cryosphere presents unique scaling challenges, particularly in polar regions where ice sheet dynamics, sea ice formation, and snow cover interact with atmospheric and oceanic processes. Ice sheet models must account for processes ranging from crystal-scale ice deformation to continent-scale ice flow, while coupling with climate models that operate on different spatial and temporal grids. The retreat of ice sheets and glaciers involves complex feedback mechanisms, including the ice-albedo feedback, where melting ice exposes darker surfaces that absorb more solar radiation, accelerating further melting.

Numerous feedback mechanisms characterize the climate system, which can either amplify (positive feedback) or dampen (negative feedback) climate changes. This feedback often exhibits nonlinear behavior, where the response is not proportional to the forcing, and may involve threshold effects or tipping points beyond which the system transitions to a different state.

The water vapor feedback exemplifies a positive feedback mechanism that operates across multiple scales. As the atmosphere warms, it can hold more water vapor. Since water vapor is a greenhouse gas, this leads to additional warming. However, the relationship between temperature and water vapor is nonlinear and depends on local conditions such as relative humidity, atmospheric stability, and cloud formation. The spatial and temporal distribution of water vapor changes affects not only local warming but also global circulation patterns through the transport of latent heat.

Cloud feedback constitutes perhaps the most significant source of uncertainty in climate projections. Clouds can both warm and cool the surface: they reflect incoming solar radiation, which cools the surface, while also trapping outgoing long-wave radiation, which warms the surface. The net effect depends on the cloud type, altitude, thickness, and particle size distribution. Low, thick clouds generally exhibit a net cooling effect, whereas high, thin clouds tend to warm the surface. Alterations in cloud properties in response to warming can either amplify or moderate climate change. However, predicting these changes requires a comprehensive understanding of the intricate interactions among atmospheric dynamics, microphysics, and thermodynamics.

Uncertainty in climate science arises from multiple sources, each presenting unique challenges for modeling and prediction. Aleatory uncertainty, stemming from the inherent randomness or chaotic nature of the climate system, sets fundamental limits on predictability. This type of uncertainty means that even with perfect knowledge of initial conditions and model physics, long-term predictions would not be perfect due to the exponential growth of small errors.

Epistemic uncertainty, arising from incomplete knowledge of climate processes and their representation in models, offers more hope for reduction through improved understanding and observations. However, the complexity of the climate system means that many processes remain poorly understood or difficult to observe directly. Deep ocean circulation, cloud microphysics, ice sheet dynamics, and ecosystem responses to environmental change all involve processes that are challenging to observe and model accurately.

Parametric uncertainty relates to the uncertainty in model parameters that cannot be directly observed or measured. Many climate model parameters are "tuned" to match observed climate statistics; however, this tuning process introduces dependencies between parameters that may not accurately reflect the true physical relationships. The high dimensionality of parameter space and computational constraints limit the extent to which parametric uncertainty can be fully explored.

Structural uncertainty arises from the choice of model structure and the mathematical representations of physical processes. Different modeling approaches may yield different results even when calibrated to the same observations, reflecting our incomplete understanding of how to best represent complex Earth system processes in mathematical form.

Traditional Climate Modeling

The development of climate models has its roots in early 20th-century efforts to understand atmospheric dynamics through mathematical representations of fluid motion. Lewis Fry Richardson's pioneering attempt at numerical weather prediction in 1922, though computationally infeasible at the time, laid the theoretical groundwork for modern climate modeling by demonstrating how differential equations describing atmospheric motion could be solved numerically.

The advent of electronic computers in the mid-20th century made the practical implementation of these ideas possible. The first successful numerical weather predictions were performed in the 1950s using simplified models that captured the essential dynamics of large-scale atmospheric motion. These early models, while primitive by today's standards, established the fundamental approach of discretizing the continuous equations of motion in space and time and solving them numerically on a computational grid.

The evolution from weather prediction models to climate models represented a significant conceptual shift. While weather models focus on predicting the specific state of the atmosphere over short time periods, climate models aim to simulate the statistical properties of the climate system over much longer periods. This shift required the inclusion of additional Earth system components, particularly the oceans, which play a crucial role in climate through their large heat capacity and slow circulation timescales.

The first coupled atmosphere-ocean climate models appeared in the 1960s and 1970s, marking a crucial milestone in climate modeling. These early coupled models, despite their simplicity, were able to simulate basic features of the global climate system and demonstrated the importance of ocean-atmosphere interactions in determining climate patterns. The inclusion of sea ice as an interactive component further enhanced model realism and underscored the importance of polar processes in the global climate.

Modern climate models are built around a dynamical core that solves the fundamental equations of fluid motion: the Navier-Stokes equations for momentum conservation, the continuity equation for mass conservation, the thermodynamic energy equation, and the ideal gas law. These equations, when applied to the atmosphere and ocean, form a system of partial differential equations that govern the evolution of velocity, temperature, pressure, and density fields.

The numerical solution of these equations requires discretization in both space and time. Spatial discretization involves dividing the Earth's surface and atmosphere into a three-dimensional grid, with typical horizontal grid spacings in current global climate models ranging from 25 to 200 kilometers. Vertical resolution varies with altitude, with higher resolution near the surface where most weather phenomena occur. Time stepping involves advancing the model state forward in discrete time intervals, typically ranging from minutes to hours, depending on the process being simulated.

However, the fundamental equations of motion alone cannot capture all the processes relevant to climate. Many critical physical processes occur at scales smaller than the model grid spacing or involve complex interactions that are not explicitly represented in the basic fluid dynamics equations. These sub-grid-scale processes must be parameterized—that is, their net effects on the resolved scales must be approximated using simplified mathematical relationships.

Parameterizations are among the most challenging aspects of climate modeling. They must capture the statistical effects of unresolved processes while remaining computationally efficient and numerically stable. The development of parameterizations requires a deep understanding of the underlying physics, extensive observational data for validation, and careful consideration of how the parameterized processes interact with the resolved dynamics.

Radiation parameterizations calculate the transfer of solar and terrestrial radiation through the atmosphere, accounting for absorption, emission, and scattering by gases, clouds, and aerosols. These calculations are fundamental to climate modeling because radiation provides the primary energy input to the climate system and determines the vertical temperature structure of the atmosphere. Radiation parameterizations must account for the wavelength dependence of radiative properties and the three-dimensional distribution of absorbing and scattering constituents.

Cloud parameterizations represent perhaps the most complex and uncertain aspect of climate modeling. Clouds form through processes involving atmospheric dynamics, thermodynamics, and microphysics that occur at scales much smaller than typical model grid spacing. Parameterizations must predict not only when and where clouds form but also their optical properties, precipitation efficiency, and effects on atmospheric heating rates. The challenge is compounded by the fact that different cloud types (cumulus, stratus, cirrus) involve different physical processes and have different climate impacts.

Convection parameterizations address the vertical transport of heat, moisture, and momentum through convective processes, including thunderstorms and cumulus clouds. Convection plays a crucial role in the tropical atmosphere, significantly influencing global circulation patterns. Parameterizations must capture both the triggering mechanisms for convection and its effects on the large-scale environment, including the redistribution of heat and moisture, as well as the formation of convective clouds.

Land surface parameterizations describe the exchange of energy, water, and momentum between the atmosphere and the land surface. These parameterizations must account for the effects of vegetation, soil properties, snow cover, and human activities on surface fluxes. The complexity of land surface processes has led to the development of sophisticated land surface models that include detailed representations of vegetation physiology, soil hydrology, and biogeochemical cycles.

Ocean models used in climate simulations solve the primitive equations of motion, adapted for oceanic flows, that account for buoyancy, rotation, and mixing processes. The ocean's role in climate arises from its large heat capacity, which allows it to store and transport vast amounts of thermal energy, and its role in the global water cycle through evaporation and the transport of water vapor by atmospheric circulation.

Ocean models must represent a wide range of physical processes, from large-scale circulation driven by wind stress and density differences to small-scale mixing processes that affect the vertical distribution of heat and tracers. The thermohaline circulation, driven by spatial variations in seawater density arising from temperature and salinity differences, operates on long timescales and plays a crucial role in climate variability and change.

Sea ice models simulate the formation, growth, melting, and motion of sea ice in polar regions. Sea ice affects climate through its high albedo, which reflects solar radiation, and its insulating properties, which affect heat exchange between the ocean and atmosphere. Sea ice models must account for thermodynamic processes such as ice growth and melting, as well as dynamic processes such as ice motion and deformation driven by winds and ocean currents.

The coupling between ocean, sea ice, and atmospheric components requires careful attention to the conservation of energy, momentum, and mass at the interfaces between model components. Flux coupling techniques ensure that the exchange of heat, moisture, and momentum between components is physically consistent and numerically stable.

Despite their sophistication, traditional climate models face several fundamental limitations that constrain their accuracy and applicability. Resolution limitations mean that many important processes cannot be explicitly resolved and must be parameterized. Representing small-scale processes through parameterizations introduces uncertainties and potential biases that can affect model predictions.

Computational constraints limit the resolution and complexity of models that can be run for climate simulations, which typically require integrations over hundreds or thousands of years. Even with modern supercomputers, compromises must be made among model resolution, complexity, and simulation length. These constraints particularly affect the representation of processes such as cloud microphysics and turbulence that occur at very small scales.

Parameterization uncertainties arise from an incomplete understanding of sub-grid-scale processes and the challenge of representing their statistical effects with simple mathematical relationships. Different modeling groups often use different parameterizations for the same processes, leading to inter-model differences in simulation results.

Tuning parameterizations to match observed climate statistics can mask underlying model deficiencies and undermine confidence in projections of future climate change.

Coupling complexity increases as more Earth system components are included in models. The interactions between atmosphere, ocean, land, ice, and biogeochemical cycles involve processes operating on vastly different timescales, creating computational and conceptual challenges. Ensuring that coupled models conserve energy and mass while maintaining numerical stability requires careful design and extensive testing.

AI in Climate Science

The integration of artificial intelligence into climate science represents a paradigm shift that promises to address many longstanding challenges in Earth system modeling and prediction. The exponential growth in available climate data, driven by satellite observations, automated measurement networks, and high-resolution model simulations, has created opportunities for data-driven approaches that were previously impossible.

Machine learning techniques excel at identifying patterns in high-dimensional data and can discover relationships that might not be apparent through traditional statistical analysis. In climate science, this capability is particularly valuable for understanding complex, nonlinear relationships between climate variables and for developing improved representations of physical processes that are difficult to model from first principles.

Advances in computational hardware have facilitated the application of AI in climate science, particularly Graphics Processing Units (GPUs), which enable the efficient training of deep neural networks on large datasets. Cloud computing platforms have made high-performance computing resources more accessible to researchers, enabling broader participation in AI-driven climate research.

The interdisciplinary nature of AI applications in climate science has fostered collaboration between computer scientists, statisticians, and Earth system scientists, leading to innovative approaches that combine domain expertise with cutting-edge machine learning techniques. This collaboration has been crucial in ensuring that AI applications in climate science are both physically meaningful and scientifically sound.

One of the most immediate applications of AI in climate science has been the discovery of patterns and relationships in observational and model data. Machine learning algorithms can identify teleconnections—correlations between climate variables at distant locations—that might be missed by traditional correlation analysis. These techniques have revealed new insights into patterns of climate variability and their driving mechanisms.

Deep learning approaches have shown particular promise for analyzing complex spatial and temporal patterns in climate data. Convolutional neural networks, initially developed for image recognition, have been adapted to identify spatial patterns in climate fields such as sea surface temperature and atmospheric pressure. Recurrent neural networks and their variants have proven effective in analyzing temporal sequences in climate data, enabling a deeper understanding of climate variability and trends.

Unsupervised learning techniques such as clustering and dimensionality reduction have enabled new approaches to climate classification and the identification of climate regimes. These methods can identify recurring patterns in high-dimensional climate data, providing insights into the underlying dynamics of the climate system. For example, self-organizing maps have been used to classify weather patterns and identify relationships between synoptic-scale circulation and local climate conditions.

Feature learning techniques enable machine learning models to automatically identify relevant variables and transformations from raw data, potentially uncovering new climate indices or process relationships that may not be apparent to human analysts. This capability is particularly valuable when dealing with high-dimensional datasets where the curse of dimensionality may limit traditional statistical techniques.

AI techniques are being increasingly used to enhance the representation of physical processes in climate models through the development of data-driven parameterizations. Traditional parameterizations are based on simplified physical theories and empirical relationships, but machine learning approaches can learn complex, nonlinear relationships directly from high-resolution simulation data or observations.

Neural network parameterizations have shown promise for representing processes such as convection, cloud microphysics, and turbulent mixing. These approaches can capture complex dependencies on environmental conditions that might be difficult to define with traditional parameterizations. However, developing physics-informed neural networks that respect conservation laws and physical constraints remains an active area of research.

The use of AI for parameterization development also raises important questions about interpretability and generalization. While neural network parameterizations may perform well when trained on specific datasets, their behavior under different climate conditions or in response to external forcings may be uncertain. Ensuring that machine learning parameterizations are robust and physically meaningful requires careful validation and testing.

Hybrid approaches that combine physical understanding with machine learning techniques offer promising pathways for parameterization development. These approaches use physical principles to constrain the structure of machine learning models, ensuring that they respect fundamental conservation laws while allowing for data-driven refinement of process representations.

Climate change is expected to alter the frequency and intensity of extreme weather events, making their detection and prediction increasingly important for climate adaptation and risk assessment. AI techniques have shown remarkable capability for identifying and predicting extreme events from climate data, often outperforming traditional statistical approaches.

Deep learning models can be trained to recognize atmospheric patterns associated with extreme events, such as hurricanes, heatwaves, and extreme precipitation. These models can identify subtle precursor patterns that might not be apparent to human analysts and can potentially provide earlier warnings of extreme events. Computer vision techniques, adapted from image recognition, have been particularly successful in identifying and tracking extreme weather phenomena in satellite imagery.

The prediction of extreme events using AI approaches often involves time series analysis and sequence modeling techniques. Long Short-Term Memory (LSTM) networks and other recurrent neural network architectures have shown promise for predicting the evolution of extreme weather systems. These approaches can capture long-range dependencies in atmospheric data that might be important for extreme event prediction.

The application of AI to extreme event prediction also presents challenges related to data imbalance, as extreme events are, by definition, rare occurrences. Techniques such as synthetic data generation, transfer learning, and ensemble methods are being developed to address these challenges and improve the reliability of AI-based extreme event predictions.

The computational cost of running comprehensive Earth system models limits their application for uncertainty quantification, parameter estimation, and scenario analysis. AI techniques offer the possibility of developing fast, accurate emulators of climate models that can approximate model behavior at a fraction of the computational cost.

Neural network emulators can be trained on the output of comprehensive climate models to discern the relationships between model inputs (such as greenhouse gas concentrations or model parameters) and outputs (such as global temperature or precipitation patterns). These emulators can subsequently be employed to explore parameter space, assess model uncertainty, or generate extensive ensembles of climate projections.

Machine learning acceleration of climate model components presents another promising application of artificial intelligence in climate modeling. Neural networks can be utilized to approximate computationally intensive model components, such as radiation calculations or chemical reaction schemes, potentially facilitating higher-resolution simulations or more comprehensive Earth system models.

The development of differentiable climate models that can be trained end-to-end using machine learning techniques represents a frontier area of research. These approaches could potentially enable automatic optimization of model parameters and structure, leading to enhanced model performance and reduced development time.

Reasoning Overview

The evolution of AI applications in climate science reflects a broader shift in machine learning from purely statistical pattern recognition toward more sophisticated reasoning capabilities. Early applications of machine learning in climate science primarily focused on regression and classification tasks, utilizing statistical relationships to predict climate variables or identify patterns in observational data.

In contrast, the ultimate objective of climate science transcends mere prediction to encompass a profound understanding of the underlying causal relationships that govern climate system behavior. This paradigm shift in causal reasoning represents a fundamental transformation in the application of AI techniques to climate challenges, moving beyond correlation-based analysis towards methodologies that can discern and harness causal relationships.

Causal reasoning in climate science requires the differentiation between correlation and causation, the identification of confounding variables, and an understanding of the mechanisms that establish causal links between causes and effects. Traditional statistical approaches often struggle to address these challenges, particularly in the presence of intricate feedback mechanisms and nonlinear relationships that characterize the climate system.

The advent of causal inference methods in machine learning has opened novel avenues for climate science applications. These methods facilitate the identification of the causal effects of external forcings on climate, the elucidation of mechanisms underlying climate variability, and the improvement of predictions by prioritizing causally relevant variables over spurious correlations.

The integration of physical knowledge into machine learning models constitutes a pivotal advancement for climate science applications. Physics-Informed Neural Networks (PINNs) seamlessly incorporate physical laws directly into the learning process, ensuring that model predictions adhere to fundamental principles such as the conservation of energy, mass, and momentum.

In climate applications, physics-informed approaches can be used to develop models that respect the governing equations of fluid motion while learning complex relationships from data. This approach combines the flexibility of machine learning with the rigor of physical modeling, potentially leading to more accurate and interpretable climate models.

Differential equation learning represents another important direction in physics-informed machine learning. These techniques can discover the mathematical relationships that govern climate processes directly from data, potentially revealing new insights into climate system dynamics or improving existing process representations.

The enforcement of physical constraints in machine learning models can be achieved through various approaches, including penalty methods that discourage violations of physical laws, hard constraints that ensure exact satisfaction of physical principles, and regularization techniques that favor solutions consistent with prior physical knowledge.

The complexity of the climate system suggests that purely data-driven or purely physics-based approaches may be insufficient for comprehensive climate modeling. Hybrid approaches that combine the strengths of both paradigms offer promising pathways for advancing climate model development.

Neural-differential equation models represent one class of hybrid approaches that use neural networks to learn unknown or uncertain components of differential equation systems. In climate applications, these models could be used to learn improved parameterizations while maintaining the physical structure of climate models.

Multi-fidelity modeling approaches combine information from multiple sources, each with varying levels of accuracy and computational cost. For example, high-resolution simulations or observations can be used to inform lower-resolution climate models, potentially improving their accuracy without proportional increases in computational cost.

Ensemble methods that combine multiple modeling approaches can harness the strengths of different techniques while mitigating the impact of individual model biases. Machine learning techniques can be employed to optimize ensemble weights or to learn nonlinear combinations of ensemble members.

Uncertainty quantification is paramount in climate science, as reliable estimates of uncertainty are crucial for informed decision-making in climate adaptation and mitigation. Bayesian approaches to machine learning provide natural frameworks for uncertainty quantification by treating model parameters as probability distributions rather than fixed values.

Bayesian neural networks can provide uncertainty estimates for climate predictions by maintaining probability distributions over network parameters. These approaches can distinguish between different sources of uncertainty, including uncertainty arising from limited training data (epistemic uncertainty) and inherent variability in the climate system (aleatory uncertainty).

Gaussian process methods offer another Bayesian approach that is particularly well-suited to climate applications involving sparse or irregular data. These methods can provide uncertainty estimates and can incorporate prior knowledge about the structure of climate relationships.

Ensemble methods and Monte Carlo approaches can be utilized to propagate uncertainty through complex modeling chains, from observational uncertainty through model parameter uncertainty to projection uncertainty. Machine learning techniques can assist in optimizing these uncertainty quantification approaches and identifying the most significant sources of uncertainty.

The application of AI in climate science raises important questions about model interpretability and explainability. Climate models are used to inform high-stakes decisions about climate policy and adaptation, making it essential that AI-based approaches can be understood and validated by domain experts.

Explainable AI techniques aim to make machine learning models more interpretable by providing insights into how they make predictions. Feature importance methods can identify which climate variables are most important for specific predictions, while attention mechanisms can highlight the spatial or temporal patterns that contribute most to model decisions.

Local interpretability methods can explain individual predictions by identifying the most relevant inputs or by approximating complex models with simpler, more interpretable models in local regions of input space. These approaches can help climate scientists understand how AI models respond to specific climate conditions or scenarios.

Global interpretability techniques aim to understand the overall behavior of machine learning models, potentially revealing general principles or relationships that govern climate system behavior. These approaches can complement traditional climate analysis by providing new perspectives on climate system dynamics.

Climate projections involve reasoning about future climate conditions under different scenarios of greenhouse gas emissions, land use change, and other human activities. AI techniques can enhance this reasoning process by improving scenario generation, enabling more efficient exploration of scenario space, and providing new approaches to scenario analysis.

Generative models can be used to create synthetic climate scenarios that are consistent with observed climate variability while exploring conditions that may not have been observed historically. These approaches can help assess climate risks under a broader range of conditions than available in the observational record.

Reinforcement learning approaches can be used to explore optimal pathways for climate mitigation or adaptation, treating climate policy as a sequential decision-making problem where actions have long-term consequences for climate outcomes.

Multi-agent modeling approaches can represent the interactions between different components of the Earth system or different human decision-makers, potentially providing insights into the complex feedback between climate change and human responses.

The convergence of artificial intelligence and climate science presents a transformative opportunity to address some of the most pressing challenges in comprehending and forecasting Earth's climate system. The inherent complexity of the climate system, characterized by its multiple scales, nonlinear interactions, and feedback mechanisms, has long posed challenges to conventional modeling approaches. The advent of AI techniques offers novel paradigms for addressing these challenges, encompassing the enhancement of process representations and the facilitation of novel forms of reasoning regarding climate system behavior.

Traditional climate modeling approaches, while foundational to our current understanding, encounter limitations in resolution, computational efficiency, and process representation that restrict their accuracy and applicability. The integration of AI techniques holds the potential to overcome many of these limitations by enabling data-driven discovery of process relationships, the development of improved parameterizations, and the creation of more efficient modeling approaches.

The evolution from statistical pattern recognition to causal reasoning and physics-informed machine learning marks a maturation of AI applications in climate science. These advanced paradigms can move beyond prediction to a true understanding of climate system behavior, leading to more reliable projections and effective climate policies.

Physical Climate Models

This chapter examines the fundamental principles underlying physical climate models and their application of deductive reasoning to understand Earth's climate system. We explore the mathematical foundations, physical principles, and computational frameworks that enable climate scientists to simulate past, present, and future climate states. The chapter covers the evolution from simple numerical weather prediction models to sophisticated Earth System Models, discussing their capabilities, limitations, and the inherent uncertainties in climate projections.

Deductive Reasoning

Deductive reasoning serves as the foundational principle in climate modelling, establishing a logical framework wherein conclusions are inevitably derived from established premises. Within the realm of climate science, this approach begins with fundamental physical laws, specifically the conservation principles of energy, mass, and momentum. It systematically applies them to understand and predict climate behavior. Unlike inductive reasoning, which generalizes from specific observations, deductive reasoning in climate modeling commences with universal physical principles and subsequently derives specific climate phenomena.

The efficacy of deductive reasoning in climate science resides in its capacity to establish a connection between localized physical processes and global climate patterns. For instance, the Stefan-Boltzmann law, which elucidates blackbody radiation, can be applied deductively to elucidate planetary energy equilibrium. Given that Earth receives approximately 1,366 W/m² of solar radiation (the solar constant) and assuming Earth's behavior as a flawless blackbody with an albedo of 0.3, we can deduce an effective radiating temperature of approximately 255 K (-18°C). This deductive approach unveils the fundamental role of atmospheric greenhouse gases in sustaining Earth's surface temperature at approximately 288 K (15°C).

Climate models employ a hierarchical application of physical laws, ranging from quantum mechanical principles governing molecular absorption and emission to macroscopic conservation laws that describe atmospheric and oceanic circulation. At the microscopic level, quantum mechanics determines how greenhouse gases absorb and emit radiation at specific wavelengths. The Beer-Lambert law describes how radiation intensity decreases exponentially with path length through an absorbing medium:

$$I(z) = I_0 \exp(-\kappa \rho z)$$

where $I(z)$ is the intensity at height z, I_0 is the initial intensity, κ is the mass absorption coefficient, and ρ is the density of the absorbing medium.

This microscopic behavior, when integrated over the entire atmospheric column and across all relevant wavelengths, produces the macroscopic radiative forcing that drives climate change. The deductive chain connects molecular physics to global temperature change through well-established mathematical relationships.

Modern climate models successfully reproduce key observational benchmarks, including the observed warming trend of approximately 0.18°C per decade since 1981, the polar amplification of warming, and the characteristic patterns of precipitation change. The ability of models to reproduce these diverse phenomena strengthens confidence in their deductive framework and underlying physical assumptions.

The climate system operates fundamentally as an energy balance system, where incoming solar radiation must be balanced by outgoing long-wave radiation for the system to remain in equilibrium. The global energy balance can be expressed as:

$$S_0(1-\alpha)/4 = \sigma T^4_e$$

where S_0 is the solar constant, α is the planetary albedo, σ is the Stefan-Boltzmann constant, and T_e is the effective radiating temperature. This simple equation encapsulates the first-order energy balance of the planet.

Radiative transfer through the atmosphere involves complex interactions between solar radiation, atmospheric constituents, and terrestrial radiation.

Chemical processes in the atmosphere also influence climate through the formation of aerosols, ozone depletion and recovery, and changes in oxidation capacity. These processes require detailed chemical kinetic modeling within Earth System Models to accurately represent atmosphere-chemistry interactions.

Climate models are sophisticated computer programs that help us understand how Earth's climate system works and predict how it might change in the future. Think of them as virtual Earths that scientists can experiment with to test different scenarios and understand complex climate processes.

Climate models are built on three fundamental conservation laws that govern all natural systems:

Energy Conservation

Energy cannot be created or destroyed, only transformed from one form to another. In climate models, this means carefully tracking all sources of energy (like sunlight) and all the ways energy is used or lost (like heat radiation back to space). Every grid point in a climate model must balance its energy budget at every time step.

Mass Conservation

Matter cannot be created or destroyed in ordinary processes. Climate models track the movement of air, water, and other substances to ensure that mass is conserved everywhere. For example, water that evaporates from the ocean must eventually fall as precipitation somewhere else.

Momentum Conservation

Moving objects tend to stay in motion unless acted upon by forces. This principle governs wind patterns, ocean currents, and other fluid motions in the climate system. The rotation of Earth adds complexity through the Coriolis effect, which causes moving air and water to curve.

The Atmosphere in Motion

Climate models divide the atmosphere into a three-dimensional grid of boxes, each representing a small volume of air. The models then solve equations that describe how temperature, pressure, humidity, and wind speed change in each box over time.

The atmosphere behaves like a fluid on a rotating sphere, creating complex circulation patterns. Models must account for processes ranging from large-scale weather patterns down to small-scale turbulence that occurs within individual grid boxes.

Turbulence and Small-Scale Processes

Many critical atmospheric processes happen on scales too small for models to resolve directly. For example, individual clouds, turbulent eddies, and convective updrafts are smaller than typical model grid boxes (which might be 50-100 kilometers across).

Climate models use "parameterizations"—simplified mathematical representations that capture the average effects of these small-scale processes. This is like trying to understand traffic flow in a city by looking only at major highways—you need rules to estimate what's happening on the side streets.

Convection and Clouds

Atmospheric convection, the process by which warm air rises, which creates clouds and storms, is crucial for the climate but challenging to model. Convection transports heat and moisture vertically much faster than other processes, redistributing energy throughout the atmosphere.

Modern models use sophisticated schemes to determine when convection will occur and how it affects temperature and humidity profiles. However, cloud formation and behavior remain among the most uncertain aspects of climate modeling.

Climate models evolved from weather prediction models, which were first developed in the 1950s. Weather models focus on predicting specific conditions over the next few days or weeks, requiring extremely accurate initial conditions and fast computation.

The European weather model, for example, divides the globe into millions of grid boxes and updates conditions every few minutes of simulated time. It can predict weather patterns about a week in advance with useful accuracy.

Climate models use similar mathematical foundations but are designed for different purposes. Instead of predicting whether it will rain next Tuesday, climate models ask questions like: "How will average rainfall patterns change over the next century?"

This shift in focus enables climate models to utilize somewhat coarser resolutions and longer time steps, but requires the inclusion of processes that become significant over longer time scales, such as changes in vegetation, ice sheets, and ocean circulation.

Components of the Modern Climate Model

The atmosphere is the fastest-changing component of the climate system. Atmospheric models simulate:

- Large-scale circulation patterns like jet streams and monsoons
- Storm systems and weather fronts
- The water cycle (evaporation, cloud formation, precipitation)
- Energy transport from the equator to the poles.

Oceans store enormous amounts of heat and transport it around the globe. Ocean models simulate:

- Major currents like the Gulf Stream and the Kuroshio Current
- Deep water formation and circulation
- Heat exchange with the atmosphere
- Sea ice formation and melting.

The ocean changes much more slowly than the atmosphere, so ocean models must run for hundreds or thousands of years to reach equilibrium.

Modern climate models "couple" atmospheric and ocean components, allowing them to exchange heat, moisture, and momentum. This coupling is crucial because the ocean and atmosphere strongly influence each other.

For example, warm ocean water provides energy for hurricanes, while strong winds can drive ocean currents. Getting this two-way interaction right is essential for realistic climate simulation.

The land surface affects climate through:

- **Energy balance**: How much sunlight is absorbed versus reflected?
- **Water cycle**: Evaporation from soil and plants.
- **Carbon cycle**: Uptake and release of CO_2 by vegetation and soils.

Advanced land models include detailed representations of vegetation, soil moisture, and even human land use changes like agriculture and urbanization.

The most advanced climate models are called Earth System Models (ESMs), which include ESMs that simulate the movement of carbon, nitrogen, and other elements through the Earth system. This includes:

- How plants absorb CO_2 during photosynthesis
- How soil organisms release CO_2 through decomposition
- How the ocean absorbs CO_2 from the atmosphere
- How these processes change as the climate changes.

Some ESMs include detailed atmospheric chemistry to simulate:

- Ozone formation and destruction
- Aerosol particles and their effects on climate
- Chemical reactions that produce or destroy greenhouse gases.

Rather than assuming vegetation remains constant, advanced models allow plant communities to change in response to climate change. Forests might expand into grasslands, or grasslands might become deserts, depending on changes in temperature and rainfall.

The newest models include ice sheet dynamics, simulating how the Greenland and Antarctic ice sheets respond to warming. This is crucial for sea level rise projections, as these ice sheets contain enough water to raise global sea levels by over 60 meters if completely melted.

Future Climate Scenarios

Climate models need assumptions about future human activities to make projections. Scientists use standardized scenarios that represent different possible futures:

Representative Concentration Pathways (RCPs) are scenarios named for their radiative forcing by 2100:
- **RCP2.6**: Strong climate action limits warming to about 2°C.
- **RCP4.5**: Moderate climate policies lead to moderate warming.
- **RCP6.0**: Limited climate action leads to significant warming.
- **RCP8.5**: Minimal climate action leads to severe warming.

Shared Socioeconomic Pathways (SSPs) are newer scenarios that consider different ways human society might develop:
- **SSP1 (Sustainability)**: Rapid social and economic development with environmental focus.
- **SSP2 (Middle Road)**: Continuation of current trends.
- **SSP3 (Regional Rivalry)**: Slow economic development, focus on security.
- **SSP4 (Inequality)**: High inequality within and between countries.
- **SSP5 (Fossil Development)**: Rapid growth fueled by fossil energy.

Sources of uncertainty include:

- **Model structure**: Different models make different assumptions about how climate processes work, leading to different results even with identical inputs.

- **Parameters**: Many processes must be simplified with adjustable parameters. Small changes in these parameters can lead to different climate sensitivity.

- **Scenarios**: Future greenhouse gas emissions depend on human choices that cannot be predicted with certainty.

- **Internal variability**: The climate system has natural fluctuations (like El Niño) that add noise to long-term trends.

One of the most important uncertainties is climate sensitivity—how much warming occurs when atmospheric CO_2 doubles. Current estimates range from 2.5°C to 4.0°C, with a best estimate around 3.0°C. This uncertainty translates directly into uncertainty about future warming.

Models are more uncertain at regional and local scales than for global averages. This is problematic because climate impacts are felt locally, but it's where models are least reliable.

Models struggle most with extreme events, such as heatwaves, droughts, and intense storms. These events often cause the greatest impacts, but they depend on rare combinations of conditions that models may not capture well.

Certain parts of the climate system may change rapidly and irreversibly once specific thresholds are crossed. Examples include:

- Arctic sea ice is disappearing permanently in summer
- Ice sheets are collapsing rapidly

- The Amazon rainforest is dying back and releasing stored carbon
- Ocean circulation patterns are shutting down.

Current models may not adequately represent these potential tipping points.

Scientists test climate models by comparing their simulations with observations of:

- Current climate patterns
- Climate variations over recent decades
- Responses to past events, like volcanic eruptions
- Paleoclimate records from ice cores and other sources.

Models that perform well on these tests are considered more reliable for future projections.

Climate models face trade-offs between:

- **Resolution**: Higher resolution captures more detail but requires more computing power.
- **Complexity**: More comprehensive models are more realistic but also more expensive and potentially error-prone.
- **Ensemble size**: Running many simulations helps quantify uncertainty, but it multiplies computational costs.

Current global climate models typically use grid boxes 50-200 km across. The next generation of "exascale" supercomputers will enable models with 1-10 km resolution, eliminating the need to parameterize many processes.

Several advances promise to improve climate modeling.

- **Machine learning**: Artificial intelligence might improve parameterizations of clouds, turbulence, and other difficult processes.

- **High resolution**: Kilometer-scale global models will explicitly simulate convection and other small-scale processes.

- **Better observations**: New satellites and measurement campaigns provide more detailed data for model development and evaluation.

- **Integrated assessment**: Coupling climate models with economic and social models to simulate human responses to climate change.

Despite decades of progress, major challenges remain, including cloud processes and their effects on climate sensitivity, the representation of extreme events, regional climate change projections, and potential tipping points and nonlinear responses.

Computational limitations requiring trade-offs between resolution, complexity, and simulation length. Climate models provide the scientific foundation for Understanding Climate Change: Models help scientists determine how much of the observed warming is due to human activities versus natural causes.

Models provide quantitative estimates of future temperature, precipitation, and sea level changes under different scenarios. Model projections drive studies of climate change impacts on agriculture, water resources, ecosystems, and human health. Models help evaluate the effectiveness of different climate policies and inform international negotiations. Probabilistic model projections support risk-based decision-making under uncertainty.

THREE

Inductive Reasoning

Climate science is one of the most complex and interdisciplinary fields of scientific inquiry, requiring sophisticated methodological approaches to understand the Earth's climate system. Among the various reasoning frameworks employed in this domain, inductive reasoning has emerged as a cornerstone methodology that enables scientists to derive general principles and patterns from specific observations and data. This chapter explores the fundamental role of inductive reasoning in climate science, examining how researchers utilize this approach to analyze historical climate data, develop predictive models, and advance our understanding of climate processes.

Inductive reasoning, fundamentally different from deductive approaches, works from the specific to the general, allowing scientists to build theories and models based on empirical observations. In climate science, this methodology proves particularly valuable given the vast temporal and spatial scales involved in climate phenomena, the complexity of Earth system interactions, and the need to make predictions about future climate states based on historical and contemporary observations.

The application of inductive reasoning in climate science has evolved significantly with technological advances, from early observational studies to sophisticated machine learning algorithms that can identify patterns in massive climate datasets. This evolution has not only enhanced our understanding of climate processes but has also improved our ability to predict future climate changes and assess their potential impacts on human and natural systems.

Unlike deductive reasoning, which moves from general premises to specific conclusions, inductive reasoning builds broader understanding through the accumulation and analysis of empirical evidence. This methodology assumes that patterns observed in specific cases can be generalized to understand broader phenomena, making it particularly well-suited for climate science applications.

Inductive reasoning, the philosophical foundation of inductive reasoning, can be traced back to Francis Bacon's scientific method. It was further developed by philosophers such as David Hume and John Stuart Mill. Hume's problem of induction highlighted the logical challenge of justifying inductive inferences, emphasizing that past observations do not guarantee future outcomes. However, in practical scientific applications, inductive reasoning offers a pragmatic approach to comprehending complex systems where controlled experiments are often impractical or impossible.

In climate science, inductive reasoning operates under the principle of uniformitarianism, which posits that the same natural processes that operated in the past continue to operate today. This principle enables scientists to utilize paleoclimate records to comprehend long-term climate variability and to project how climate systems may respond to future forcing conditions. While the uniformitarian assumption is generally valid for many climate processes, it must be carefully applied, particularly when considering unprecedented conditions such as current atmospheric greenhouse gas concentrations.

Methodological Framework

The application of inductive reasoning in climate science follows a systematic methodological framework that begins with observation and data collection. Scientists gather empirical evidence from various sources, including instrumental measurements, paleoclimate proxies, and satellite observations. This evidence forms the foundation for identifying patterns, relationships, and trends within climate data.

Pattern recognition represents a crucial component of inductive climate analysis. Scientists examine spatial and temporal variations in climate variables, seeking to identify recurring patterns that might indicate underlying physical processes. These patterns can range from seasonal cycles and interannual variability to longer-term trends and regime shifts. The identification of such patterns often leads to the formulation of hypotheses about the mechanisms driving observed climate variations.

Statistical analysis plays a central role in the inductive reasoning process, providing quantitative methods for testing the significance and robustness of observed patterns. Climate scientists employ various statistical techniques, from basic descriptive statistics to advanced multivariate analyses, to extract meaningful signals from noisy climate data. These statistical methods help distinguish between genuine climate signals and random variability, ensuring that inductive conclusions are based on statistically significant evidence.

Hypothesis Generation and Testing

Inductive reasoning in climate science involves an iterative process of hypothesis generation and testing. Initial observations and pattern identification lead to the formulation of preliminary hypotheses about climate processes or relationships. These hypotheses are then tested against additional data, either through analysis of independent datasets or through the collection of new observations.

The hypothesis testing process in climate science often involves multiple lines of evidence. For example, a hypothesis about the relationship between solar variability and climate might be tested using paleoclimate records, instrumental observations, and climate model simulations. The convergence of evidence from different sources strengthens the inductive conclusions and increases confidence in the proposed relationships.

However, the complexity of the climate system means that inductive reasoning in this field must account for multiple confounding factors and feedback mechanisms. Climate scientists must carefully consider alternative explanations for observed patterns and work to isolate the effects of specific variables or processes. This requirement has led to the development of sophisticated statistical techniques and modeling approaches designed to disentangle complex climate relationships.

Historical climate data analysis forms the bedrock of climate science, providing the empirical foundation upon which our understanding of

Earth's climate system is built. This analysis encompasses multiple timescales, from recent instrumental records spanning decades to centuries, to paleoclimate reconstructions extending back millions of years. Through inductive analysis of these historical records, scientists have identified fundamental patterns of climate variability and change that inform our understanding of climate processes and guide predictions of future climate states.

The systematic analysis of historical climate data began in earnest during the 19th century with the establishment of organized meteorological observations. However, the true power of inductive reasoning in climate science emerged as longer-term datasets became available and analytical techniques became more sophisticated. Today, historical climate data analysis combines traditional statistical methods with advanced computational approaches to extract meaningful patterns from increasingly complex and voluminous datasets.

One of the key insights derived through inductive analysis of historical climate data is the recognition of climate as a complex system characterized by multiple modes of variability operating on different timescales. From short-term weather fluctuations to long-term climate trends, historical data analysis has revealed the hierarchical nature of climate variability and the importance of understanding climate behavior across multiple temporal and spatial scales.

Paleoclimate records offer a comprehensive temporal perspective on climate variability, which is essential for understanding natural climate variations and situating recent climate changes within a historical context. These records are derived from various proxy indicators that preserve information about past climate conditions, including tree rings, ice cores, coral reefs, lake sediments, and marine sediments. Each proxy type offers unique advantages and limitations, necessitating careful interpretation and cross-validation to ensure the reliability of climate reconstructions.

Tree ring chronologies represent one of the most widely used paleoclimate proxies, providing annual resolution records extending back thousands of years. The width, density, and cellular characteristics of tree rings respond to various climate variables, particularly temperature and precipitation. Through inductive analysis of tree ring patterns across multiple sites and species, scientists have developed regional and hemispheric climate reconstructions that reveal patterns of drought, temperature variability, and extreme events over centuries to millennia.

Ice core records from polar regions and high-altitude glaciers offer another crucial paleoclimate archive, preserving atmospheric composition and climate conditions in annual layers of accumulated ice and snow. The analysis of ice core chemistry, including greenhouse gas concentrations, atmospheric dust levels, and isotopic compositions, has provided fundamental insights into past climate states and abrupt climate changes. Inductive analysis of ice core records has revealed the existence of rapid climate transitions, the relationship between atmospheric composition and climate, and the regional patterns of climate response to external forcing.

Marine sediment cores provide the longest-term paleoclimate records, extending back millions of years and offering insights into climate behavior under different boundary conditions. The analysis of microfossils, sediment composition, and chemical proxies in marine cores has revealed long-term climate trends, ice age cycles, and the relationship between ocean circulation and global climate. Through inductive analysis of marine paleoclimate records, scientists have developed an understanding of climate sensitivity, the role of feedback mechanisms, and the behavior of the climate system under extreme conditions.

Pattern Recognition and Climate Variability

Inductive analysis of paleoclimate records has revealed fundamental patterns of climate variability that operate across multiple timescales. These patterns include regular cycles driven by orbital variations, irregular oscillations associated with internal climate dynamics, and long-term trends related to external forcing factors. The identification and characterization of these patterns through paleoclimate analysis has been crucial for understanding natural climate variability and distinguishing it from anthropogenic climate change.

One of the most significant discoveries from paleoclimate inductive analysis is the recognition of rapid climate transitions and threshold behavior in the climate system. Analysis of ice core records has revealed that past climate changes often occurred as rapid transitions between relatively stable climate states, rather than gradual linear changes. This finding has important implications for understanding climate sensitivity and the potential for abrupt climate change in the future.

The analysis of paleoclimate records has also revealed the existence of persistent climate patterns and modes of variability that operate on decadal to centennial timescales. These include patterns such as the Medieval Climate Anomaly and the Little Ice Age, which demonstrate the capacity for sustained climate anomalies that can persist for centuries. Understanding these natural climate variations is essential for distinguishing between natural and anthropogenic influences on recent climate change.

The systematic collection of instrumental climate data began in the 17th and 18th centuries with the development of meteorological instruments and the establishment of observational networks. Early observations were often sporadic and geographically limited, but the gradual expansion of observational networks during the 19th and 20th centuries provided increasingly comprehensive coverage of global climate conditions.

The establishment of national meteorological services during the 19th century marked a significant milestone in climate data collection, leading to the standardization of observational practices and the systematic archiving of climate records. International cooperation through organizations such as the World Meteorological Organization has further enhanced the quality and consistency of global climate observations, enabling more reliable inductive analyses of climate trends and variability.

Modern instrumental records provide high-quality, high-resolution data on multiple climate variables, including temperature, precipitation, atmospheric pressure, humidity, wind speed and direction, and cloud cover. These records, while relatively short compared to paleoclimate timescales, offer the precision and accuracy necessary for detecting subtle climate changes and trends. The analysis of instrumental records has been crucial for documenting recent climate change and attributing observed changes to specific forcing factors.

Inductive analysis of instrumental climate records relies heavily on statistical methods designed to extract meaningful signals from noisy observational data. Climate data are characterized by high levels of natural variability across multiple timescales, requiring sophisticated statistical techniques to identify significant trends and patterns. These methods must account for various sources of uncertainty, including measurement errors, spatial and temporal sampling biases, and changes in observational practices over time.

Trend analysis represents one of the fundamental applications of statistical methods to instrumental climate records. Linear trend analysis provides a simple measure of long-term change in climate variables, while more sophisticated methods can detect nonlinear trends, trend breaks, and changes in variability. The statistical significance of observed trends is assessed using various techniques that account for the temporal correlation structure of climate data and the potential for multiple testing issues.

Extreme value analysis has emerged as a crucial application of statistical methods to instrumental climate records, focusing on the behavior of climate extremes, such as heatwaves, droughts, and heavy precipitation events. These analyses offer insights into changes in the frequency and intensity of extreme events, which often have more significant societal and ecological impacts than changes in mean climate conditions. Inductive analysis of extreme events has revealed significant changes in extreme temperature and precipitation patterns consistent with expectations from greenhouse warming.

Regional and Global Pattern Analysis

The analysis of instrumental climate records has revealed complex spatial patterns of climate variability and change that reflect the influence of various physical processes and feedback mechanisms. These patterns include the differential response of land and ocean temperatures to greenhouse gas forcing, the Arctic amplification of warming, and regional patterns of precipitation change associated with shifts in atmospheric circulation patterns.

Principal component analysis and other multivariate statistical techniques have been widely applied to identify and characterize the dominant patterns of climate variability in instrumental records. These analyses have revealed the importance of large-scale climate oscillations such as the El Niño-Southern Oscillation, the Atlantic Multidecadal Oscillation, and the Pacific Decadal Oscillation in driving regional climate variations. Understanding these patterns and their interactions is crucial for interpreting observed climate changes and predicting future climate variations.

The analysis of instrumental records has also provided important insights into the attribution of observed climate changes to specific forcing factors. Through comparison of observed patterns of climate change with the expected patterns from different forcing mechanisms, scientists have been able to attribute recent climate warming primarily to increasing greenhouse gas concentrations. This attribution analysis represents a sophisticated application of inductive reasoning that combines observational evidence with theoretical understanding of climate processes.

The advent of satellite observations in the latter half of the 20th century revolutionized climate monitoring and analysis, providing global, continuous observations of Earth's climate system with unprecedented spatial and temporal coverage. Satellite observations complement ground-based measurements by offering uniform global coverage, including remote regions such as the polar areas and oceans that are poorly sampled by conventional observational networks.

Satellite measurements encompass a wide range of climate variables and Earth system components, including atmospheric temperature profiles, precipitation, cloud properties, sea surface temperatures, sea ice extent, land surface temperatures, vegetation indices, and atmospheric compositions. These observations provide crucial data for understanding climate processes, validating climate models, and monitoring climate change on regional and global scales.

The long-term consistency and calibration of satellite observations present unique challenges for climate analysis. Satellite instruments have limited lifetimes, requiring careful intercalibration between successive satellites to maintain long-term climate records. Additionally, satellite orbits can drift over time, introducing potential biases in the observational record. Addressing these challenges requires sophisticated data processing techniques and careful validation against other observational datasets.

Global Climate Monitoring and Analysis

Satellite observations have provided fundamental insights into global climate processes and changes through inductive analysis of multidecadal observational records. Temperature measurements from satellite microwave sounders have provided an independent validation of surface warming trends documented in ground-based observations, while also revealing important differences in warming rates between the surface and different atmospheric levels.

Satellite measurements of precipitation have revealed global patterns of precipitation change and variability, including the intensification of the global water cycle and regional shifts in precipitation patterns. These observations have been crucial for understanding changes in extreme precipitation events and for validating climate model predictions of hydrological cycle changes under greenhouse warming.

The monitoring of polar regions through satellite observations has been particularly important for documenting rapid changes in Arctic and Antarctic climate conditions. Satellite measurements of sea ice extent, ice sheet mass balance, and polar temperature changes have provided compelling evidence for rapid climate change in polar regions and have helped to quantify the contribution of ice sheet melting to sea level rise.

The full value of satellite observations for climate analysis is realized through their integration with ground-based observational networks. This integration involves careful comparison and validation of satellite and ground-based measurements, as well as the development of merged datasets that combine the advantages of both observational approaches.

Satellite observations provide essential spatial context for interpreting ground-based measurements, helping to assess the representativeness of point measurements and to understand regional patterns of climate variability. Conversely, ground-based observations provide crucial validation and calibration data for satellite measurements, particularly for long-term climate trend analysis.

The integration of satellite and ground-based observations has enabled the development of comprehensive global climate datasets that support a wide range of climate research applications. These integrated datasets provide the observational foundation for validating climate models, assessing climate impacts, and attributing climate change. Through inductive analysis of these comprehensive observational datasets, scientists have developed an increasingly sophisticated understanding of climate processes and changes.

The Emergence of Computational Climate Science

The integration of machine learning techniques into climate science represents a paradigmatic shift in how researchers approach the analysis of complex climate data and the development of predictive models. As climate datasets have grown exponentially in size and complexity, traditional statistical methods have reached their limits in extracting meaningful patterns and relationships from high-dimensional climate data. Machine learning provides powerful tools for pattern recognition, dimensionality reduction, and nonlinear modeling, which are particularly well-suited to the challenges of climate data analysis.

The application of machine learning in climate science adheres to the fundamental principles of inductive reasoning, utilizing empirical data to identify patterns and relationships that can be generalized to new situations. However, machine learning extends traditional inductive approaches by enabling the analysis of much larger and more complex datasets than would be feasible with conventional statistical methods. This capability has opened new avenues for climate research and has led to discoveries that would have been impossible using traditional analytical approaches.

Machine learning algorithms excel at identifying subtle patterns and nonlinear relationships in climate data that traditional statistical analyses might miss. These capabilities are particularly valuable in climate science, where complex interactions between different components of the Earth system can produce nonlinear responses and emergent behaviors. By applying machine learning techniques to climate data, researchers can uncover hidden relationships and develop more accurate predictive models of climate behavior.

Supervised learning algorithms have found widespread application in climate science for both regression and classification problems. In regression applications, these algorithms are used to predict continuous climate variables, such as temperature, precipitation, or atmospheric pressure, based on predictor variables like atmospheric circulation patterns, sea surface temperatures, or greenhouse gas concentrations. These predictive models enable researchers to understand the relationships between different climate variables and to develop empirical forecasting tools.

Linear regression models, while relatively simple, have proven valuable for establishing baseline relationships between climate variables and for identifying significant predictors of climate variations. Multiple linear regression allows researchers to examine the simultaneous influence of several predictor variables on climate outcomes, while techniques such as ridge regression and LASSO help address issues of multicollinearity and overfitting that are common in climate applications.

Nonlinear regression techniques, including polynomial regression, spline methods, and kernel regression, provide greater flexibility for capturing complex relationships between climate variables. These methods are particularly valuable for modeling climate processes that exhibit threshold behavior or nonlinear responses to forcing factors. For example, nonlinear regression models have been used to characterize the relationship between atmospheric CO2 concentrations and global temperature, revealing the logarithmic relationship predicted by radiative transfer theory.

More sophisticated supervised learning algorithms, such as support vector machines, random forests, and gradient boosting methods, have shown exceptional performance in climate prediction applications. These algorithms can capture complex, high-dimensional relationships between predictor and response variables, making them particularly well-suited for climate problems involving multiple interacting factors. Random forest algorithms, in particular, have proven effective for climate classification problems, such as identifying climate zones or predicting the occurrence of extreme weather events.

Artificial neural networks represent one of the most powerful classes of supervised learning algorithms applied in climate science. Feed-forward neural networks have been used extensively for climate prediction and pattern recognition applications, demonstrating the ability to capture complex nonlinear relationships that are difficult to model using traditional statistical methods. These networks can learn intricate mappings between input climate variables and target outcomes, making them valuable tools for empirical climate modeling.

Recurrent neural networks (RNNs) and their advanced variants, such as Long Short-Term Memory (LSTM) networks and Gated Recurrent Units (GRUs), have shown particular promise for modeling sequential climate data. These architectures are specifically designed to handle temporal dependencies and can capture long-term memory effects that are important in climate systems. LSTM networks have been successfully applied to problems such as seasonal climate prediction, drought forecasting, and the modeling of climate teleconnections.

Convolutional neural networks (CNNs) have emerged as powerful tools for analyzing spatial climate data, such as satellite imagery and gridded climate datasets. These networks can automatically learn spatial features and patterns from climate data, making them valuable for tasks such as cloud classification, precipitation estimation from satellite data, and the identification of weather patterns. The ability of CNNs to capture spatial relationships makes them particularly well-suited for climate applications involving geospatial data.

Ensemble methods, which combine predictions from multiple individual models, have become increasingly important in climate science applications of supervised learning. These methods can improve prediction accuracy and provide estimates of prediction uncertainty by leveraging the strengths of different individual models while mitigating their weaknesses. Ensemble approaches are particularly valuable in climate applications, where prediction uncertainty is a critical consideration for decision-making.

Bootstrap aggregating (bagging) methods, such as random forests, create ensembles by training multiple models on different subsets of the training data. This approach helps reduce overfitting and provides more robust predictions, particularly important when dealing with the limited sample sizes that are common in climate applications. The variable importance measures provided by random forest algorithms also offer valuable insights into which climate variables are most important for specific prediction tasks.

Boosting methods, such as AdaBoost and gradient boosting, create ensembles by sequentially training models that focus on correcting the errors of previous models. These methods have shown excellent performance in climate applications, particularly for complex prediction tasks involving multiple interacting variables. Gradient boosting machines have been successfully applied to problems such as temperature and precipitation forecasting, extreme event prediction, and climate model bias correction.

Unsupervised Learning for Pattern Detection

Unsupervised learning techniques play a crucial role in climate science by enabling researchers to identify patterns and structures in climate data without prior knowledge of specific outcomes or categories. Clustering algorithms are particularly valuable for identifying distinct climate regimes, weather patterns, or climate zones based solely on the characteristics of the data. These techniques follow the principles of inductive reasoning by allowing patterns to emerge from the data rather than imposing predetermined categories.

K-means clustering has been widely applied in climate science for identifying distinct climate states or regimes. This algorithm partitions climate data into k clusters based on similarity in multi-dimensional space, helping researchers identify characteristic patterns of atmospheric circulation, ocean conditions, or regional climate variations. K-means clustering has been used to classify El Niño and La Niña events, identify drought patterns, and characterize different phases of climate oscillations.

Hierarchical clustering methods provide alternative approaches that can reveal nested structures and relationships within climate data. These methods create tree-like structures (dendrograms) that show how different climate patterns or regions are related to each other. Hierarchical clustering has been particularly useful for identifying climate regions, classifying weather types, and understanding the relationships between different climate phenomena.

More advanced clustering techniques, such as Gaussian mixture models and density-based clustering (DBSCAN), offer greater flexibility for identifying clusters with complex shapes and handling noise in climate data. These methods have been applied to problems such as identifying tropical cyclone tracks, classifying cloud types from satellite imagery, and detecting anomalous climate conditions.

The high dimensionality of many climate datasets presents significant challenges for analysis and visualization. Dimensionality reduction techniques provide powerful tools for identifying the most important patterns and relationships in high-dimensional climate data while reducing computational complexity and enabling visualization of complex datasets.

Principal Component Analysis (PCA) remains one of the most widely used dimensionality reduction techniques in climate science. PCA identifies the directions of maximum variance in climate data, allowing researchers to capture the most important patterns of variability with a reduced number of variables. In climate applications, PCA has been used to identify dominant patterns of sea surface temperature variability, characterize modes of atmospheric circulation, and reduce the dimensionality of climate model output for analysis.

Independent Component Analysis (ICA) offers an alternative approach for identifying statistically independent components in climate data. Unlike PCA, which focuses on variance, ICA seeks to find components that are as statistically independent as possible. This approach has proven valuable for separating different physical processes that contribute to observed climate patterns, such as distinguishing between forced and natural climate variations.

Non-linear dimensionality reduction techniques, such as t-SNE (t-Distributed Stochastic Neighbor Embedding) and UMAP (Uniform Manifold Approximation and Projection), have gained popularity for visualizing complex climate datasets. These methods can reveal nonlinear relationships and cluster structures that are not apparent in linear projections, making them valuable for exploratory analysis of climate data.

Anomaly Detection

Anomaly detection represents an important application of unsupervised learning in climate science, focusing on the identification of unusual or extreme climate conditions that deviate significantly from normal patterns. These techniques are particularly valuable for identifying extreme weather events, detecting climate regime shifts, and monitoring for unprecedented climate conditions.

Statistical approaches to anomaly detection in climate data often rely on threshold-based methods that identify observations exceeding certain percentile values or standard deviation limits. While simple, these approaches can be effective in detecting extreme events, such as heatwaves, droughts, or heavy precipitation events. However, they may miss more subtle anomalies or fail to account for the temporal and spatial correlations inherent in climate data.

Machine learning approaches to anomaly detection offer more sophisticated capabilities for identifying complex patterns of anomalous behavior. One-class Support Vector Machines (SVMs) and isolation forests are examples of machine learning algorithms specifically designed for anomaly detection that have been applied to climate data. These methods can learn the characteristics of normal climate behavior and identify observations that deviate significantly from these learned patterns.

Autoencoder neural networks provide another powerful approach for climate anomaly detection. These networks learn to compress and reconstruct climate data, with large reconstruction errors indicating anomalous conditions. Variational autoencoders extend this approach by learning probabilistic representations of climate data, enabling the quantification of anomaly severity and uncertainty.

Deep Neural Networks (DNNs)

Deep Neural Networks have emerged as transformative tools in climate science, offering unprecedented capabilities for modeling complex, nonlinear relationships in climate data. The deep architecture of these networks, with multiple hidden layers, enables them to learn hierarchical representations of climate features, from simple patterns in individual layers to complex interactions in deeper layers. This hierarchical learning capability is particularly valuable in climate science, where phenomena often involve interactions across multiple scales and processes.

Feed-forward deep neural networks have been successfully applied to a wide range of climate problems, from downscaling global climate model output to local scales, to predicting climate variables from large-scale circulation patterns. These networks can learn complex mappings between input and output variables without requiring explicit specification of the functional relationships, making them valuable for problems where the underlying physics are poorly understood or highly complex.

Convolutional Neural Networks (CNNs) have revolutionized the analysis of gridded climate data and satellite imagery. The convolutional layers in these networks can automatically learn spatial features and patterns, such as weather fronts, cloud formations, or temperature gradients, without manual feature engineering. Applications include precipitation estimation from satellite imagery, tropical cyclone detection and tracking, and the identification of atmospheric rivers and other weather patterns.

Recurrent Neural Networks (RNNs) and their variants, particularly LSTM and GRU networks, have shown exceptional performance in modeling temporal sequences in climate data. These networks can capture long-term dependencies and memory effects that are crucial for understanding climate processes. Applications include seasonal climate prediction, modeling of climate oscillations such as ENSO, and the prediction of extreme weather events based on precursor conditions.

Transfer learning has emerged as a powerful technique in climate science applications of deep learning, allowing researchers to leverage knowledge learned from one climate problem to solve related problems.

This approach is particularly valuable in climate science, where labeled training data can be scarce or expensive to obtain. By starting with networks pre-trained in related tasks, researchers can achieve better performance with smaller datasets and reduced computational requirements.

Pre-trained models developed for general computer vision tasks have been successfully adapted for climate applications involving satellite imagery and gridded data. These models, initially trained on large datasets of natural images, can be fine-tuned for specific climate tasks such as cloud classification, land use detection, or weather pattern recognition. The features learned by these pre-trained models often transfer well to climate applications, providing a solid foundation for further learning.

Domain adaptation techniques allow deep learning models trained on one climate dataset to be applied to different regions or time periods. This capability is particularly valuable for climate applications, where models trained on historical data need to be applied to future conditions or models developed for one geographic region need to be applied to other areas. Techniques such as adversarial training and domain-adaptive neural networks have shown promise for these applications.

The "black box" nature of deep neural networks presents challenges for their application in climate science, where understanding the physical basis for predictions is often as important as prediction accuracy itself. Researchers have developed various techniques for interpreting and explaining the behavior of deep learning models in climate applications, helping to build trust in these models and gain insights into underlying climate processes.

Gradient-based attribution methods, such as Integrated Gradients and Gradient×Input, help identify which input variables most strongly influence network predictions. In climate applications, these methods can reveal which atmospheric variables, spatial regions, or temporal periods are most important for specific predictions, providing insights into the physical mechanisms underlying model behavior.

Layer-wise Relevance Propagation (LRP) and SHAP (SHapley Additive exPlanations) values provide alternative approaches for explaining deep learning model predictions. These methods decompose model predictions into contributions from individual input features, allowing researchers to understand how different climate variables contribute to specific outcomes. Such interpretability is crucial for building confidence in deep learning models and for identifying potential biases or limitations.

Attention mechanisms, incorporated into neural network architectures, provide built-in interpretability by highlighting which parts of the input data the network focuses on when making predictions. In climate applications, attention mechanisms can reveal which spatial regions or temporal periods are most relevant for specific predictions, providing valuable insights into climate processes and patterns.

One of the primary advantages of inductive approaches in climate science lies in their capacity for data-driven discovery, allowing researchers to uncover patterns and relationships that might not be apparent through theoretical analysis alone. This empirical foundation enables climate scientists to identify novel phenomena, unexpected connections between variables, and previously unknown modes of climate variability. The data-driven nature of inductive reasoning is particularly valuable in climate science, where the complexity of the

Earth system often produces emergent behaviors that are difficult to predict from first principles.

Inductive approaches have led to numerous important discoveries in climate science, from the identification of climate oscillations such as the El Niño-Southern Oscillation to the recognition of abrupt climate transitions in paleoclimate records. These discoveries often emerged from careful analysis of observational data, with patterns becoming apparent only after extensive empirical investigation. The ability to let data guide the discovery process, rather than being constrained by preexisting theoretical frameworks, has been crucial for advancing understanding of climate processes.

The machine learning revolution has further enhanced the data-driven discovery capabilities of inductive approaches. Advanced algorithms can identify subtle patterns and complex relationships in massive climate datasets that would be impossible to detect using traditional analytical methods. These capabilities have led to new insights into climate predictability, improved understanding of climate teleconnections, and better characterization of extreme weather events. The ability to process and analyze increasingly large and complex climate datasets ensures that inductive approaches will continue to drive new discoveries in climate science.

Inductive approaches demonstrate remarkable flexibility and adaptability, allowing researchers to adjust their methods and conclusions as new data becomes available. This characteristic is particularly valuable in climate science, where observational capabilities are constantly improving and new datasets are regularly becoming available. Unlike rigid theoretical frameworks that may resist modification, inductive approaches can readily incorporate new information and adapt to changing understanding of climate processes.

The adaptive nature of inductive reasoning enables climate scientists to refine their understanding progressively as more data becomes available. Early hypotheses based on limited data can be tested and refined as additional observations are collected, leading to an increasingly sophisticated understanding of climate phenomena. This iterative process of hypothesis refinement is fundamental to scientific progress and is particularly well-suited to the challenges of climate research, where many phenomena operate on timescales longer than individual research careers.

Machine learning applications exemplify this flexibility, with algorithms that can continuously learn and improve their performance as new training data becomes available. Online learning algorithms can update their parameters in real-time as new observations are collected, ensuring that predictive models remain current and accurate. This adaptability is crucial for climate applications, where the underlying relationships between variables may evolve over time due to changing boundary conditions or non-stationary climate behavior.

Inductive approaches provide strong empirical validation for climate science conclusions by grounding them directly in observational evidence. This empirical foundation enhances the credibility and robustness of research findings, particularly important in a field where conclusions often have significant policy and societal implications. The requirement for empirical support helps ensure that climate science conclusions are based on solid evidence rather than theoretical speculation alone.

The emphasis on empirical validation in inductive approaches promotes rigorous testing of hypotheses against multiple lines of evidence. Climate scientists using inductive methods typically validate their findings using independent datasets, different analytical techniques, and various temporal or spatial scales. This comprehensive validation process helps identify robust patterns and relationships while filtering out spurious correlations or methodological artifacts.

Statistical significance testing and uncertainty quantification are integral components of inductive climate research, providing objective measures of confidence in research findings. These quantitative assessments enable researchers to distinguish between genuine climate signals and random variability, ensuring that conclusions are statistically sound. The probabilistic framework inherent in many inductive approaches also enables explicit quantification of uncertainty, crucial for informing decision-making under uncertainty.

Limitations and Challenges

One of the fundamental limitations of inductive approaches in climate science is the challenge of distinguishing correlation from causation. While inductive methods excel at identifying patterns and relationships in data, they cannot definitively establish causal relationships without additional theoretical or experimental evidence. This limitation is particularly problematic in climate science, where understanding causal mechanisms is often crucial for prediction and decision-making.

The complex nature of the climate system, with numerous interacting components and feedback mechanisms, makes it particularly difficult to establish causation from observational data alone. Variables that appear correlated may be responding to common forcing factors, may be linked through complex indirect pathways, or may be related only coincidentally. Distinguishing between these possibilities requires careful analysis and often additional evidence from theoretical understanding or physical modeling.

Machine learning algorithms, while powerful for pattern recognition, are particularly susceptible to identifying spurious correlations in large datasets. The ability of these algorithms to find complex patterns in high-dimensional data can lead to overfitting, where models learn relationships that are specific to the training data but do not generalize to new situations. Addressing this challenge requires careful validation procedures, regularization techniques, and integration with a physical understanding of climate processes.

The reliability and validity of inductive climate research depend critically on the quality and availability of observational data. Poor data quality, including measurement errors, calibration problems, or systematic biases, can lead to erroneous conclusions and misleading patterns. Climate datasets often suffer from various quality issues, including instrumental errors, spatial and temporal sampling biases, and changes in measurement procedures over time.

Historical climate datasets present particular challenges for inductive analysis, as measurement techniques, instrumentation, and observational practices have evolved significantly over time. These changes can introduce artificial trends or discontinuities that may be mistaken for genuine climate signals. Homogenization procedures can address some of these issues, but uncertainties remain, particularly for longer-term trend analysis.

Spatial and temporal coverage limitations also constrain inductive climate research. Many regions of the world, particularly polar areas and developing countries, have limited observational coverage, potentially biasing global analyses. Temporal coverage is often insufficient for studying long-term climate variations, with instrumental records covering only the past few centuries at most. These limitations can lead to an incomplete understanding of climate variability and may result in conclusions that are not globally representative.

The Earth's climate system represents one of the most complex systems studied by science, with numerous interacting components operating across multiple temporal and spatial scales. This complexity presents significant challenges for inductive approaches, which may struggle to capture the full range of interactions and feedback mechanisms operating in the climate system. Linear statistical methods, in particular, may fail to capture nonlinear relationships and threshold behaviors that are important in climate dynamics.

The high dimensionality of climate data presents additional challenges for inductive analysis. Climate datasets often involve thousands or millions of variables, creating computational and statistical challenges for traditional analytical methods. The "curse of dimensionality" can make it difficult to identify meaningful patterns in high-dimensional data, particularly when sample sizes are limited relative to the number of variables.

Temporal and spatial scale interactions present another challenge for inductive climate analysis. Climate phenomena operate across a wide range of scales, from local weather events to global climate patterns, and across timescales from hours to millennia. Understanding how processes at different scales interact and influence each other requires sophisticated analytical approaches that can handle multi-scale relationships.

Inductive approaches in climate science face several statistical and methodological limitations that can affect the reliability and interpretability of research findings. Many climate datasets exhibit non-stationary behavior, with statistical properties that change over time due to external forcing or internal climate dynamics. Traditional statistical methods often assume stationarity, potentially leading to incorrect conclusions when applied to non-stationary climate data.

Temporal autocorrelation is prevalent in climate data, with observations at adjacent time points exhibiting greater similarity than would be anticipated by chance. This autocorrelation diminishes the effective sample size for statistical analyses and can result in an overestimation of statistical significance if not adequately accounted for. Similarly, spatial autocorrelation in gridded climate datasets can lead to inflated significance levels and erroneous conclusions regarding the strength of relationships.

Multiple testing issues frequently arise in climate data analysis, where researchers may test numerous hypotheses concurrently or examine relationships across numerous spatial locations or time periods. Without proper correction for multiple comparisons, the probability of identifying spurious significant results substantially increases. This issue is particularly problematic in exploratory data analysis and in studies involving a substantial number of climate variables or spatial locations.

The limited sample sizes available for many climate phenomena present additional statistical challenges. Long-term climate variations, extreme events, and paleoclimate reconstructions often involve small sample sizes that restrict statistical power and augment uncertainty in parameter estimates. These limitations are particularly problematic for comprehending rare events or long-term trends, where the signal-to-noise ratio may be low.

The most effective climate science research often combines inductive and deductive approaches, leveraging the strengths of both methodologies while mitigating their individual limitations. This integration enables researchers to ground empirical patterns in physical understanding while using observational evidence to test and refine theoretical models. The combination of approaches provides a more robust foundation for climate science conclusions than either approach alone.

Physical climate models represent sophisticated deductive tools that encode our theoretical understanding of climate processes. However, these models require extensive validation against observational data to ensure their reliability and accuracy. Inductive analysis of observational data provides crucial benchmarks for model evaluation, helping to identify model biases, calibrate model parameters, and assess model performance under different conditions.

Conversely, physical understanding can guide and constrain inductive analyses, helping to ensure that identified patterns are physically plausible and meaningful. Theoretical knowledge can inform the selection of variables for analysis, suggest appropriate temporal and spatial scales for investigation, and help interpret the physical significance of empirical relationships. This guidance is particularly valuable for avoiding spurious correlations and focusing on relationships that are likely to be robust and generalizable.

Inductive approaches play a crucial role in evaluating process-based climate models, providing observational benchmarks against which model performance can be assessed. This evaluation process involves comparing model simulations with observational data across multiple variables, spatial scales, temporal scales, and climatic conditions. The systematic comparison of models with observations helps identify model strengths and weaknesses and guides model development priorities.

Pattern-based evaluation approaches focus on assessing whether climate models can reproduce the spatial and temporal patterns of variability observed in the real climate system. These evaluations examine model performance in simulating phenomena such as seasonal cycles, interannual variability, spatial patterns of climate change, and extreme events. The ability to reproduce observed patterns provides confidence in model representations of underlying physical processes.

Process-oriented evaluation approaches go beyond pattern matching to assess whether models reproduce observed relationships between different climate variables and processes. These evaluations examine model performance in simulating phenomena such as cloud-radiation interactions, precipitation processes, ocean-atmosphere coupling, and feedback mechanisms. This type of evaluation provides more stringent tests of model physics, helping to identify specific areas for model improvement.

Emergent constraints represent an innovative approach that combines inductive analysis of observational data with ensemble climate model simulations to constrain projections of future climate change. This approach identifies relationships between observable climate characteristics and model sensitivity to external forcing, using these relationships to reduce uncertainty in climate projections. Emergent constraints have been successfully applied to constrain climate sensitivity, cloud feedbacks, and regional climate projections.

The identification of emergent constraints requires extensive inductive analysis of both observational data and climate model simulations. Researchers examine relationships between current climate characteristics and model responses to external forcing across large ensembles of model simulations. Observable quantities that show strong correlations with model sensitivity can then be used to weight model projections based on their agreement with observations.

Model selection and weighting approaches use observational data to assess the relative reliability of different climate models for specific applications. Rather than treating all models equally, these approaches weight model contributions to ensemble projections based on their historical performance in simulating relevant climate characteristics. This observationally-based weighting can improve the reliability of climate projections and provide more realistic estimates of projection uncertainty.

Artificial Intelligence and Advanced Analytics

The continued development of artificial intelligence and advanced analytics presents exciting opportunities for enhancing inductive approaches in climate science. Next-generation machine learning algorithms, including deep learning architectures, reinforcement learning, and causal inference methods, offer improved capabilities for analyzing complex climate data and identifying subtle patterns and relationships.

Causal inference methods represent a particularly promising development for addressing one of the key limitations of traditional inductive approaches. These methods, including techniques such as instrumental variables, propensity score matching, and causal graphical models, provide frameworks for inferring causal relationships from observational data. The application of these methods to climate data could help address fundamental questions about climate causation and improve our understanding of climate processes.

Explainable AI techniques are becoming increasingly important for climate applications of machine learning, addressing concerns about the "black box" nature of complex algorithms. These techniques enable researchers to understand how machine learning models make predictions, identify which variables are most important for specific outcomes, and assess whether model behavior is consistent with physical understanding. The development of climate-specific explainable AI methods could enhance the credibility and acceptance of machine learning approaches in climate science.

The explosion of climate data from observations, models, and reanalysis products presents both opportunities and challenges for inductive climate research. High-resolution climate models, comprehensive Earth system models, and extensive observational datasets are generating petabytes of climate data that require new analytical approaches and computational infrastructure. Big data technologies and high-performance computing platforms provide the necessary tools for analyzing these massive datasets.

Cloud computing platforms and distributed processing frameworks enable climate researchers to access powerful computational resources and analyze large datasets without requiring substantial local infrastructure investments. These platforms facilitate collaborative research and enable smaller research groups to tackle problems that previously required supercomputing resources. The democratization of access to computational resources could accelerate progress in data-intensive climate research.

Real-time data processing and analysis capabilities are becoming increasingly important for climate monitoring and prediction applications. The ability to process streaming climate data from satellites, weather stations, and other observational platforms in real-time enables rapid detection of climate anomalies, improved weather and climate prediction, and timely warnings of extreme events. These capabilities require sophisticated data processing pipelines and automated analysis systems.

The future of inductive climate research increasingly depends on interdisciplinary collaboration, bringing together expertise from climate science, statistics, computer science, and other relevant fields. This collaboration is essential for developing new analytical methods, addressing methodological challenges, and ensuring that technical advances are appropriately applied to climate problems.

The integration of social sciences with physical climate research presents opportunities for a more comprehensive understanding of climate impacts and adaptation. Inductive analysis of socioeconomic data, combined with physical climate information, can provide insights into climate vulnerability, adaptation effectiveness, and the human dimensions of climate change. These interdisciplinary approaches are essential for developing actionable climate information for decision-making.

Citizen science initiatives and community-based monitoring programs are generating new sources of climate data that can complement traditional observational networks. These programs engage broader communities in climate research and can provide valuable data from regions or phenomena that are poorly covered by conventional monitoring systems. The integration of citizen science data with traditional climate datasets requires careful quality control and validation, but offers opportunities for enhanced spatial and temporal coverage.

The application of inductive reasoning in climate science represents a fundamental approach to understanding Earth's complex climate system through empirical observation and data analysis. This chapter has explored the multifaceted role of inductive methods in climate research, from the philosophical foundations that underpin empirical climate science to the cutting-edge machine learning algorithms that are revolutionizing climate data analysis.

The historical development of climate science demonstrates the crucial importance of inductive approaches in building our understanding of climate processes and variability. The systematic analysis of paleoclimate records has revealed the natural baseline of climate variability and provided essential context for understanding recent climate changes. Instrumental observations have documented unprecedented recent warming and enabled detailed analysis of climate trends and patterns. Satellite observations have revolutionized our ability to monitor global climate conditions and have provided crucial data for understanding rapid climate changes in polar regions and other remote areas.

The integration of machine learning techniques into climate science has dramatically expanded the capabilities of inductive approaches, enabling the analysis of massive, high-dimensional datasets and the identification of complex patterns that would be impossible to detect using traditional methods. Supervised learning algorithms have improved climate prediction capabilities, while unsupervised learning techniques have revealed new insights into climate variability and extreme events. Deep neural networks have demonstrated exceptional performance in modeling complex climate relationships and processing spatial and temporal climate data.

However, this exploration has also highlighted important limitations and challenges associated with inductive approaches in climate science. The fundamental challenge of distinguishing correlation from causation remains a significant concern, particularly when using machine learning algorithms that can identify spurious patterns in large datasets. Data quality issues, coverage limitations, and the complexity of the climate system all present ongoing challenges for inductive climate research.

The future success of inductive approaches in climate science depends on addressing these limitations while capitalizing on emerging opportunities. The integration of inductive and deductive approaches provides a pathway for combining the pattern-recognition capabilities of empirical methods with the explanatory power of physical understanding. This integration is essential for developing climate science that is both empirically grounded and physically meaningful.

The continued development of artificial intelligence and advanced analytics presents exciting opportunities for enhancing inductive climate research. Causal inference methods offer the potential to address fundamental questions about climate causation, while explainable AI techniques can help build trust in complex machine learning models. The growth of big data and high-performance computing capabilities will enable analysis of increasingly large and complex climate datasets.

Interdisciplinary collaboration will be essential for realizing the full potential of inductive approaches in climate science. The integration of expertise from multiple fields, including statistics, computer science, and social sciences, is crucial for developing robust analytical methods and ensuring that climate research addresses the full range of societal needs.

Inductive reasoning has been, and will continue to be, indispensable to climate science. The empirical foundation provided by inductive approaches gives climate science its credibility and ensures that our understanding of climate processes is grounded in observational reality. As we face the challenges of understanding and predicting future climate change, the data-driven insights provided by inductive methods will be crucial for informing both scientific knowledge and societal responses.

The evolution from simple statistical analysis of climate observations to sophisticated machine learning algorithms represents a remarkable transformation in the tools available for climate research. However, the fundamental principles of inductive reasoning—careful observation, pattern recognition, hypothesis testing, and empirical validation—

remain as relevant today as they were at the dawn of modern climate science.

Looking ahead, the continued advancement of inductive approaches in climate science will require maintaining the careful balance between methodological innovation and scientific rigor. The powerful tools of modern data science must be applied thoughtfully, with appropriate attention to their limitations and with integration into the broader framework of physical understanding. By maintaining this balance, inductive approaches will continue to drive progress in climate science and contribute to our ability to understand and respond to the challenges of climate change.

The journey from early barometric observations to contemporary machine learning applications illustrates the remarkable progress that inductive approaches have enabled in climate science. This progress provides a foundation of knowledge and a set of analytical tools that position climate science to address the complex challenges of understanding and predicting climate change in an era of unprecedented environmental change. The future of climate science will undoubtedly continue to rely on the empirical insights and data-driven discoveries that are the hallmarks of inductive reasoning, ensuring that our understanding of Earth's climate system remains firmly grounded in observational reality while reaching toward ever more sophisticated theoretical understanding.

FOUR

Casual Reasoning in Climate Science

Causal reasoning represents one of the most fundamental challenges in climate science, where understanding the complex web of cause-and-effect relationships is essential for accurate prediction, attribution, and policy formulation. This chapter provides a comprehensive examination of causal reasoning methodologies in climate science, covering theoretical fundamentals, advanced inference techniques, discovery methods, and the critical challenge of spurious correlation elimination. We explore how modern causal reasoning frameworks can be applied to climate systems, from large-scale atmospheric dynamics to sub-grid scale processes, providing climate scientists with the theoretical foundation and practical tools necessary for robust causal analysis.

Introduction

Climate systems represent some of the most complex causal networks in natural science, characterized by nonlinear interactions, feedback loops, multi-scale processes, and emergent behaviors that span temporal scales from milliseconds to millennia and spatial scales from molecular to planetary. Traditional correlation-based approaches, while valuable for identifying statistical relationships, often fall short in establishing the causal mechanisms that drive climate phenomena. The distinction between correlation and causation becomes particularly critical when addressing questions of climate attribution, understanding tipping points, and developing effective mitigation strategies.

The challenge of causal reasoning in climate science is compounded by several factors: the impossibility of controlled experiments at planetary scales, the presence of confounding variables across multiple scales, the nonstationary nature of climate systems, and the inherent complexity of Earth system interactions. These challenges necessitate sophisticated methodological approaches that can extract causal insights from observational data while accounting for the unique characteristics of climate systems.

This chapter introduces state-of-the-art causal reasoning frameworks specifically adapted for climate science applications. We begin with fundamental concepts of causality theory, progress through advanced inference techniques, and conclude with practical applications to climate system analysis. Throughout, we emphasize the integration of physical understanding with statistical methodology, recognizing that effective causal reasoning in climate science requires both domain expertise and methodological rigor.

Fundamentals of Causal Reasoning

Causal reasoning in climate science builds upon several philosophical traditions, most notably the counterfactual theory of causation developed by David Lewis and the interventionist framework proposed by James Woodward. The counterfactual approach defines causation in terms of what would have happened under different circumstances: X causes Y if Y would not have occurred in the nearest possible world where X did not occur. In climate science, this translates to questions such as "Would the observed warming have occurred without anthropogenic greenhouse gas emissions?"

The interventionist framework, more directly applicable to scientific practice, defines causal relationships through the concept of manipulation: X causes Y if an intervention that changes X would produce a corresponding change in Y, holding all other relevant factors constant. While direct manipulation of climate variables is often impossible, the interventionist framework provides a conceptual foundation for understanding causal relationships and designing observational studies that can approximate experimental conditions.

Modern causal reasoning relies heavily on graphical models, particularly directed acyclic graphs (DAGs), which provide a formal language for representing causal assumptions and deriving testable implications. In the climate science context, a DAG represents variables as nodes and causal relationships as directed edges, with the crucial constraint that no variable can be its own ancestor (the acyclic property).

Consider a simple climate example where we wish to understand the relationship between sea surface temperature (SST), atmospheric CO_2

concentration, and precipitation patterns. A possible DAG might represent:

$$CO_2 \rightarrow SST \rightarrow Precipitation$$
$$CO_2 \rightarrow Precipitation$$

This structure encodes the assumptions that CO_2 affects both SST and precipitation directly, while SST also affects precipitation. The graph immediately reveals testable implications: controlling for CO_2, SST, and precipitation should remain associated, but controlling for both CO_2 and SST, no additional association should exist.

The mathematical framework extends to structural equation models (SEMs), which quantify the relationships encoded in DAGs. For our climate example:

$$SST = f_1(CO_2, U_1)$$
$$Precipitation = f_2(CO_2, SST, U_2)$$

where f_1 and f_2 represent functional relationships and U_1, U_2 represent unmeasured influences. These equations allow us to calculate the causal effect of interventions, such as the expected change in precipitation from a given increase in CO_2 concentration.

Climate systems exhibit complex temporal dynamics that pose unique challenges for causal reasoning. The principle that causes precede effects provides a fundamental constraint, but climate systems involve feedback loops, delayed responses, and multi-scale interactions that complicate temporal analysis.

Consider the relationship between Arctic sea ice extent and global temperature. While reduced sea ice (through albedo feedback) can amplify warming, increased temperatures also drive ice loss, creating a positive feedback loop. The temporal signature of these interactions—ice loss typically lagging temperature increases by several months, while albedo effects operate on shorter timescales—provides crucial information for causal inference.

Time series causal analysis in climate science must account for:

- **Lag structures**: Physical processes operate on different timescales, from radiative forcing (days) to ice sheet dynamics (centuries).
- **Seasonality and trends**: Climate variables exhibit strong seasonal cycles and long-term trends that can confound causal relationships.
- **Regime changes**: Climate systems can undergo sudden transitions that alter causal relationships
- **Memory effects**: Past states influence current dynamics through various physical mechanisms.

Climate causation operates across multiple spatial scales, from local microclimates to global teleconnections. Spatial autocorrelation—the tendency for nearby locations to have similar climate characteristics—violates the independence assumptions of many statistical methods and can lead to spurious causal inferences.

The concept of spatial causation in climate science involves several key considerations:

- **Scale dependence**: Causal relationships may differ across spatial scales. For example, the relationship between precipitation and vegetation may be positive at local scales (vegetation benefits from water) but negative at regional scales (forests can reduce regional precipitation through moisture recycling patterns).

- **Teleconnections:** Distant regions can be causally connected through atmospheric or oceanic pathways. The El Niño-Southern Oscillation (ENSO) exemplifies such teleconnections, where sea surface temperature anomalies in the tropical Pacific influence weather patterns globally.

- **Spatial confounding:** Geographic variables such as latitude, elevation, and proximity to water bodies can confound relationships between climate variables, requiring careful statistical control or stratification.

Climate systems exhibit diverse types of causal relationships, each requiring specific analytical approaches:

- Direct causation involves immediate physical mechanisms linking cause and effect. For example, increased atmospheric CO_2 concentrations directly enhance the greenhouse effect, leading to increased surface temperatures through radiative forcing.

- Mediated causation operates through intermediate variables. The effect of solar variability on surface temperature is mediated through changes in stratospheric ozone, atmospheric chemistry, and circulation patterns.

- Interactive causation occurs when multiple causes combine non-additively to produce effects. The impact of aerosols on climate depends on their interaction with cloud formation processes, which in turn depend on humidity, temperature, and atmospheric dynamics.

- Threshold causation involves nonlinear responses where small changes in causes can produce large effects once critical thresholds are exceeded. Ice sheet dynamics exemplify this type, where gradual warming can trigger rapid ice loss once critical temperature thresholds are crossed.

- Reciprocal causation characterizes feedback systems where variables simultaneously influence each other. The carbon cycle involves reciprocal causation between atmospheric CO_2 concentrations, terrestrial vegetation, and ocean chemistry.

Feedback loops represent a fundamental aspect of climate causation, creating complex networks of interdependent relationships. Positive feedbacks amplify changes, while negative feedbacks provide stabilizing influences.

Ice-albedo feedback exemplifies positive feedback: as ice melts, darker surfaces are exposed, absorbing more solar radiation, leading to further warming and more ice loss. This feedback operates at multiple scales, from local snow patches to continental ice sheets.

Water vapor feedback represents another crucial positive feedback: warmer air holds more water vapor, and since water vapor is a greenhouse gas, this amplifies initial warming. The magnitude of this feedback depends on complex interactions between convection, cloud formation, and atmospheric circulation.

Cloud feedbacks involve both positive and negative components. Low clouds generally cool the surface by reflecting solar radiation, while high clouds warm the surface by trapping outgoing longwave radiation. Changes in cloud properties with warming involve complex interactions between microphysics, dynamics, and thermodynamics.

Carbon cycle feedbacks link climate change to biogeochemical processes. Warming can reduce carbon storage in soils and vegetation while increasing plant growth in some regions, creating complex spatial and temporal patterns of feedback.

Climate systems exhibit emergent properties—characteristics that arise from interactions among system components but are not predictable from knowledge of individual components alone. These emergent properties pose particular challenges for causal reasoning because they cannot be understood through reductionist approaches.

Atmospheric circulation patterns emerge from the interaction of thermal gradients, rotation, and topography. While individual components follow well-understood physical laws, the resulting circulation patterns—such as jet streams, storm tracks, and monsoon systems—represent emergent phenomena with their own causal properties.

Tipping points represent emergent threshold behaviors where gradual changes in forcing can trigger rapid, potentially irreversible changes in system state. The collapse of ice sheets, dieback of forests, or shutdown of ocean circulation represent examples where understanding causation requires recognizing emergent system-level properties.

Synchronization phenomena emerge when different components of the climate system become phase-locked or correlated despite having different natural frequencies. The synchronization between ENSO and the annual cycle represents one such emergent property with important implications for predictability and causal understanding.

Climate causation involves interactions across multiple spatial and temporal scales, creating a hierarchical structure of causal relationships. Understanding these scale interactions is crucial for developing comprehensive causal models.

Upscaling involves processes where local-scale phenomena influence larger-scale patterns. Convective clouds, driven by local heating, can organize into mesoscale systems that influence synoptic weather patterns. The causal chain from surface heating to global circulation patterns exemplifies multiscale causation.

Downscaling describes how large-scale patterns influence local processes. Global circulation patterns determine regional precipitation patterns, which in turn influence local ecosystem dynamics and surface energy balance.

Scale separation occurs when processes on different scales operate independently, allowing for simplified causal analysis. The assumption of scale separation underlies many climate modeling approaches but may break down during extreme events or regime transitions.

Cross-scale coupling represents situations where processes on different scales directly interact, creating complex causal networks. The interaction between tropical cyclones (synoptic scale) and convective processes (mesoscale) exemplifies such coupling.

Inference Techniques

While true randomized controlled trials are impossible for most climate phenomena, natural experiments provide opportunities for causal inference. Volcanic eruptions represent natural experiments where random timing and magnitude of aerosol injection allow estimation of climate sensitivity. The eruption of Mount Pinatubo in 1991 provided a natural experiment for understanding aerosol-climate interactions, with the random timing helping to separate volcanic effects from other climate drivers.

Regression discontinuity designs exploit arbitrary thresholds in policy or natural systems. Environmental regulations that apply above certain pollution thresholds create quasi-experimental conditions for studying pollution-climate relationships.

Instrumental variables identify exogenous variation in explanatory variables. Solar irradiance variations, being driven by solar physics rather than terrestrial processes, can serve as instruments for studying climate sensitivity.

Most climate causal inference relies on observational data, requiring sophisticated methods to account for confounding and selection bias.

Propensity score methods help control for confounding by balancing treatment groups on observed covariates. In climate applications, propensity scores can help compare regions with similar characteristics except for the variable of interest.

Difference-in-differences approaches compare changes over time between treatment and control groups. This method has been applied to study the effects of environmental policies on regional climate by comparing policy and non-policy regions before and after implementation.

Synthetic control methods create counterfactual scenarios by constructing synthetic control units from weighted combinations of untreated units. This approach has been used to study the climatic effects of large-scale land use changes by creating synthetic regions that match treated regions on pre-treatment characteristics.

Granger causality provides a statistical framework for causal inference in time series data based on predictability: X Granger-causes Y if past values of X improve the prediction of Y beyond what can be achieved using past values of Y alone.

In climate applications, Granger causality has been used to study:

- Relationships between climate indices (ENSO, NAO, PDO)
- Interactions between atmospheric and oceanic variables
- Coupling between different components of the Earth system.

Transfer entropy extends Granger causality by measuring the reduction in uncertainty about future states of Y given knowledge of past states of X, accounting for nonlinear relationships and non-Gaussian distributions common in climate data.

Convergent cross mapping addresses the challenge of distinguishing correlation from causation in nonlinear deterministic systems, particularly relevant for climate applications where variables may be synchronized due to common forcing rather than direct causation.

Modern machine learning techniques offer powerful tools for causal inference in complex, high-dimensional climate datasets.

Causal discovery algorithms automatically learn causal structure from data using various statistical tests and assumptions. The PC algorithm, GES algorithm, and constraint-based methods have been applied to climate data to discover causal networks.

Deep learning for causal inference includes methods such as:

- Causal convolutional networks that learn temporal causal relationships

- Variational auto-encoders for causal inference that separate causal and confounding factors
- Adversarial learning approaches that learn representations invariant to confounding.

Bayesian networks provide a probabilistic framework for representing and reasoning about causal relationships under uncertainty, particularly valuable for climate applications where uncertainty quantification is crucial.

Climate science offers the unique opportunity to incorporate physical knowledge into causal inference, improving both accuracy and interpretability.

Process-based constraints use physical understanding to constrain causal relationships. For example, energy conservation principles constrain possible relationships between radiative forcing and temperature response. Mechanistic modeling combines statistical causal inference with physical process models, allowing researchers to test causal hypotheses against both observational data and physical theory. Hybrid statistical-physical models integrate data-driven causal discovery with physics-based constraints, providing more robust causal inferences than purely statistical or purely physical approaches.

Discovery Methods

Constraint-based methods discover causal structure by testing conditional independence relationships implied by different causal graphs.

PC Algorithm: The Peter-Clark algorithm learns causal structure through a series of conditional independence tests. In climate applications, the PC algorithm has been used to discover causal networks among climate variables, revealing unexpected connections and validating known relationships.

The algorithm proceeds in phases, starts with a complete undirected graph, removes edges between conditionally independent variables, orients edges using rules based on conditional independence patterns, and applies additional orientation rules to maximize causal information.

Fast Causal Inference (FCI): Extends PC to handle latent confounding, common in climate systems where many relevant variables are unobserved.

PCMCI Algorithm: Specifically designed for time series data, combining PC with momentary conditional independence testing to handle temporal dependencies and autocorrelation.

Score-based methods evaluate different causal structures using goodness-of-fit measures and select the structure with the best score.

Greedy Equivalence Search (GES): Uses a Bayesian information criterion to score different causal structures, searching through the space of possible graphs using greedy optimization.

Bayesian approaches: Place prior distributions over causal structures and use Markov Chain Monte Carlo methods to sample from the posterior distribution, providing uncertainty quantification for discovered relationships.

Additive Noise Models (ANMs) assume that effects are generated as smooth functions of causes plus independent additive noise. ANMs exploit asymmetries in regression to determine causal direction.

Linear Non-Gaussian Acyclic Models (LiNGAM) use non-Gaussianity to identify causal direction in linear relationships, particularly useful for climate variables that often exhibit non-Gaussian distributions. Post-Nonlinear Models handle nonlinear relationships with nonlinear noise, extending causal discovery to more complex climate relationships. Minimum Description Length selects causal structures that provide the most compressed representation of the data, balancing model complexity with explanatory power. Transfer Entropy Networks construct causal networks based on information transfer between variables, particularly useful for studying climate teleconnections and regime transitions.

Modern causal discovery increasingly combines multiple approaches to leverage their respective strengths. Constraint-Score Hybrid uses constraint-based methods to determine the graph skeleton and score-based methods for edge orientation. Physics-Guided Discovery incorporates physical constraints and domain knowledge to guide the discovery process, improving accuracy and interpretability in climate applications.

Scale Processes

Climate models operate on discrete grids with typical resolutions ranging from hundreds of kilometers for global models to several kilometers for high-resolution regional models. However, many crucial physical processes occur at smaller scales and must be parameterized rather than explicitly resolved. Understanding the causal relationships involving these sub-grid scale processes presents unique challenges and opportunities.

Convective processes exemplify the sub-grid scale challenge. Individual convective clouds may be only a few kilometers in diameter, but their collective effects drive precipitation patterns, heat transport, and atmospheric circulation at much larger scales. The causal relationship between large-scale atmospheric conditions and convective activity involves complex interactions across scales.

Turbulent mixing in the atmosphere and ocean occurs at scales much smaller than typical model grids but fundamentally affects heat, moisture, and momentum transport. Understanding how small-scale turbulence causally influences large-scale circulation patterns requires sophisticated theoretical and observational approaches.

Cloud microphysics involves processes at micrometer scales that determine cloud properties and precipitation efficiency. The causal chain from aerosol particles through droplet formation to precipitation involves multiple-scale interactions that challenge traditional modeling approaches.

Parameterizations represent sub-grid scale processes in terms of resolved-scale variables, essentially encoding causal relationships between scales. However, these relationships are often based on empirical correlations rather than fundamental causal understanding.

Convective parameterizations typically relate convective activity to large-scale thermodynamic conditions through relationships such as:

Convective Activity = f(CAPE, Wind Shear, Moisture,...)

where Convective Available Potential Energy (CAPE) and other variables represent resolved-scale conditions. While these relationships may be statistically robust, they may not capture the true causal mechanisms governing convection.

Boundary layer parameterizations relate surface fluxes to near-surface gradients through relationships that assume steady-state conditions and local equilibrium. These assumptions may break down during rapidly evolving conditions, leading to incorrect causal inferences.

Cloud parameterizations face the challenge of representing complex microphysical processes through statistical relationships. The causal relationship between aerosol concentrations and cloud properties involves nonlinear processes that are difficult to capture in simple parameterizations.

Understanding causality in the presence of sub-grid scale processes requires methods that can handle scale interactions and emergent behaviors.

Multiscale decomposition methods separate variability at different scales, allowing for scale-specific causal analysis. Wavelet analysis, empirical mode decomposition, and other techniques can isolate processes operating at different scales.

Coarse-graining approaches systematically reduce the resolution of high-resolution data or models to understand how causal relationships change with scale. These approaches can reveal whether causal relationships identified at fine scales remain valid at coarser scales.

Scale-bridging methods attempt to connect processes across scales through theoretical or statistical relationships. Homogenization theory, multiscale asymptotics, and other mathematical approaches provide frameworks for understanding cross-scale causation.

Sub-grid scale processes can give rise to emergent causal relationships that are not present in the underlying fine-scale dynamics.

Collective behavior emerges when many individual sub-grid elements interact to produce large-scale patterns. Convective organization represents one example where individual clouds interact to create mesoscale patterns with their own causal properties.

Critical phenomena can emerge from sub-grid scale processes, leading to threshold behaviors and regime transitions. The onset of deep convection represents a critical phenomenon where small changes in large-scale conditions can trigger dramatic changes in precipitation and circulation.

Self-organization in sub-grid scale processes can lead to emergent spatial and temporal patterns. Hurricane formation exemplifies self-organization where initial disturbances organize into coherent structures through scale interactions.

High-resolution observations provide crucial constraints on causal relationships involving sub-grid scale processes. Satellite observations offer global coverage at increasingly fine spatial and temporal resolution, allowing for statistical analysis of scale interactions and causal relationships. Aircraft observations provide detailed profiles through clouds and boundary layers, revealing the vertical structure of causal relationships between different atmospheric variables. Ground-based remote sensing systems such as radars and lidars offer continuous monitoring of atmospheric processes at fine spatial and temporal scales. Large eddy simulations explicitly resolve sub-grid scale processes over limited domains, providing detailed information about causal mechanisms that can be used to evaluate and improve parameterizations.

Correlations Elimination

Spurious correlations, statistical associations that do not reflect causal relationships, present a major challenge in climate science due to the complex, interconnected nature of Earth system components.

Common forcing represents a primary source of spurious correlations. Multiple climate variables may respond to the same forcing (e.g., solar variability, volcanic eruptions, greenhouse gas increases), creating statistical associations without direct causal links between the variables themselves.

Seasonal cycles create spurious correlations between variables that follow similar annual patterns but are not causally related. Temperature and daylight hours are correlated not because one causes the other directly, but because both respond to the Earth's orbital cycle.

Long-term trends can induce spurious correlations between variables that exhibit similar trends over time. The correlation between global CO_2 concentration and global sea level reflects both direct causation (thermal expansion) and indirect effects through ice sheet dynamics.

Spatial autocorrelation creates spurious correlations when nearby locations share similar climate characteristics due to geographic proximity rather than causal relationships.

Measurement artifacts can induce spurious correlations through systematic errors, instrument drift, or changes in observational networks over time.

Partial correlation analysis removes the influence of confounding variables by conditioning on them. If the correlation between X and Y disappears after conditioning on Z, this suggests that Z may be a common cause of both X and Y.

Principal component analysis can reveal whether correlations result from a small number of common factors (suggesting common forcing) or from complex causal relationships involving multiple independent processes.

Granger causality testing helps distinguish genuine causal relationships from spurious correlations by testing whether one variable improves the prediction of another beyond what can be achieved using the target variable's own history.

Randomization tests create null distributions by randomly permuting time series or spatial patterns to test whether observed correlations exceed what would be expected by chance.

Cross-validation approaches test whether correlations identified in one dataset or time period generalize to independent data, helping to identify overfitted or spurious relationships.

Physical understanding provides powerful constraints for identifying spurious correlations and validating causal relationships.

Energy balance constraints limit possible relationships between radiative forcing and temperature response, helping to identify unrealistic correlations in observational data. Mass conservation constrains relationships involving water vapor, precipitation, and atmospheric moisture transport. Dynamical consistency requires that identified causal relationships be consistent with known atmospheric and oceanic dynamics. Thermodynamic constraints limit possible relationships between temperature, pressure, and moisture variables.

Scale consistency requires that causal relationships operate through plausible physical mechanisms at appropriate spatial and temporal scales.

Lag analysis examines whether correlations persist when variables are shifted in time. Genuine causal relationships should show maximum correlation at physically plausible time lags.

Lead-lag analysis tests whether one variable consistently leads another, providing evidence for causal direction.

Event coincidence analysis examines whether extreme events in different variables occur together more often than expected by chance, while accounting for temporal clustering and persistence.

Phase relationship analysis examines the phase relationships between oscillatory components of different variables to identify causal connections versus common forcing.

Robust identification of spurious correlations requires triangulation across multiple approaches:

Cross-dataset validation tests whether relationships identified in one dataset are reproducible in independent observations.

Multi-method convergence examines whether different causal inference methods yield consistent conclusions.

Process-based validation tests whether identified causal relationships are consistent with detailed process models and physical understanding.

Scale-dependent analysis examines whether causal relationships remain consistent across different spatial and temporal scales.

Atlantic Multidecadal Oscillation (AMO) versus Anthropogenic Warming: Early studies identified correlations between AMO and North Atlantic temperatures, but subsequent analysis revealed that much of this correlation reflected different responses to common forcing by aerosols and greenhouse gases rather than genuine oscillatory behavior.

Solar Activity and Climate: Many claimed correlations between solar variability and climate have been shown to be spurious, resulting from selective time periods, multiple testing, or failure to account for other climate forcings.

Urban Heat Island versus Global Warming: Claims that global warming is an artifact of urban heat island effects have been refuted through careful analysis that accounts for station location, measurement changes, and spatial patterns of warming.

CO_2 Fertilization versus Vegetation Trends: Correlations between atmospheric CO_2 and vegetation greenness can be spurious if they don't account for simultaneous changes in temperature, precipitation, and land use.

Future Directions

Earth System Models (ESMs) provide unique opportunities for causal inference by allowing for controlled experiments impossible in the real world. However, these models also introduce their own challenges for causal reasoning.

Model-based causal inference uses ESM experiments to test causal hypotheses. Single forcing experiments, where only one climate forcing is varied while others remain constant, provide clear tests of causal relationships. The Climate Model Intercomparison Project (CMIP) historical and detection/attribution experiments exemplify this approach.

Ensemble methods quantify uncertainty in causal inferences by running multiple model realizations with slightly different initial conditions or parameter values. Ensemble spread provides information about the robustness of identified causal relationships.

Perturbed physics ensembles systematically vary model parameters to explore how causal relationships depend on model formulation and to quantify structural uncertainty.

Model hierarchy approaches use models of varying complexity to understand causal mechanisms. Simple models may reveal fundamental causal relationships, while complex models test whether these relationships hold under realistic conditions.

Deep learning for climate causation leverages the ability of deep neural networks to learn complex nonlinear relationships from high-dimensional data. Convolutional neural networks can learn spatial patterns of causation, while recurrent networks can capture temporal dependencies.

Causal representation learning aims to learn representations of climate data that separate causal factors from confounding factors, improving both causal inference and prediction accuracy.

Physics-informed neural networks incorporate physical constraints into machine learning models, potentially improving causal inference by ensuring that learned relationships respect known physical laws.

Interpretable machine learning develops methods to understand and visualize the causal relationships learned by complex machine learning models, bridging the gap between prediction accuracy and causal understanding.

Bayesian causal inference provides natural frameworks for quantifying uncertainty in causal relationships through posterior distributions over causal structures and parameters.

Conformal prediction offers model-agnostic methods for quantifying uncertainty in causal predictions, providing prediction intervals that are guaranteed to contain the true causal effect with specified probability.

Sensitivity analysis examines how causal conclusions depend on model assumptions, particularly assumptions about unmeasured confounding.

Multi-model approaches combine causal inferences from different models or methods to provide more robust uncertainty quantification than any single approach.

Extreme event attribution represents one of the most active areas of climate causal inference, seeking to quantify the contribution of anthropogenic climate change to specific extreme weather events.

Compound events involve multiple interacting climate extremes (e.g., concurrent heat and drought), requiring sophisticated causal analysis to understand the mechanisms driving these interactions.

Tipping point detection uses causal inference methods to identify early warning signals of critical transitions in climate systems.

Rare event simulation develops methods to study the causal mechanisms of extremely rare but high-impact climate events through specialized modeling approaches.

Causal decision theory provides frameworks for making optimal decisions under uncertainty about causal relationships, particularly relevant for climate policy applications.

Value of information analysis quantifies the value of additional observational or experimental information for reducing uncertainty in causal relationships.

Robust decision-making develops strategies that perform well across multiple possible causal structures, acknowledging uncertainty in our understanding of climate causation.

Adaptive management uses causal inference to learn about climate relationships through policy interventions, treating policy implementation as natural experiments.

Case Studies

Single event attribution applies causal inference methods to determine whether anthropogenic climate change affected the probability or intensity of specific extreme weather events. The 2003 European heat wave represents a landmark case where multiple lines of evidence converged to demonstrate substantial anthropogenic influence.

Multi-event attribution examines causal patterns across multiple events to identify common causal mechanisms and improve attribution confidence. Analysis of global heat extremes has revealed consistent patterns of anthropogenic influence across different regions and time periods.

Compound event attribution addresses complex events involving multiple climate variables. Hurricane Harvey (2017) involved extreme precipitation enhanced by anomalously warm sea surface temperatures, requiring attribution analysis of both the meteorological pattern and the thermodynamic enhancement.

Process-based evaluation uses causal understanding to evaluate climate models based on their representation of physical mechanisms rather than just statistical performance. Models that reproduce observations for the right physical reasons are more credible for future projections.

Emergent constraint approaches use causal relationships between observable quantities and future projections to constrain model projections. The relationship between present-day cloud properties and climate sensitivity exemplifies this approach.

Attribution-based evaluation tests whether models can reproduce the observed causal relationships between different climate forcings and responses, providing stringent tests of model physical realism.

Sectoral impact attribution applies causal inference to understand how climate change affects specific sectors such as agriculture, water resources, and human health. Understanding causal mechanisms improves the credibility and usefulness of impact assessments.

Early warning systems use causal understanding of climate precursors to develop improved predictions of extreme events. Understanding the causal chain from large-scale circulation patterns to local extremes improves prediction skill.

Adaptation planning relies on causal understanding of climate risks to design effective adaptation measures. Understanding why certain regions are vulnerable to specific climate impacts informs targeted adaptation strategies.

Limitations

The high dimensionality of climate data challenges many causal inference methods that assume small numbers of variables. Climate systems involve thousands of interacting variables across multiple scales.

Nonlinear dynamics violate the linear assumptions of many causal inference methods. Climate systems exhibit threshold behaviors, regime transitions, and chaotic dynamics that complicate causal analysis.

Non-stationarity means that causal relationships may change over time as the climate system evolves, requiring methods that can detect and account for time-varying causation.

Missing data and irregular sampling complicate causal inference, particularly for paleoclimate applications where proxy data provide incomplete information about past climate states.

Scale dependence of causal relationships means that conclusions valid at one scale may not apply at other scales, requiring careful consideration of the appropriate scale for causal analysis.

Emergent causation challenges reductionist approaches to causal understanding, requiring new conceptual frameworks for understanding system-level causal properties.

Multiple realizability means that similar climate phenomena may result from different causal mechanisms in different contexts, complicating efforts to identify universal causal laws.

Computational costs of sophisticated causal inference methods can be prohibitive for large climate datasets, requiring the development of computationally efficient algorithms.

Data quality issues, including systematic errors, inhomogeneities, and bias, can lead to incorrect causal inferences, requiring careful data preprocessing and quality control.

Communication challenges arise when translating complex causal analyses into actionable information for decision makers, requiring the development of effective science communication strategies.

Causal reasoning represents both one of the greatest challenges and one of the most promising opportunities in climate science. The complex, multiscale, and interconnected nature of Earth system processes demands sophisticated approaches that go beyond traditional correlation-based analysis to establish genuine cause-and-effect relationships. This chapter has provided a comprehensive framework for understanding and applying causal reasoning methods in climate science, from fundamental theoretical concepts to advanced computational techniques.

The integration of multiple methodological approaches—combining observational causal inference, physics-based constraints, machine learning techniques, and model-based experiments—offers the most promising path forward for robust causal understanding. No single method can address all the challenges posed by climate systems, but the convergence of evidence across multiple approaches can provide compelling support for causal conclusions.

Several key principles emerge from our analysis:

- **Physical plausibility must constrain statistical inference**: While data-driven methods can reveal unexpected relationships, causal claims in climate science must ultimately be grounded in physical understanding. The most robust causal inferences combine statistical evidence with mechanistic understanding.
- **Scale matters**: Causal relationships in climate systems are inherently scale-dependent, requiring careful consideration of the spatial and temporal scales at which causal claims are made. Methods that can handle multi-scale interactions and emergent behaviors will be increasingly important.

- **Uncertainty quantification is essential:** Given the complexity of climate systems and the limitations of observational data, all causal inferences must be accompanied by honest assessments of uncertainty. Bayesian approaches and ensemble methods provide valuable frameworks for quantifying and communicating uncertainty.

- **Integration across disciplines is crucial:** Effective causal reasoning in climate science requires collaboration between statisticians, computer scientists, climate modelers, observational scientists, and domain experts. The most significant advances will come from truly interdisciplinary efforts.

Looking forward, several areas show particular promise for advancing causal reasoning in climate science. The explosion of high-resolution observational data from satellites, ground-based networks, and field campaigns provides unprecedented opportunities for causal analysis. Advanced machine learning techniques, particularly when combined with physical constraints, offer powerful tools for discovering causal relationships in high-dimensional climate data. The continuing improvement in Earth system models, including higher resolution and more comprehensive process representation, enhances our ability to test causal hypotheses through controlled experiments.

The urgency of climate change makes robust causal understanding not just a scientific goal but a societal imperative. Decisions about mitigation and adaptation strategies depend critically on our understanding of how human activities cause climate change and how climate change causes impacts on natural and human systems. The methods and principles outlined in this chapter provide the foundation for the kind of rigorous causal analysis that can support evidence-based climate policy.

As climate science continues to evolve, causal reasoning will undoubtedly play an increasingly central role. The convergence of big data, advanced computing, and sophisticated statistical methods creates unprecedented opportunities for causal discovery. At the same time, the growing recognition of climate systems as complex adaptive systems challenges us to develop new conceptual frameworks for understanding causation in these systems.

The future of causal reasoning in climate science lies not in any single methodological approach, but in the skillful integration of multiple approaches guided by physical understanding and motivated by the practical needs of society. By embracing this multifaceted approach, climate science can continue to advance our causal understanding of the Earth system and provide the robust foundation needed for addressing one of the greatest challenges of our time.

FIVE

ML and AI in Monitoring

The intersection of artificial intelligence and climate science presents one of the most promising frontiers in our endeavor to comprehend and forecast Earth's intricate climate system. As climate data volumes continue to expand exponentially and computational capabilities advance, machine learning techniques have emerged as indispensable tools for extracting meaningful patterns from extensive datasets, enhancing prediction accuracy, and expediting scientific discovery. This chapter delves into the state-of-the-art applications of neural network architectures in climate science, elucidating how these potent computational models are transforming our approach to climate prediction, pattern recognition, and system comprehension.

The climate system is characterized by nonlinear dynamics, multi-scale interactions, and intricate feedback mechanisms that operate across temporal scales ranging from seconds to millennia and spatial scales from micrometers to global dimensions. Traditional physics-based models, while foundational to climate science, encounter computational constraints and parametrization challenges when attempting to capture the full complexity of these interactions. Machine learning approaches provide complementary capabilities, excelling at pattern recognition, nonlinear mapping, and data-driven discovery of relationships that may be challenging to express analytically.

Modern climate science increasingly relies on hybrid approaches that combine the interpretability and physical consistency of process-based models with the pattern recognition capabilities and computational efficiency of machine learning algorithms. This integration has led to breakthrough applications in weather forecasting, climate projection, extreme event prediction, and the discovery of previously unknown climate phenomena. The neural network architectures discussed in this chapter—convolutional neural networks (CNNs), recurrent neural networks (RNNs), and transformer models—each bring unique strengths to different aspects of climate modeling and analysis.

Neural Network Architectures in Climate Science

Neural networks have found extensive application in climate science due to their ability to learn complex, nonlinear relationships from data without requiring explicit mathematical formulations of underlying processes. The universal approximation theorem provides the theoretical foundation for their effectiveness, stating that feedforward networks with appropriate architectures can approximate any continuous function to arbitrary precision given sufficient data and computational resources.

In climate applications, neural networks serve multiple roles: as surrogate models for computationally expensive physical simulations, as pattern recognition tools for identifying climate modes and extremes, as data assimilation algorithms for integrating observations with model predictions, and as discovery engines for uncovering hidden relationships in climate data. The choice of architecture depends critically on the nature of the climate problem, the structure of available data, and the desired balance between accuracy, interpretability, and computational efficiency.

Multi-layer perceptrons (MLPs) represent the foundational architecture for many climate applications. Their fully connected structure makes them particularly suitable for problems involving tabular climate data, statistical downscaling, and the development of parametrization schemes for physical processes that are unresolved in global climate models. In statistical downscaling applications, MLPs learn relationships between large-scale atmospheric variables and local-scale climate variables, enabling the translation of coarse-resolution global model output to fine-scale regional predictions relevant for impact assessment.

Recent advances in MLP architectures for climate applications include the development of residual connections that facilitate training of deeper networks, attention mechanisms that allow models to focus on relevant input features, and ensemble approaches that quantify prediction uncertainty. Climate-specific innovations include the incorporation of physical constraints through custom loss functions, the use of transfer learning to leverage knowledge across different climate regions, and the development of interpretability techniques that reveal which large-scale patterns most strongly influence local climate variability.

The inherent uncertainty in climate systems necessitates robust approaches to uncertainty quantification in neural network applications. Ensemble methods, including Bayesian neural networks, Monte Carlo dropout, and deep ensembles, have emerged as essential tools for quantifying predictive uncertainty in climate applications. These approaches provide not only point estimates but also confidence intervals that are crucial for climate risk assessment and decision-making under uncertainty.

Bayesian neural networks treat network weights as probability distributions rather than point estimates, enabling principled uncertainty quantification through the posterior distribution over model parameters. In climate applications, this approach has proven valuable for quantifying uncertainty in precipitation predictions, temperature projections, and extreme event probabilities. The computational overhead of Bayesian inference can be mitigated through variational approaches and modern scalable inference algorithms.

Convolutional Neural Networks have revolutionized the analysis of spatially structured climate data, leveraging their ability to detect local patterns and hierarchical features through the application of learnable convolution filters. The translation-invariant nature of convolutions makes CNNs particularly well-suited for climate applications where similar patterns may appear at different spatial locations, such as cloud formations, precipitation systems, and atmospheric waves.

The hierarchical feature extraction capability of CNNs aligns naturally with the multi-scale nature of climate phenomena. Lower layers detect local features such as gradients and edges in meteorological fields, while deeper layers combine these features to recognize larger-scale patterns like cyclones, frontal systems, and teleconnection patterns. This hierarchical processing mirrors the scale interactions inherent in climate systems, where local processes aggregate to form regional patterns that in turn influence global climate variability.

Modern CNN architectures employed in climate science extend far beyond basic convolution-pooling structures. U-Net architectures, originally developed for biomedical image segmentation, have found extensive application in climate data analysis for tasks requiring precise spatial localization, such as cloud detection, precipitation nowcasting, and the identification of extreme weather events. The skip connections in U-Net architectures preserve fine-scale spatial information while enabling the network to learn global context, a crucial capability for climate applications where both local details and large-scale patterns are important.

ResNet architectures, with their residual connections enabling the training of very deep networks, have proven particularly effective for complex climate pattern recognition tasks. Climate-specific modifications include the incorporation of dilated convolutions to capture multi-scale temporal and spatial dependencies, the use of separable convolutions to reduce computational requirements while maintaining representational capacity, and the integration of attention mechanisms that allow models to focus on climatologically relevant regions and time periods.

The unique characteristics of climate data have motivated several domain-specific innovations in CNN architectures. Spherical CNNs address the challenges associated with the spherical geometry of global climate data, avoiding the distortions inherent in map projections and providing more natural representations for global-scale phenomena. These architectures use spherical harmonics and icosahedral grids to maintain the geometric properties of Earth's surface throughout the convolution operations.

Climate data often exhibits strong seasonal cycles and long-term trends that standard CNN architectures struggle to capture effectively. Temporal convolutional networks (TCNs) extend CNNs to handle temporal dependencies through dilated causal convolutions, enabling the modeling of relationships across multiple time scales while maintaining computational efficiency. These architectures have proven particularly effective for seasonal climate prediction and the detection of climate change signals in observational records.

CNNs have achieved remarkable success in numerical weather prediction, often matching or exceeding the performance of traditional physics-based models for specific forecast tasks. The European Centre for Medium-Range Weather Forecasts has successfully deployed CNN-based post-processing systems that correct systematic biases in ensemble forecasts, improving both accuracy and reliability. These systems learn relationships between model predictions and subsequent observations, automatically adapting to model biases and seasonal variations in forecast skill.

In climate prediction applications, CNNs excel at pattern recognition tasks that inform long-range forecasting. The identification of El Niño/Southern Oscillation (ENSO) patterns from sea surface temperature anomalies, the detection of atmospheric rivers from integrated water vapor fields, and the classification of weather regimes from circulation patterns all benefit from the spatial pattern recognition capabilities of CNNs. These applications often require careful attention to data preprocessing, including detrending to focus on variability rather than long-term change, and the use of anomaly fields to emphasize patterns relative to climatological expectations.

Recurrent Neural Networks address the fundamental temporal nature of climate systems through architectures specifically designed to process sequential data and model temporal dependencies. Unlike feedforward networks that treat each input independently, RNNs maintain hidden states that carry information from previous time steps, enabling them to capture the memory effects and temporal correlations that are pervasive in climate systems.

The climate system exhibits temporal dependencies across multiple scales, from diurnal cycles and weather patterns operating on daily timescales to seasonal cycles, interannual variability associated with phenomena like ENSO, and multidecadal oscillations such as the Atlantic Multidecadal Oscillation. RNN architectures provide mechanisms for modeling these diverse temporal scales through their recurrent connections and memory capabilities, making them particularly valuable for climate prediction applications that require an understanding of how past conditions influence future states.

Long Short-Term Memory networks represent a major advancement in recurrent architectures, addressing the vanishing gradient problem that limited the ability of traditional RNNs to capture long-term dependencies. The sophisticated gating mechanisms of LSTM networks—forget gates, input gates, and output gates—provide fine-grained control over information flow, enabling the selective retention of relevant information across extended time sequences while discarding irrelevant details.

In climate applications, LSTM networks have proven particularly effective for modeling phenomena with complex temporal structures.

Seasonal climate prediction benefits from LSTM's ability to maintain information about slowly varying boundary conditions, such as sea surface temperatures and soil moisture, that influence regional climate over monthly to seasonal timescales. The forget gates allow the network to discard short-term weather variability while retaining the longer-term signals relevant for seasonal prediction, effectively filtering signal from noise in the temporal domain.

Gated Recurrent Units offer a simplified alternative to LSTM networks while maintaining much of their capacity for modeling long-term dependencies. With fewer parameters and computational requirements than LSTM networks, GRUs provide an efficient option for climate applications where computational resources are constrained or where simpler architectures may provide better generalization. The reset and update gates in GRU architectures provide mechanisms for controlling information flow that are well-suited to climate prediction tasks.

Climate-specific applications of GRU networks include the modeling of hydrological systems, where the networks learn relationships between precipitation inputs and streamflow outputs while accounting for the complex temporal dynamics of watershed processes. The simplified architecture of GRUs makes them particularly suitable for ensemble-based approaches, where multiple networks with different initializations provide uncertainty estimates for hydrological predictions.

Bidirectional RNN architectures process temporal sequences in both forward and backward directions, providing access to both past and future context when analyzing each time step. While future information is not available in real-time prediction applications, bidirectional RNNs excel in climate analysis tasks where the goal is to understand temporal patterns in historical data or to perform temporal interpolation and quality control of observational records.

Climate reanalysis applications benefit significantly from bidirectional processing, as the assimilation of observations from future time steps can improve the estimation of atmospheric states at earlier times. Similarly, the identification of climate trends and the detection of changepoints in climate time series benefit from the ability to consider both preceding and subsequent patterns when characterizing temporal evolution.

Sequence-to-sequence (seq2seq) architectures, comprising encoder and decoder RNNs, provide powerful frameworks for climate prediction tasks that involve mapping from input sequences to output sequences of potentially different lengths. The encoder RNN processes historical climate data to create a compressed representation of the system state, while the decoder RNN generates future predictions conditioned on this encoded representation.

Attention mechanisms enhance seq2seq architectures by allowing the decoder to selectively focus on different parts of the input sequence when generating each element of the output sequence. In climate applications, attention mechanisms enable models to adaptively weight the importance of different historical time periods, identifying the specific past conditions that are most relevant for predicting future climate states. This capability is particularly valuable for seasonal prediction, where the relative importance of different lead times varies depending on the predicted variable and the time of year.

Transformer Models

Transformer architectures have emerged as revolutionary tools in climate science, leveraging self-attention mechanisms to model complex relationships across both spatial and temporal dimensions without the sequential processing constraints of RNNs or the spatial locality assumptions of CNNs. The attention mechanism enables transformers to directly model dependencies between any pair of positions in input sequences, making them particularly powerful for capturing the teleconnections and non-local interactions that characterize climate systems.

The mathematical foundation of self-attention provides climate models with unprecedented flexibility in learning which spatial locations and temporal periods are most relevant for specific prediction tasks. Unlike convolution operations that are limited to local neighborhoods or recurrent connections that process information sequentially, attention mechanisms can immediately access information from any part of the input, enabling the direct modeling of phenomena such as the influence of tropical sea surface temperatures on mid-latitude weather patterns.

Vision Transformers adapt the transformer architecture to image-like data by treating climate fields as sequences of spatial patches, applying self-attention mechanisms to capture relationships between different regions of climate datasets. This approach has proven particularly effective for global climate modeling tasks, where the spherical nature of Earth requires models to understand how conditions in distant regions influence local climate through atmospheric and oceanic teleconnections.

Climate-specific modifications to ViT architectures include the development of hierarchical patch structures that capture multi-scale spatial relationships, the incorporation of geographical embeddings that encode Earth's spherical geometry, and the use of time-aware positional encodings that account for seasonal cycles and long-term climate trends. These adaptations enable ViTs to excel at tasks such as global precipitation prediction, where tropical convection patterns influence precipitation in remote regions through atmospheric wave propagation.

The extension of transformer architectures to handle both spatial and temporal dimensions simultaneously represents a significant advancement for climate modeling applications. Spatiotemporal transformers can model the complex evolution of climate patterns by treating climate data as sequences of spatial fields, applying attention mechanisms across both space and time to capture the full range of climate system interactions.

These architectures prove particularly valuable for extreme weather prediction, where the development of events like hurricanes, heat waves, and atmospheric rivers involves complex interactions between local conditions and large-scale atmospheric patterns that evolve over multiple time scales. The attention mechanism enables the model to identify the specific combinations of spatial patterns and temporal evolution that precede extreme events, providing both improved prediction accuracy and enhanced scientific understanding of extreme weather development.

The development of large-scale pre-trained transformer models specifically for climate applications represents an emerging frontier in climate AI. These foundation models, trained on comprehensive climate datasets spanning multiple decades and variables, develop rich representations of climate system behavior that can be fine-tuned for specific downstream tasks with relatively small amounts of additional training data.

Climate foundation models offer several advantages over task-specific architectures: they capture general climate system dynamics that transfer across different prediction problems, they provide robust representations that improve performance in data-sparse regions and time periods, and they enable rapid development of specialized applications through transfer learning. Recent examples include models pre-trained on global reanalysis data that achieve state-of-the-art performance when fine-tuned for regional weather prediction, seasonal forecasting, and climate impact assessment.

Multimodal Transformers for Integrated Climate Analysis

The integration of diverse climate data sources—satellite observations, ground-based measurements, model output, and ancillary datasets—benefits from multimodal transformer architectures that can jointly process heterogeneous information types. These models learn aligned representations across different data modalities, enabling improved analysis and prediction through the synergistic combination of complementary information sources.

Applications of multimodal transformers in climate science include the fusion of satellite precipitation estimates with ground-based gauge observations to produce improved precipitation analyses, the integration of atmospheric and oceanic observations for enhanced seasonal prediction, and the combination of climate model output with impact-relevant socioeconomic data for comprehensive risk assessment. The attention mechanism enables these models to automatically learn which data sources are most informative for different prediction tasks and geographical regions.

Case Studies

Seasonal climate prediction represents one of the most successful applications of machine learning in climate science, with neural network approaches consistently achieving skill levels comparable to or exceeding traditional dynamical models. The seasonal prediction problem is particularly well-suited to machine learning approaches because it involves identifying slowly evolving boundary conditions—such as sea surface temperature patterns, soil moisture, and snow cover—that provide predictability beyond the chaotic limit of weather forecasting.

Deep learning models for seasonal prediction typically employ hybrid architectures that combine the spatial pattern recognition capabilities of CNNs with the temporal modeling strengths of RNNs or transformers. These models are trained on comprehensive datasets spanning multiple decades, learning relationships between large-scale climate patterns and regional seasonal anomalies. Successful implementations include the prediction of summer monsoon rainfall over South Asia, winter temperature patterns over North America, and the seasonal evolution of Arctic sea ice extent.

The incorporation of physics-informed constraints in seasonal prediction models has led to significant improvements in both accuracy and interpretability. These constraints include the enforcement of conservation laws, the incorporation of known teleconnection patterns, and the use of physically motivated loss functions that penalize predictions inconsistent with established climate dynamics. Such approaches ensure that learned relationships remain consistent with fundamental climate principles while benefiting from the pattern recognition capabilities of neural networks.

Machine learning approaches have achieved remarkable success in the prediction and early detection of extreme weather and climate events. The spatial and temporal pattern recognition capabilities of deep learning models enable the identification of precursor conditions that lead to extremes, often revealing previously unknown relationships between large-scale climate patterns and local extreme events.

Hurricane intensity prediction has benefited significantly from CNN-based approaches that analyze satellite imagery to estimate current intensity and predict future intensification. These models learn to recognize the complex cloud patterns and atmospheric structures associated with different intensity levels, achieving accuracy levels that rival traditional statistical-dynamical approaches while providing predictions in real-time. The incorporation of environmental variables such as sea surface temperature, wind shear, and atmospheric stability further improves prediction skill.

Heat wave prediction represents another successful application area, with machine learning models learning to identify the atmospheric circulation patterns that lead to persistent high-pressure systems and associated temperature extremes. These models typically employ long-lead prediction capabilities, providing early warning of potentially dangerous heat events several weeks in advance. The combination of meteorological predictors with urban heat island effects and demographic vulnerability data enables comprehensive heat risk assessment.

Drought prediction and monitoring applications leverage the ability of machine learning models to integrate diverse data sources and identify complex relationships between meteorological, hydrological, and agricultural variables. These models typically combine precipitation and temperature observations with soil moisture, vegetation indices, and hydrological model output to provide comprehensive drought characterization.

LSTM and transformer architectures prove particularly effective for drought applications due to the inherently temporal nature of drought development and recovery. These models learn the complex relationships between precipitation deficits, evapotranspiration, soil moisture depletion, and vegetation stress that characterize different types of drought. The attention mechanisms in transformer models enable automatic identification of the most relevant time periods and geographical regions for drought prediction in specific locations.

Satellite-based drought monitoring applications employ CNN architectures to process vegetation indices, soil moisture retrievals, and land surface temperature data. These models learn to recognize the spatial patterns associated with drought impacts across different land cover types and climatic regions, providing near-real-time drought monitoring capabilities with global coverage.

Statistical downscaling represents one of the most mature applications of machine learning in climate science, with neural network approaches providing efficient alternatives to computationally expensive dynamical downscaling methods. These applications bridge the gap between coarse-resolution global climate models and fine-resolution regional information needed for impact assessment and adaptation planning.

Deep learning downscaling models typically employ hierarchical architectures that first learn relationships between large-scale atmospheric patterns and regional climate variability, then apply additional processing to capture fine-scale spatial details influenced by topography, land use, and coastal effects. Super-resolution CNN architectures, adapted from computer vision applications, prove particularly effective for spatial downscaling tasks that require generating high-resolution climate fields from coarse-resolution input data.

Temporal downscaling applications employ RNN and transformer architectures to disaggregate monthly or seasonal climate predictions to daily or hourly time scales. These models learn the statistical relationships between large-scale climate conditions and the frequency, timing, and intensity of precipitation events, enabling the generation of high-temporal-resolution weather sequences consistent with predicted seasonal climate anomalies.

The modeling of ocean-atmosphere interactions represents a frontier application for machine learning in climate science, with neural networks providing novel approaches for understanding and predicting coupled system behavior. These interactions occur across multiple time scales, from air-sea exchange processes operating on hourly time scales to decadal variations in ocean circulation that influence global climate patterns.

Neural network models of air-sea interaction typically focus on specific components of the coupled system, such as the relationship between sea surface temperatures and surface heat fluxes, the influence of ocean currents on atmospheric boundary layer properties, or the feedback between wind stress and ocean surface waves. CNN architectures excel at capturing the spatial patterns of these interactions, while RNN and transformer models handle the temporal evolution and memory effects inherent in coupled ocean-atmosphere processes.

ENSO prediction represents a particularly successful application of machine learning to ocean-atmosphere interaction modeling. Deep learning models trained on tropical Pacific sea surface temperature patterns, thermocline depth variations, and atmospheric circulation indices achieve prediction skill comparable to sophisticated coupled general circulation models while requiring orders of magnitude less computational resources. These models learn to recognize the complex spatial and temporal patterns associated with El Niño and La Niña development, providing reliable predictions up to 12-18 months in advance.

Arctic regions, experiencing rapid climate change and representing critical components of the global climate system, present unique challenges and opportunities for machine learning applications. The sparse observational coverage, extreme seasonal variations, and complex feedback processes in Arctic regions require specialized approaches that leverage the pattern recognition and extrapolation capabilities of neural networks.

Sea ice prediction represents a key application area, with CNN models learning to predict ice extent, thickness, and motion from satellite observations and atmospheric forcing data. These models capture the complex relationships between ice dynamics, thermodynamics, and atmospheric forcing that govern sea ice evolution, providing improved seasonal predictions of Arctic sea ice conditions. The incorporation of ice age and thickness information enables more accurate predictions of ice survival through the summer melt season.

Permafrost modeling applications employ deep learning approaches to predict permafrost temperature profiles and active layer thickness from surface climate data and soil properties. These models learn the complex relationships between air temperature variations, snow cover, vegetation effects, and subsurface thermal processes that control permafrost dynamics. The temporal memory capabilities of RNN architectures prove particularly important for capturing the lagged response of permafrost to surface climate variations.

Future Directions

Physics-Informed Neural Networks represent a paradigm shift in the application of machine learning to climate science, embedding physical laws directly into neural network architectures through modified loss functions that enforce conservation principles, boundary conditions, and known physical relationships. This approach addresses one of the primary limitations of traditional machine learning applications in climate science: the potential for models to learn relationships that violate fundamental physical principles.

In climate applications, PINNs have shown particular promise for modeling processes where observations are sparse but physical understanding is strong. Applications include the modeling of atmospheric wave propagation, where networks learn solutions to wave equations while fitting observational data, and the simulation of oceanic circulation patterns subject to conservation of mass and momentum.

The incorporation of physical constraints often leads to improved extrapolation capabilities and more robust performance when applied to conditions outside the training data range.

The integration of physics-based models with machine learning components represents an active area of research that leverages the complementary strengths of both approaches. Physics-based models provide interpretability, physical consistency, and well-understood behavior, while machine learning components offer improved parameterizations, bias correction capabilities, and enhanced pattern recognition.

Successful hybrid approaches include the use of neural networks to improve subgrid-scale parameterizations in climate models, machine learning-based bias correction of numerical weather prediction output, and the development of neural network emulators for computationally expensive components of Earth system models. These approaches maintain the physical realism of traditional models while benefiting from the flexibility and efficiency of machine learning techniques.

The development of robust uncertainty quantification methods for machine learning applications in climate science remains a critical research priority. Climate predictions must include reliable uncertainty estimates to support decision-making under uncertainty, and model interpretability is essential for building scientific understanding and trust in AI-based climate predictions.

Recent advances include the development of Bayesian deep learning approaches that provide principled uncertainty quantification, the use of ensemble methods that quantify model uncertainty through multiple predictions, and the application of explainable AI techniques that reveal which input features most strongly influence predictions. Climate-specific innovations include the development of physics-constrained uncertainty quantification methods and interpretability techniques that highlight climatologically relevant patterns and relationships.

The computational requirements of modern deep learning models present significant challenges for operational climate prediction applications, particularly for real-time forecasting and ensemble-based uncertainty quantification. Research in efficient architectures focuses on developing models that maintain prediction accuracy while reducing computational requirements through techniques such as network pruning, quantization, and knowledge distillation.

Edge computing applications enable the deployment of machine learning models for climate applications in resource-constrained environments, such as remote weather stations and mobile monitoring platforms. These applications require highly efficient models that can operate with minimal computational resources while maintaining acceptable prediction accuracy.

Federated learning approaches enable the training of machine learning models across distributed climate datasets without requiring data centralization. This approach is particularly valuable for climate applications involving sensitive or proprietary data, international collaborations, and situations where bandwidth limitations constrain data transfer.

Climate-specific federated learning applications include the development of global weather prediction models trained across multiple national weather services, collaborative drought monitoring systems that leverage distributed agricultural data, and privacy-preserving approaches to climate impact assessment that utilize sensitive socioeconomic datasets.

The integration of machine learning and artificial intelligence into climate science has fundamentally transformed our ability to understand, predict, and respond to climate variability and change. The neural network architectures explored in this chapter—CNNs for spatial pattern recognition, RNNs for temporal modeling, and transformers for complex relationship modeling—each contribute unique capabilities that address different aspects of climate system complexity.

The success of these approaches stems from their ability to complement traditional physics-based methods, providing enhanced pattern recognition capabilities, improved computational efficiency, and novel insights into climate system behavior. As climate data volumes continue to grow and computational capabilities advance, machine learning methods will play increasingly central roles in climate science, from operational weather prediction to long-term climate projection and impact assessment.

Future developments in climate AI will likely focus on the integration of physics-based understanding with machine learning flexibility, the development of more interpretable and trustworthy AI systems, and the creation of foundation models that can be adapted to diverse climate prediction challenges. The continued collaboration between climate scientists, machine learning researchers, and domain experts will be essential for realizing the full potential of AI in advancing climate science and supporting climate adaptation and mitigation efforts.

The case studies presented demonstrate the breadth and depth of successful machine learning applications in climate science, from seasonal prediction and extreme event forecasting to the modeling of complex ocean-atmosphere interactions. These applications illustrate not only the technical capabilities of modern AI systems but also their potential to provide actionable information for climate risk management and adaptation planning.

As we advance into an era of unprecedented climate change, the tools and techniques described in this chapter will play crucial roles in enhancing our scientific understanding of climate system behavior, improving the accuracy and reliability of climate predictions, and supporting evidence-based decision-making for climate adaptation and mitigation. The continued evolution of machine learning capabilities, combined with growing climate datasets and computational resources, promises to further accelerate progress in climate science and our collective ability to address the climate challenge.

Six

Extreme Events and Emission Monitoring

Climate change manifests most prominently through extreme weather events and altered atmospheric composition, rendering the detection, prediction, and monitoring of these phenomena crucial components of climate science and policy. This chapter delves into the application of advanced artificial intelligence and machine learning techniques to two interconnected facets of climate research: the analysis and prediction of extreme weather events, and the monitoring and assessment of greenhouse gas emissions. These applications represent some of the most societally pertinent and technically demanding challenges in contemporary climate science, necessitating sophisticated approaches capable of addressing the rarity, complexity, and high-stakes nature of extreme events while providing accurate, real-time monitoring of global carbon cycles.

Extreme weather events, by their very definition, occur infrequently but have disproportionate impacts on human societies and natural systems. Traditional statistical approaches often encounter challenges due to the limited sample sizes inherent in extreme event analysis, while physics-based models face computational constraints when attempting to resolve the multi-scale processes that drive extreme events. Machine learning approaches offer unique advantages for extreme event applications, including the capacity to learn from limited data through transfer learning, to identify subtle precursor patterns that may not be discernible through conventional analysis, and to provide rapid, automated detection and early warning capabilities.

Simultaneously, the monitoring of greenhouse gas emissions has become increasingly critical as nations and organizations seek to track progress toward climate goals and identify emission sources with unprecedented precision. Satellite-based monitoring systems generate vast quantities of data that require sophisticated analysis techniques to extract actionable information about emission sources, transport patterns, and temporal variability. AI-powered approaches enable the processing of these large datasets in near real-time, the integration of multiple observation types, and the development of emission attribution systems that can identify specific sources and quantify their contributions to atmospheric greenhouse gas concentrations.

The integration of extreme event analysis and emissions monitoring reflects the interconnected nature of climate system components. Extreme events both respond to and influence atmospheric composition through processes such as wildfire emissions, drought-induced changes in ecosystem carbon uptake, and flood-related methane emissions from wetlands and agricultural systems. Understanding these interactions requires sophisticated modeling frameworks that can simultaneously track atmospheric composition changes and extreme event occurrence, providing insights into climate system feedbacks and helping to inform both mitigation and adaptation strategies.

The detection and prediction of extreme weather events represents one of the most challenging applications in climate science, requiring methods that can identify rare events with potentially catastrophic consequences while maintaining low false alarm rates. Extreme events are characterized by their location in the statistical tails of climate distributions, their often compound nature involving multiple coincident hazards, and their dependence on processes operating across multiple spatial and temporal scales. Traditional approaches based on threshold exceedance or return period analysis provide important baseline capabilities but often fail to capture the complex, multivariate nature of extreme events or to leverage the wealth of information available in modern climate datasets.

Machine learning approaches to extreme event detection and prediction leverage several key advantages over traditional methods. Deep learning models can automatically identify complex spatial and temporal patterns associated with extreme events without requiring explicit specification of these patterns by human experts. Ensemble methods provide robust uncertainty quantification that is essential for extreme event applications where false alarms and missed events carry significant costs. Transfer learning techniques enable models trained in data-rich regions or time periods to be applied in situations where extreme event samples are limited. Multi-modal approaches can integrate diverse data sources, from satellite observations to social media feeds, providing comprehensive situational awareness for extreme event monitoring and response.

The evaluation of extreme event detection and prediction systems requires specialized metrics that account for the rarity and high impact of these events. Traditional accuracy measures can be misleading when applied to highly imbalanced datasets where extreme events represent a small fraction of total observations. Instead, extreme event applications typically employ metrics such as the Critical Success Index, which balances hits against false alarms and misses, or probability-based measures that evaluate the reliability and sharpness of probabilistic forecasts. The temporal and spatial scales of evaluation must also be carefully considered, as the utility of extreme event predictions depends critically on providing actionable information at lead times and spatial resolutions relevant for emergency management and risk reduction.

Convolutional Neural Networks have proven particularly effective for extreme event detection applications that involve analyzing spatially structured climate data. The hierarchical feature extraction capabilities of CNNs enable the identification of multi-scale patterns associated with extreme events, ranging from local-scale signatures, such as convective instability indicators, to synoptic-scale patterns, including atmospheric blocking configurations. State-of-the-art CNN architectures for extreme event detection employ attention mechanisms that allow models to focus on the most relevant spatial regions and variables, residual connections that enable training of very deep networks capable of capturing complex pattern hierarchies, and multi-scale processing that explicitly handles the scale interactions inherent in extreme weather development.

Recent innovations in CNN architectures for extreme event applications include the development of spatially adaptive convolution operations that adjust their receptive fields based on local data characteristics, enabling more effective processing of phenomena that exhibit scale-dependent behavior. Capsule networks represent another promising development, providing improved handling of spatial hierarchies and part-whole relationships that are important for understanding the structural organization of extreme weather systems. The integration of physics-informed constraints in CNN architectures ensures that learned patterns remain consistent with fundamental atmospheric dynamics while benefiting from the pattern recognition capabilities of deep learning.

Recurrent Neural Networks and their variants address the inherently temporal nature of extreme event development and evolution. Long Short-Term Memory networks excel at capturing the extended temporal dependencies that characterize many extreme events, such as the slow buildup of atmospheric blocking patterns that lead to persistent heat waves or the multi-week evolution of drought conditions. The gating mechanisms in LSTM architectures enable selective retention of information across multiple time scales, allowing models to distinguish between short-term weather variability and the longer-term patterns that provide predictability for extreme events.

Transformer architectures have emerged as particularly powerful tools for extreme event prediction, leveraging self-attention mechanisms to model complex relationships between different spatial locations and temporal periods without the sequential processing constraints of RNNs. The ability of transformers to directly model long-range dependencies makes them especially suitable for extreme event applications where precursor conditions may occur weeks or months before event onset. Vision transformers adapted for climate applications can process global weather patterns as sequences of spatial patches, identifying teleconnection patterns and remote influences that contribute to extreme event development.

Compound extreme events, involving multiple coincident or sequential hazards, represent some of the most impactful and challenging phenomena in climate risk assessment. These events can involve combinations of meteorological extremes, such as concurrent heat waves and droughts, or cascading impacts where one extreme event triggers secondary hazards, such as wildfire-induced debris flows following extreme precipitation. The detection and prediction of compound events requires sophisticated approaches that can model complex dependencies between different hazard types while accounting for their joint probability distributions and potential interaction effects.

Machine learning approaches to compound event analysis typically employ multivariate techniques that can capture complex statistical dependencies between different extreme event types. Copula-based methods provide flexible frameworks for modeling joint probability distributions of extreme events, while vine copula approaches enable the modeling of higher-dimensional dependencies involving multiple hazard types. Deep learning models can learn these complex dependencies directly from data, automatically identifying the combinations of conditions that lead to compound extremes without requiring explicit specification of dependence structures.

Graph neural networks represent an emerging approach for compound event modeling that explicitly represents the network of interactions between different components of the climate system. These models treat climate variables as nodes in a graph, with edges representing causal relationships or statistical dependencies. The message-passing mechanisms in graph neural networks enable information to propagate through the network, capturing how disturbances in one component of the climate system can cascade through interconnected pathways to produce compound extremes in distant locations or at later times.

The temporal evolution of compound events often involves complex feedback processes where the occurrence of one extreme modifies the probability of subsequent extremes. Drought conditions, for example, can increase fire risk while simultaneously reducing atmospheric moisture transport, affecting precipitation patterns and potentially reinforcing drought conditions. Dynamic Bayesian networks provide frameworks for modeling these evolving dependencies, while neural ordinary differential equations offer continuous-time approaches that can capture the smooth evolution of compound event probabilities.

The spatial heterogeneity of extreme event characteristics necessitates approaches that can adapt models trained in one region to perform effectively in other geographical areas with different climatic conditions, topography, and extreme event characteristics. Transfer learning techniques enable the leveraging of knowledge gained from data-rich regions to improve extreme event detection and prediction in areas with limited observational records or different extreme event regimes.

Domain adaptation methods address the challenge of applying extreme event models across different climate regions by learning representations that are invariant to regional differences while preserving the information necessary for extreme event detection. Adversarial training approaches can learn to remove region-specific features from model representations, creating models that generalize across different geographical areas. Multi-task learning frameworks train models to simultaneously perform extreme event detection across multiple regions, encouraging the learning of generalizable features while allowing for region-specific adaptations.

The incorporation of physical constraints and climate knowledge in transfer learning applications helps ensure that adapted models remain physically reasonable when applied to new regions. Physics-informed transfer learning approaches use known atmospheric dynamics to guide the adaptation process, ensuring that model behavior remains consistent with fundamental physical principles across different climate regimes. Uncertainty quantification becomes particularly important in transfer learning applications, as model confidence may vary significantly when applied to regions or conditions that differ substantially from training data.

Hurricanes and Tropical Cyclones

Tropical cyclone detection and tracking represents one of the most mature and successful applications of machine learning in extreme weather analysis. The distinctive spatial patterns and evolutionary characteristics of tropical cyclones make them particularly amenable to automated detection using computer vision techniques, while their significant societal impacts provide strong motivation for improved prediction capabilities. Modern machine learning approaches to hurricane detection and tracking leverage high-resolution satellite imagery, numerical weather prediction model output, and multi-sensor observations to provide accurate, real-time monitoring of tropical cyclone activity across global ocean basins.

Convolutional Neural Networks trained on satellite imagery have achieved remarkable success in automated hurricane detection, often exceeding the accuracy of traditional detection algorithms while providing more consistent and objective assessments. These models learn to recognize the characteristic spiral structure, eye formation, and cloud patterns associated with tropical cyclones at different intensity levels and developmental stages. The incorporation of multiple satellite channels, including infrared, visible, and microwave observations, enables robust detection capabilities that are less sensitive to time of day, cloud cover, and atmospheric conditions that can affect single-channel approaches.

Advanced CNN architectures for hurricane detection employ several domain-specific innovations that improve performance for tropical cyclone applications. Multi-scale processing enables the simultaneous detection of the compact inner core structure and the broader circulation patterns that characterize tropical cyclones. Attention mechanisms allow models to focus on the most relevant spatial regions and atmospheric features, automatically adapting to different storm characteristics and environmental conditions. Temporal consistency constraints ensure that detected storms exhibit realistic movement and intensity evolution, reducing false detections and improving tracking accuracy.

The integration of numerical weather prediction model output with satellite observations provides enhanced detection capabilities that leverage both observational accuracy and model-based understanding of atmospheric dynamics. Ensemble-based approaches use multiple detection models trained on different data sources or with different architectures to provide robust detection capabilities and uncertainty quantification. These ensemble methods can identify situations where detection confidence is low, flagging potential storms that require additional analysis or triggering enhanced observational strategies.

Hurricane intensity estimation and prediction represent a particularly challenging aspect of tropical cyclone forecasting, with significant implications for storm surge prediction, evacuation planning, and impact assessment. Traditional intensity estimation methods rely primarily on satellite-based techniques that analyze cloud top temperatures, wind shear measurements, and structural characteristics to infer maximum sustained winds and central pressure. Machine learning approaches offer enhanced capabilities for intensity estimation through their ability to learn complex relationships between observable characteristics and storm intensity while integrating multiple data sources and accounting for environmental influences.

Deep learning models for intensity estimation typically employ CNN architectures that process multi-channel satellite imagery to estimate current storm intensity and predict future intensity changes. These models learn to recognize subtle cloud patterns, eye characteristics, and structural features that correlate with different intensity levels, often achieving accuracy levels that rival or surpass those of operational analysis techniques. The incorporation of environmental data such as sea surface temperatures, wind shear, and atmospheric stability provides additional predictive capability for intensity forecasting applications.

Recent advances in hurricane intensity prediction include the development of sequence-to-sequence models that predict intensity evolution over multiple time steps, enabling forecasts of rapid intensification and weakening events that are critical for emergency planning. These models employ LSTM or transformer architectures to capture the temporal dependencies involved in intensity changes, learning relationships between current storm characteristics, environmental conditions, and future intensity evolution.

The prediction of rapid intensification events represents a particular focus area due to their significant impact on forecast accuracy and emergency preparedness. Machine learning models for rapid intensification prediction typically employ ensemble approaches that provide probabilistic forecasts of intensification likelihood, enabling more nuanced risk assessment than traditional deterministic approaches. Feature importance analysis reveals which combinations of storm and environmental characteristics are most predictive of rapid intensification, providing insights that inform both operational forecasting and scientific understanding of tropical cyclone dynamics.

Multi-modal approaches to intensity prediction integrate satellite observations with aircraft reconnaissance data, ocean observations, and numerical model output to provide comprehensive assessments of storm intensity and evolution potential. These models learn to weight different data sources based on their reliability and relevance for different storm situations, automatically adapting to data availability and quality variations that are common in operational environments.

Storm surge represents the most dangerous aspect of many tropical cyclones, responsible for the majority of hurricane-related fatalities and causing extensive coastal damage. The prediction of storm surge requires sophisticated modeling that accounts for storm characteristics, coastal geometry, bathymetry, and astronomical tides. Machine learning approaches to storm surge prediction offer computational efficiency advantages over traditional physics-based models while enabling rapid ensemble-based uncertainty quantification and real-time updating as storm characteristics evolve.

Neural network models for storm surge prediction typically employ hybrid architectures that combine the spatial processing capabilities of

CNNs with the temporal modeling strengths of RNNs to predict surge heights and inundation patterns based on storm track, intensity, and coastal characteristics. These models learn relationships between storm parameters and surge response that account for nonlinear interactions between storm size, forward speed, approach angle, and coastal geometry. The incorporation of high-resolution digital elevation models and bathymetric data enables detailed prediction of inundation extent and depth across complex coastal landscapes.

Transfer learning approaches enable storm surge models trained in one coastal region to be adapted for application in other areas with different coastal characteristics. These methods learn generalizable relationships between storm characteristics and surge response while accounting for regional differences in coastal geometry, bathymetry, and tidal ranges. Domain adaptation techniques ensure that transferred models remain accurate when applied to coastal regions with different characteristics from their training data.

Real-time storm surge prediction systems employ ensemble neural networks that provide probabilistic surge forecasts with quantified uncertainty. These systems update predictions as new storm information becomes available, providing emergency managers with continuously refined assessments of surge risk and inundation potential. The computational efficiency of neural network approaches enables high-resolution ensemble predictions that would be computationally prohibitive using traditional physics-based surge models.

The integration of social vulnerability and infrastructure data with physical surge predictions enables a comprehensive impact assessment that considers both hazard intensity and community resilience.

Machine learning models can learn relationships between physical surge characteristics and various impact metrics, including building damage, infrastructure disruption, and evacuation requirements. These integrated approaches provide decision-support tools that help emergency managers optimize resource allocation and response strategies.

Hurricane track prediction has seen significant improvements through the application of machine learning techniques that can identify subtle patterns in atmospheric flow and storm behavior that influence future movement. Track prediction models must account for the complex interactions between tropical cyclone circulation and the large-scale atmospheric flow, including steering currents, beta drift effects, and interactions with topographic features. Machine learning approaches offer enhanced capability for identifying these complex relationships and providing probabilistic track forecasts with well-calibrated uncertainty estimates.

Ensemble neural networks for track prediction typically employ multiple model architectures and training datasets to provide robust uncertainty quantification. These ensemble approaches recognize that track prediction uncertainty arises from multiple sources, including observational uncertainty in current storm position and intensity, uncertainty in atmospheric flow patterns, and model uncertainty in the relationships governing storm movement. By explicitly modeling these uncertainty sources, ensemble methods provide probabilistic track forecasts that better support risk-based decision making.

Graph neural networks represent an innovative approach to track prediction that models the tropical cyclone as a node in a dynamic network of atmospheric interactions. These models explicitly represent the relationships between storm circulation and environmental flow patterns, enabling more sophisticated modeling of storm-environment interactions that influence track behavior. The message-passing mechanisms in graph neural networks allow information about large-scale atmospheric patterns to influence local storm behavior predictions, capturing teleconnections and remote influences that traditional models may miss.

Long-range track prediction, extending beyond the traditional 5-day forecast horizon, represents a frontier application where machine learning approaches show particular promise. Extended-range track prediction requires models that can capture the slowly evolving atmospheric patterns that influence storm behavior over weekly to seasonal time scales. Transformer architectures, with their ability to model long-range dependencies, have shown success in extended-range applications, providing track guidance that helps inform seasonal hurricane risk assessment and climate adaptation planning.

The verification and calibration of probabilistic track forecasts requires specialized approaches that account for the spatial and temporal correlation structure of track errors. Machine learning models for track prediction must be carefully calibrated to ensure that predicted uncertainty levels accurately reflect actual forecast skill, enabling reliable risk assessment and decision support. Post-processing techniques, including quantile regression and distributional modeling, provide methods for calibrating track forecast uncertainty and ensuring reliable probabilistic predictions.

Droughts and Floods

Drought represents one of the most complex and impactful extreme events, characterized by multiple dimensions including meteorological, agricultural, hydrological, and socioeconomic aspects that evolve over different spatial and temporal scales. Unlike rapid-onset events such as hurricanes, drought develops slowly through the accumulation of precipitation deficits and the gradual depletion of water stores in soil, groundwater, and surface water systems. This complex temporal evolution and multi-faceted nature make drought detection and characterization particularly well-suited to machine learning approaches that can integrate diverse data sources and identify subtle patterns across multiple variables and time scales.

Traditional drought indices, such as the Standardized Precipitation Index and Palmer Drought Severity Index, provide valuable baseline measures but often capture only single aspects of drought conditions and may not reflect the full complexity of drought impacts on different sectors and systems. Machine learning approaches enable the development of more comprehensive drought characterization methods that can integrate meteorological, hydrological, agricultural, and remote sensing data to provide multidimensional assessments of drought conditions and impacts.

Deep learning models for drought detection typically employ architectures that can handle the multi-scale spatial and temporal patterns associated with drought development and propagation. Convolutional neural networks process gridded datasets of precipitation, temperature, soil moisture, and vegetation indices to identify spatial patterns of drought development. Recurrent neural networks capture the temporal evolution of drought conditions, learning to distinguish between short-term dry spells and the sustained precipitation deficits that characterize true drought conditions.

Attention-based architectures provide particular advantages for drought applications by enabling models to automatically identify the most relevant spatial regions and temporal periods for characterizing drought conditions in specific locations. These models can learn to weight different data sources and time periods based on their relevance for different types of drought and impact sectors, providing more nuanced and context-specific drought assessments.

The integration of satellite remote sensing data provides unprecedented capabilities for drought monitoring at global scales with high spatial and temporal resolution. Machine learning models can process multiple satellite-derived variables, including vegetation indices, land surface temperature, soil moisture retrievals, and evapotranspiration estimates, to provide comprehensive assessments of drought conditions across different land cover types and climate regions. These models learn to recognize the spectral and temporal signatures associated with different drought severities and impact types, enabling near real-time drought monitoring with global coverage.

Flash floods represent one of the most dangerous weather-related hazards, developing rapidly in response to intense precipitation events and causing significant damage to life and property. The rapid onset and localized nature of flash floods make them particularly challenging for traditional forecasting approaches, which often lack the spatial and temporal resolution necessary to capture the small-scale processes that drive flash flood development. Machine learning approaches offer enhanced capabilities for flash flood prediction through their ability to process high-resolution data streams, identify complex relationships between meteorological and hydrological variables, and provide real-time risk assessments.

The prediction of flash floods requires models that can rapidly process diverse data sources and identify the combinations of conditions that lead to dangerous runoff and flooding. These conditions include not only precipitation intensity and duration but also antecedent soil moisture, topographic characteristics, land use patterns, and drainage network properties. Machine learning models can automatically learn these complex relationships from historical data, identifying subtle patterns and thresholds that may not be apparent through traditional analysis methods.

Convolutional neural networks for flash flood prediction typically process high-resolution precipitation observations and forecasts along with static geographic data such as digital elevation models, soil properties, and land use classifications. These models learn to recognize the spatial patterns of precipitation that, combined with specific landscape characteristics, are most likely to produce dangerous flash flooding. The incorporation of radar-based precipitation estimates provides the high spatial and temporal resolution necessary for effective flash flood prediction at local scales.

Real-time flash flood warning systems employ streaming data architectures that can process continuous data feeds from weather radar, rain gauges, stream gauges, and satellite observations. Machine learning models integrated into these systems provide automated threat detection capabilities that can issue warnings within minutes of hazardous conditions developing. These systems typically employ ensemble approaches that provide probabilistic flood risk assessments, enabling more nuanced risk communication and decision support.

The incorporation of social media and crowdsourced data provides additional capabilities for flash flood detection and impact assessment. Natural language processing techniques can analyze social media posts to identify flood-related reports and extract information about flood extent, depth, and impacts. Computer vision methods can analyze user-submitted photographs and videos to assess flood conditions and validate model predictions. These crowdsourced approaches provide valuable real-time information that can complement traditional observational systems and improve situational awareness during flash flood events.

Urban environments present unique challenges for flood prediction due to the complex interactions between natural hydrological processes and engineered infrastructure systems. Urban floods can result from multiple causes, including overwhelmed stormwater systems, riverine flooding, coastal storm surge, and groundwater emergence, often involving compound events where multiple flood sources occur simultaneously. Machine learning approaches to urban flood modeling offer enhanced capabilities for integrating diverse data sources and modeling the complex interactions between meteorological forcing, urban infrastructure, and flood response.

Graph neural networks provide particularly powerful frameworks for urban flood modeling by explicitly representing the network structure of urban drainage systems and the spatial relationships between different components of the urban environment. These models treat urban areas as networks of interconnected nodes representing drainage infrastructure, land use areas, and flood-prone locations, with edges representing flow pathways and hydraulic connections. The message-passing mechanisms in graph neural networks enable information about upstream conditions to propagate through the network, capturing the cascade of impacts that characterize urban flood development.

The integration of Internet of Things sensor networks with machine learning models provides unprecedented capabilities for real-time urban flood monitoring and prediction. Smart city infrastructure increasingly includes dense networks of water level sensors, flow meters, and precipitation gauges that generate continuous data streams about urban hydrological conditions. Machine learning models can process these data streams in real-time to provide early warning of flood conditions and optimal control of stormwater infrastructure such as retention ponds, pumping stations, and storm gates.

Digital twin approaches combine real-time sensor data with detailed urban models to provide comprehensive flood prediction and management capabilities. These systems employ machine learning models trained on historical data and continuously updated with real-time observations to predict flood development and evaluate the effectiveness of different flood management strategies. The integration of hydraulic models with machine learning components enables physically consistent flood predictions while benefiting from the pattern recognition and computational efficiency advantages of artificial intelligence approaches.

Climate change adaptation applications of urban flood modeling focus on assessing how changing precipitation patterns and extreme event characteristics will affect urban flood risk. Machine learning models trained on current climate conditions can be adapted to future climate scenarios through transfer learning approaches that account for changing statistical relationships between meteorological forcing and flood response. These applications provide critical information for urban planning and infrastructure design under changing climate conditions.

Regional-scale drought and flood prediction requires models that can capture the large-scale atmospheric and oceanic patterns that influence regional hydrological conditions while providing predictions at spatial and temporal scales relevant for water resource management and agricultural planning. These applications typically involve prediction time horizons ranging from seasonal to annual scales, requiring models that can leverage slowly varying boundary conditions such as sea surface temperatures, soil moisture, and snow cover to provide predictability beyond the weather time scale.

Seasonal drought prediction models typically employ hybrid architectures that combine the pattern recognition capabilities of CNNs with the temporal modeling strengths of RNNs or transformers. These models learn relationships between large-scale climate patterns, such as El Niño/Southern Oscillation indices, sea surface temperature anomalies, and atmospheric circulation patterns, and regional drought conditions. The incorporation of land surface variables such as soil moisture and vegetation conditions provides additional predictability sources that are particularly important for agricultural drought applications.

Continental-scale flood prediction systems employ machine learning models that can process vast datasets of meteorological observations and forecasts to identify regions at elevated flood risk. These models typically focus on riverine flooding associated with large-scale precipitation events, snowmelt, or persistent wet patterns. The computational efficiency of machine learning approaches enables the processing of ensemble forecast datasets to provide probabilistic flood risk assessments across large geographical areas.

Transfer learning approaches enable regional drought and flood prediction models to leverage information from multiple geographical regions and climate regimes. These methods learn generalizable relationships between large-scale climate patterns and regional hydrological conditions while accounting for regional differences in climate sensitivity, land surface characteristics, and hydrological response. Cross-regional validation approaches ensure that transferred models maintain accuracy when applied to regions with different climate characteristics from their training data.

The integration of socioeconomic and agricultural data with physical drought and flood predictions enables a comprehensive impact assessment that considers both hazard characteristics and community vulnerability. Machine learning models can learn relationships between physical drought and flood conditions and various impact metrics, including agricultural losses, water supply disruptions, and economic impacts. These integrated approaches provide decision-support tools that help water managers, agricultural producers, and emergency planners optimize resource allocation and risk management strategies.

Heatwaves and Cold Spells

Temperature extremes, including both heatwaves and cold spells, represent critical components of climate risk that have significant impacts on human health, energy systems, agriculture, and natural ecosystems. The detection and attribution of temperature extremes requires sophisticated approaches that can distinguish between natural climate variability and anthropogenic climate change influences while accounting for the multiple spatial and temporal scales over which temperature extremes develop and persist. Machine learning approaches offer enhanced capabilities for extreme temperature analysis through their ability to identify complex patterns in large climate datasets and to model the nonlinear relationships between different climate system components that influence extreme temperature occurrence.

The detection of temperature extremes involves challenges related to the definition of extreme events, which can vary depending on geographical location, season, and impact sector. Traditional approaches based on fixed temperature thresholds or statistical percentiles may not adequately capture the relative nature of extreme events or their impacts on adapted systems. Machine learning approaches enable more sophisticated extreme event detection that can account for local climate conditions, seasonal cycles, and adaptation levels while maintaining consistency across different regions and time periods.

Convolutional neural networks for extreme temperature detection typically process gridded temperature datasets along with related meteorological variables to identify spatial patterns associated with extreme events. These models learn to recognize the characteristic atmospheric circulation patterns, such as atmospheric blocking configurations or persistent ridge patterns, that lead to sustained temperature extremes. The incorporation of multiple variables, including geopotential heights, wind patterns, and moisture content, enables more robust detection that captures the synoptic-scale processes driving extreme temperatures.

Attribution analysis, which seeks to quantify the influence of anthropogenic climate change on specific extreme events, represents a particularly challenging application where machine learning methods show significant promise. Traditional attribution approaches rely on large ensembles of climate model simulations to estimate the probability of extreme events under different scenarios. Machine learning approaches can enhance attribution analysis by identifying the specific patterns and processes associated with extreme events and by quantifying how these patterns have changed under anthropogenic forcing.

Causal inference methods provide frameworks for attribution analysis that can identify the causal relationships between anthropogenic forcing and extreme event characteristics. These approaches employ techniques such as do-calculus and causal discovery algorithms to distinguish between correlation and causation in climate data, enabling more robust attribution statements. The integration of observational data with climate model output through transfer learning approaches provides enhanced capabilities for attribution analysis that leverage both observational accuracy and model-based understanding of the climate system response to forcing.

The prediction of heat-related health impacts requires models that can translate meteorological conditions into physiologically relevant measures of heat stress while accounting for population vulnerability, adaptation measures, and healthcare system capacity. Traditional heat stress indices, such as the heat index and wet-bulb globe temperature, provide valuable baseline measures but may not fully capture the complexity of human thermal response or the factors that influence population vulnerability to heat-related illness.

Machine learning approaches to heat stress prediction offer enhanced capabilities through their ability to integrate diverse data sources and learn complex relationships between meteorological conditions, environmental factors, and health outcomes. These models can process meteorological variables such as temperature, humidity, wind speed, and solar radiation along with urban heat island effects, air quality conditions, and population characteristics to provide comprehensive heat risk assessments.

Deep learning models for heat stress prediction typically employ architectures that can handle the multi-scale spatial patterns associated with heat exposure and the temporal evolution of heat stress conditions. Urban-scale models must account for the significant spatial variability in heat exposure within cities, incorporating factors such as building density, vegetation cover, surface materials, and shade availability. These models learn to recognize the combinations of meteorological and urban environmental factors that produce dangerous heat stress conditions in different parts of urban areas.

The integration of real-time health surveillance data with meteorological observations enables the development of models that can predict heat-related health impacts with improved accuracy and timeliness. These models learn relationships between heat stress conditions and various health outcomes, including emergency department visits, hospital admissions, and mortality rates. Machine learning approaches can identify vulnerable populations and geographic areas that experience disproportionate health impacts from heat events, enabling targeted intervention and resource allocation strategies.

Early warning systems for heat-related health impacts employ machine learning models that provide probabilistic forecasts of health risk levels based on meteorological predictions and population vulnerability characteristics. These systems typically provide warnings at multiple temporal scales, from short-term alerts for imminent dangerous conditions to seasonal outlooks that inform public health planning and resource allocation. The integration of uncertainty quantification enables more nuanced risk communication that accounts for forecast confidence levels.

Temperature extremes have significant impacts on agricultural systems through their effects on crop growth, development, and yield. Heat stress can reduce crop yields through multiple pathways, including reduced photosynthesis, increased respiration, accelerated senescence, and impaired reproductive processes. Cold spells can cause frost damage, delay planting and harvesting, and reduce crop survival. Machine learning approaches to agricultural impact assessment offer enhanced capabilities for predicting these impacts and informing adaptation strategies through their ability to integrate diverse data sources and model complex crop-environment interactions.

Crop yield prediction models employ machine learning architectures that can process meteorological data, remote sensing observations, and management information to predict agricultural productivity under different temperature extreme scenarios. These models learn relationships between weather conditions, crop development stages, and yield outcomes that account for the nonlinear and threshold responses characteristic of crop systems. The incorporation of remote sensing data provides real-time information about crop conditions and stress levels, enhancing prediction accuracy.

Process-based crop models provide a mechanistic understanding of crop responses to environmental conditions but often require extensive parameterization and computational resources. Machine learning approaches can enhance process-based models by providing data-driven parameterizations, bias correction capabilities, and efficient emulation of computationally expensive model components. Hybrid approaches that combine process-based understanding with machine learning flexibility provide improved prediction capabilities while maintaining interpretability and physical realism.

Regional agricultural impact assessment requires models that can scale from field-level crop responses to regional agricultural productivity assessments. These models must account for the spatial variability in crop types, management practices, soil conditions, and climate exposure while providing predictions at scales relevant for food security and economic analysis. Transfer learning approaches enable models trained in data-rich agricultural regions to be adapted for application in areas with limited observational data.

Climate change adaptation applications focus on assessing how changing extreme temperature characteristics will affect agricultural productivity and identifying effective adaptation strategies. Machine learning models can evaluate the effectiveness of different adaptation measures, such as modified planting dates, crop variety selection, and irrigation strategies, under projected climate conditions. These applications provide critical information for agricultural planning and food security assessment under changing climate conditions.

Cold waves and extreme cold events present significant challenges for energy systems, transportation infrastructure, and human health, particularly in regions where such events are infrequent and systems are not fully adapted to extreme cold conditions. The analysis and prediction of cold waves requires models that can capture the atmospheric circulation patterns and air mass characteristics that lead to sustained cold conditions while accounting for the impacts of these events on various infrastructure and societal systems.

The detection of cold wave events involves challenges related to the relative nature of extreme cold, which must be defined in terms of local climate conditions and adaptation levels. Machine learning approaches enable more sophisticated cold wave detection that accounts for factors such as seasonal timing, duration, and intensity while maintaining consistency across different climate regions. These models can learn to recognize the characteristic atmospheric patterns associated with cold air outbreaks, including Arctic air mass movements, polar vortex disruptions, and persistent trough patterns.

Energy system impact prediction represents a critical application for cold wave analysis, as extreme cold events can lead to surges in heating demand that stress electricity generation and distribution systems. Machine learning models for energy demand prediction during cold waves learn relationships between temperature conditions, building characteristics, and energy consumption patterns. These models must account for nonlinear relationships between temperature and energy demand, including threshold effects where demand increases rapidly below certain temperature levels.

The integration of weather prediction models with energy system models enables a comprehensive assessment of the impacts of cold waves on energy infrastructure. Machine learning approaches can identify the meteorological conditions most likely to cause energy system stress and provide early warning of potential supply-demand imbalances. These models support energy system operators in optimizing generation scheduling, demand response programs, and emergency preparedness measures.

Infrastructure vulnerability assessment during cold waves requires models that can predict the impacts of extreme cold on various infrastructure systems, including transportation, water supply, and telecommunications. Machine learning models can learn relationships between cold wave characteristics and infrastructure performance, identifying vulnerable components and informing resilience planning. The integration of infrastructure monitoring data with meteorological observations provides enhanced capabilities for real-time impact assessment and response coordination.

Uncertainty Quantification in Extreme Events

The inherent uncertainty in extreme event prediction necessitates sophisticated approaches to uncertainty quantification that can provide decision-makers with reliable assessments of prediction confidence and risk levels. Traditional deterministic forecasting approaches, while valuable for providing single-valued predictions, often fail to capture the full range of possible outcomes and may provide false confidence in situations where prediction uncertainty is high. Probabilistic forecasting methods address these limitations by providing complete probability distributions over possible outcomes, enabling risk-based decision making and more robust emergency planning.

The sources of uncertainty in extreme event prediction are multiple and complex, including observational uncertainty in initial conditions, model uncertainty in representing physical processes, and scenario uncertainty related to future emission pathways and adaptation measures. Bayesian approaches provide principled frameworks for representing and propagating these different uncertainty sources through prediction systems. Deep learning models can incorporate Bayesian treatments through techniques such as variational inference, Monte Carlo dropout, and ensemble methods that provide posterior distributions over model predictions.

Ensemble forecasting represents one of the most successful approaches to uncertainty quantification in extreme event prediction. Traditional ensemble methods, based on multiple runs of numerical weather prediction models with perturbed initial conditions or model physics, provide estimates of forecast uncertainty through the spread of ensemble members. Machine learning approaches enhance ensemble forecasting through post-processing techniques that can calibrate ensemble predictions, correct systematic biases, and provide improved uncertainty estimates.

Neural network ensemble methods employ multiple model architectures, training procedures, or data samples to generate diverse predictions that capture different aspects of prediction uncertainty. Deep ensemble methods train multiple neural networks with different random initializations to capture uncertainty arising from the optimization process. Bayesian neural networks treat network weights as probability distributions, providing principled uncertainty quantification through the posterior distribution over model parameters. These approaches enable the quantification of both epistemic uncertainty (model uncertainty) and aleatoric uncertainty (data uncertainty), providing comprehensive uncertainty estimates for extreme event prediction.

Extreme Value Theory provides the mathematical foundation for analyzing rare events and has been extensively developed for climate applications. The integration of EVT with machine learning approaches offers enhanced capabilities for extreme event analysis by combining the theoretical rigor of EVT with the pattern recognition capabilities of modern AI systems. This integration is particularly valuable for extreme event applications where the rarity of events makes traditional machine learning approaches challenging due to limited training data.

Generalized Extreme Value distributions and Peaks-Over-Threshold models provide established frameworks for modeling extreme event statistics, but these traditional approaches often assume stationarity and may not capture the complex dependencies between extreme events and environmental conditions. Machine learning approaches can enhance EVT applications by providing non-stationary models where distribution parameters vary as functions of covariates, enabling the modeling of how extreme event characteristics change with environmental conditions or anthropogenic forcing.

Neural network implementations of extreme value models employ architectures that can learn complex relationships between environmental covariates and extreme value distribution parameters. These models can capture nonlinear relationships between climate variables and extreme event characteristics while maintaining the theoretical foundation provided by extreme value theory. The incorporation of physical constraints ensures that learned relationships remain consistent with established extreme value principles while benefiting from the flexibility of neural network approaches.

Deep learning approaches to extreme value analysis typically employ specialized loss functions based on extreme value likelihood functions, ensuring that models are optimized for extreme event prediction rather than overall accuracy measures, which non-extreme conditions can dominate. These approaches often employ importance sampling or other techniques to ensure adequate representation of extreme events in training datasets, addressing the class imbalance problems that are inherent in extreme event applications.

Monte Carlo methods provide powerful frameworks for uncertainty quantification in extreme event prediction through the generation of large ensembles of possible scenarios that capture the full range of potential outcomes. These approaches are particularly valuable for compound event analysis, where the joint probability distributions of multiple variables are complex and may not be well-represented by analytical approaches. Machine learning models can enhance Monte Carlo applications by providing efficient generators for extreme event scenarios and by enabling the exploration of high-dimensional uncertainty spaces.

Generative adversarial networks represent an emerging approach for extreme event scenario generation that can learn to produce realistic extreme event scenarios from historical data. These models employ adversarial training procedures where a generator network learns to produce synthetic extreme event scenarios while a discriminator network learns to distinguish between real and synthetic events. The resulting generator can produce large ensembles of realistic extreme event scenarios for uncertainty quantification and risk assessment applications.

Variational auto-encoders provide alternative approaches to extreme event scenario generation that can learn compressed representations of extreme event patterns and generate new scenarios by sampling from learned latent spaces. These models are particularly valuable for applications involving high-dimensional data, such as spatial patterns of extreme precipitation or temperature, where traditional Monte Carlo approaches may be computationally prohibitive.

Physics-informed generative models incorporate physical constraints and conservation laws into scenario generation procedures, ensuring that synthetic extreme event scenarios remain physically realistic while exploring the full range of possible outcomes. These approaches combine the efficiency of generative modeling with the physical realism required for climate applications, providing enhanced capabilities for uncertainty quantification and risk assessment.

Bayesian methods provide comprehensive frameworks for extreme event prediction that can integrate multiple sources of information while providing principled uncertainty quantification. These approaches treat all model parameters as probability distributions and update these distributions as new information becomes available, providing dynamic prediction systems that can adapt to changing conditions and incorporate new observational data.

Bayesian neural networks for extreme event prediction employ variational inference or Markov Chain Monte Carlo methods to approximate posterior distributions over network weights. These approaches provide prediction intervals and probability distributions that quantify both model uncertainty and data uncertainty. The incorporation of informative priors based on physical understanding can improve prediction performance in data-sparse situations and ensure that model behavior remains physically reasonable.

Hierarchical Bayesian models enable the sharing of information across multiple extreme event prediction tasks, allowing models trained on data from one region or event type to inform predictions for other situations. These approaches are particularly valuable for rare extreme events where data limitations make single-task learning challenging. Multi-task learning within Bayesian frameworks enables the leveraging of information across different but related prediction problems while maintaining appropriate uncertainty quantification.

Sequential Bayesian updating provides frameworks for real-time extreme event prediction that can continuously incorporate new observations and update prediction distributions as conditions evolve. These approaches are particularly valuable for rapidly evolving extreme events where early warning systems must provide continuously updated risk assessments based on the latest available information.

Modern early warning systems must address the increasing complexity of climate-related hazards, including single extreme events, compound events involving multiple coincident hazards, and cascading events where one extreme triggers secondary impacts. The development of multi-hazard early warning systems requires sophisticated architectures that can simultaneously monitor multiple hazard types, assess their potential interactions, and provide integrated risk communications that support effective decision-making across different sectors and time scales.

Machine learning approaches enable the development of integrated early warning systems that can process diverse data streams and provide unified threat assessments across multiple hazard types. These systems typically employ modular architectures where specialized models for different hazard types are integrated through ensemble methods or multi-task learning frameworks. The integration enables the identification of compound and cascading hazard scenarios that might be missed by single-hazard approaches while maintaining the specialized capabilities required for effective individual hazard prediction.

Graph neural networks provide particularly powerful frameworks for multi-hazard early warning by explicitly modeling the relationships and dependencies between different hazard types and impact sectors. These models treat hazards, vulnerable systems, and impact pathways as nodes in a network, with edges representing causal relationships and interaction effects. The message-passing mechanisms enable information about one hazard type to influence predictions for related hazards, capturing the cascading and compounding effects that characterize many extreme events.

Real-time data fusion represents a critical component of multi-hazard early warning systems, requiring approaches that can integrate observations from multiple sensor types, satellite platforms, and monitoring networks. Machine learning models for data fusion learn to optimally combine information from different sources while accounting for varying data quality, temporal resolution, and spatial coverage. Attention mechanisms enable models to adaptively weight different data sources based on their reliability and relevance for specific hazard situations.

The effectiveness of early warning systems depends critically on their ability to provide timely and accurate alerts based on real-time monitoring of hazard conditions. Modern monitoring systems must process continuous data streams from multiple sources, including weather observations, satellite imagery, social media feeds, and sensor networks, to provide situational awareness and trigger appropriate warning actions. Machine learning approaches offer enhanced capabilities for real-time monitoring through their ability to process high-volume data streams and identify complex patterns indicative of developing hazard conditions.

Streaming data architectures enable the continuous processing of real-time observations for hazard detection and characterization. These systems typically employ edge computing approaches that perform initial data processing and pattern recognition at or near data collection points, reducing latency and bandwidth requirements while enabling rapid response to developing hazard conditions. Machine learning models deployed at edge nodes can perform initial hazard detection and classification, triggering more detailed analysis when potential threats are identified.

Anomaly detection algorithms play a crucial role in early warning systems by identifying unusual patterns or conditions that may indicate developing hazard situations. These approaches learn normal patterns of variability from historical data and flag situations where current conditions deviate significantly from expected ranges. Machine learning anomaly detection methods can identify subtle patterns that may not trigger traditional threshold-based warning systems while providing robust performance across different environmental conditions and seasonal variations.

Alert generation systems must balance the competing objectives of providing timely warnings while minimizing false alarms that can reduce public trust and response effectiveness. Machine learning approaches enable the development of sophisticated alert generation algorithms that can optimize this trade-off through the use of cost-sensitive learning approaches that explicitly account for the relative costs of missed events versus false alarms. These systems can automatically adjust alert thresholds based on current conditions, forecast confidence, and the potential consequences of different decision outcomes.

Traditional hazard-focused early warning systems provide information about physical hazard characteristics but may not effectively communicate the potential impacts and risks associated with extreme events. Impact-based forecasting represents an evolution toward early warning systems that provide information about expected impacts on specific sectors, infrastructure systems, and vulnerable populations. Machine learning approaches enable the development of impact-based forecasting systems that can learn complex relationships between hazard characteristics and various impact metrics while accounting for vulnerability and exposure factors that influence impact severity.

Impact prediction models typically employ multi-modal architectures that integrate hazard forecasts with information about exposed systems, vulnerability characteristics, and protective measures. These models learn relationships between hazard intensity, duration, and spatial extent and various impact metrics, including infrastructure damage, service disruptions, health impacts, and economic losses. The incorporation of vulnerability data enables models to provide spatially explicit impact predictions that account for differences in adaptive capacity and exposure across different communities and regions.

Risk communication represents a critical component of impact-based early warning systems, requiring approaches that can translate complex technical information into actionable guidance for different user communities. Natural language generation techniques enable the automatic creation of customized warning messages that are tailored to specific audiences and communication channels. These systems can generate technical briefings for emergency managers, public warnings for general audiences, and specialized guidance for critical infrastructure operators, each optimized for the information needs and communication preferences of different user groups.

Visualization and decision-support tools provide enhanced capabilities for risk communication through interactive displays that enable users to explore different scenarios and understand the uncertainty associated with impact predictions. Machine learning approaches can personalize these visualizations based on user roles, decision contexts, and past interaction patterns, providing more effective risk communication that supports informed decision-making under uncertainty.

The evaluation of early warning system performance requires sophisticated approaches that can assess multiple dimensions of system effectiveness, including detection accuracy, timeliness, false alarm rates, and user response outcomes. Traditional evaluation metrics based solely on hazard prediction accuracy may not capture the full value of early warning systems, which must be evaluated in terms of their ability to support effective decision-making and risk reduction outcomes.

Machine learning approaches enable the development of comprehensive evaluation frameworks that can learn relationships between warning system characteristics and user response outcomes. These models can identify the warning message features, timing characteristics, and communication channels that are most effective for different user communities and decision contexts. The insights gained from these analyses can inform continuous improvement efforts that optimize early warning system design and operation.

User feedback integration represents a critical component of early warning system evaluation and improvement. Machine learning models can analyze user feedback data to identify systematic biases or performance issues while accounting for the subjective nature of user experiences and the varying contexts in which warnings are received and acted upon. Natural language processing techniques enable the analysis of qualitative feedback to identify themes and patterns that inform system improvement efforts.

Adaptive learning approaches enable early warning systems to continuously improve their performance through the incorporation of new data and feedback about system effectiveness. These approaches can automatically adjust model parameters, update training datasets, and refine warning generation algorithms based on observed system performance and changing environmental conditions. The integration of online learning techniques enables systems to adapt to evolving hazard characteristics and user needs without requiring complete model retraining.

Emissions Tracking and Carbon Monitoring

The monitoring of greenhouse gas emissions from space represents one of the most rapidly advancing applications of machine learning in climate science, offering unprecedented capabilities for tracking emission sources, quantifying emission rates, and attributing emissions to specific activities and facilities. Satellite-based emission monitoring systems leverage observations from multiple satellite platforms that measure atmospheric concentrations of greenhouse gases at different spatial and temporal scales, from global background monitoring to high-resolution plume detection for individual emission sources.

Machine learning approaches for satellite-based emission monitoring must address several technical challenges, including the separation of emission signals from atmospheric background concentrations, the attribution of observed concentration enhancements to specific sources, and the quantification of emission rates from concentration observations. These challenges require sophisticated approaches that can model atmospheric transport processes, account for measurement uncertainties, and integrate observations from multiple satellite sensors with different characteristics and capabilities.

Convolutional neural networks for emission source detection process satellite imagery and atmospheric concentration data to identify and characterize emission plumes and source locations. These models learn to recognize the spatial patterns associated with different types of emission sources, from large power plants and industrial facilities to smaller distributed sources such as urban areas and agricultural operations. The incorporation of multiple satellite sensors, including both greenhouse gas measurements and ancillary data such as aerosol optical depth and nitrogen dioxide concentrations, enables more robust source detection and characterization.

Deep learning approaches to emission quantification typically employ physics-informed architectures that incorporate an understanding of atmospheric transport processes while learning from observational data. These models must account for complex relationships between emission rates, meteorological conditions, and observed atmospheric concentrations, requiring approaches that can handle the nonlinear and time-varying nature of atmospheric transport. The integration of numerical weather prediction model output provides enhanced capabilities for emission quantification by providing meteorological context for atmospheric transport modeling.

Methane represents a particularly important target for satellite-based emission monitoring due to its high global warming potential and the significant uncertainties in current emission inventories. Machine learning approaches for methane monitoring focus on the detection and quantification of emission sources, including both persistent sources such as oil and gas facilities and landfills, and episodic sources such as pipeline leaks and venting events. The identification of super-emitter sources, which contribute disproportionately to total emissions, represents a particular priority for methane monitoring applications.

Satellite-based methane monitoring systems typically employ hyperspectral imaging sensors that measure methane absorption features in the shortwave infrared portion of the electromagnetic spectrum. Machine learning models for methane detection process hyperspectral data to identify methane enhancements above background levels while accounting for atmospheric and surface interference effects. Advanced preprocessing techniques, including atmospheric correction and noise reduction algorithms, enable the detection of relatively small methane plumes that traditional analysis methods might miss.

Point source detection algorithms employ computer vision techniques adapted for atmospheric applications to identify and characterize individual methane emission sources. These algorithms must distinguish between methane plumes and various interference sources, including water vapor variability, surface reflectance features, and sensor noise. Machine learning approaches can learn to recognize the characteristic spectral and spatial signatures of methane plumes while filtering out false detections caused by other atmospheric and surface phenomena.

Emission rate quantification for methane sources requires models that can relate observed atmospheric concentrations to source emission rates while accounting for atmospheric transport and dispersion processes. Machine learning approaches typically employ hybrid models that combine physics-based understanding of atmospheric transport with data-driven approaches that can learn from observational data. These models must account for the influence of meteorological conditions, topography, and atmospheric stability on plume transport and dispersion.

Time series analysis of methane observations enables the identification of temporal patterns in emission behavior, including diurnal cycles, seasonal variations, and long-term trends. Machine learning models for temporal analysis can identify periodic patterns associated with operational activities, detect anomalous emission events, and quantify changes in emission rates over time. These capabilities are particularly valuable for monitoring the effectiveness of emission reduction measures and identifying facilities with degrading emission control performance.

Carbon dioxide monitoring from satellite platforms presents additional challenges compared to methane monitoring due to the relatively small enhancements of CO_2 concentrations above high atmospheric background levels and the need to separate anthropogenic emissions from natural flux variability. Machine learning approaches for CO_2 monitoring must address these challenges through sophisticated signal processing and source attribution techniques that can identify anthropogenic emission signals amidst large natural variability.

Inverse modeling approaches use atmospheric CO_2 observations to estimate surface flux patterns, employing optimization techniques to find flux distributions that best match observed atmospheric concentrations while accounting for atmospheric transport uncertainties. Machine learning approaches enhance inverse modeling through improved representation of prior flux information, more sophisticated treatment of transport uncertainties, and enhanced optimization algorithms that can handle high-dimensional flux estimation problems.

Natural flux modeling represents a critical component of anthropogenic CO_2 monitoring systems, as accurate quantification of anthropogenic emissions requires accounting for natural CO_2 exchanges from ecosystems. Machine learning models for natural flux estimation typically integrate satellite observations of vegetation activity, meteorological data, and ecosystem characteristics to estimate photosynthesis and respiration fluxes. These models must account for the complex dependencies of ecosystem CO_2 fluxes on environmental conditions while providing estimates at the spatial and temporal scales required for emission verification applications.

Urban CO_2 monitoring represents an emerging application that focuses on quantifying emissions from cities and metropolitan areas. These applications require models that can integrate satellite observations with urban-scale emission inventories and atmospheric transport modeling to provide city-scale emission estimates. Machine learning approaches can learn relationships between urban characteristics, activity patterns, and CO_2 emissions, enabling the development of improved urban emission estimation methods and the verification of city-level emission reporting.

The development of automated carbon accounting systems represents a critical advancement in enabling widespread, accurate, and cost-effective carbon footprint analysis across different sectors and scales. Traditional carbon accounting approaches often rely on manual data collection and analysis processes that are time-consuming, expensive, and prone to errors or inconsistencies. Machine learning approaches offer enhanced capabilities for carbon accounting through their ability to process diverse data sources, identify patterns in activity data, and provide automated calculations with uncertainty quantification.

Automated carbon accounting systems typically employ multi-modal machine learning architectures that can process diverse data types, including energy consumption records, transportation data, purchasing records, and activity monitoring data. These systems learn relationships between observable activities and associated carbon emissions while accounting for the complex dependencies between different emission sources and activity types. Natural language processing techniques enable the analysis of text-based data sources, such as purchase orders and activity descriptions, to extract emission-relevant information that can be incorporated into carbon accounting calculations.

Machine learning approaches for carbon accounting must address several technical challenges, including the attribution of emissions to specific activities, the handling of missing or incomplete data, and the quantification of uncertainties in emission calculations. Probabilistic models provide frameworks for uncertainty quantification that can propagate uncertainties from activity data through emission calculations to provide confidence intervals for carbon footprint estimates. These approaches are particularly valuable for comparative assessments and decision-making applications where understanding the reliability of carbon footprint estimates is critical.

Real-time carbon monitoring systems employ streaming data architectures that can continuously process activity data and provide updated carbon footprint estimates as new information becomes available. These systems are particularly valuable for applications involving dynamic emission sources, such as transportation systems or manufacturing facilities, where emission patterns may vary significantly over time. Machine learning models for real-time monitoring can identify anomalous emission patterns and provide alerts when carbon footprint levels exceed predetermined thresholds.

Life Cycle Assessment represents a comprehensive approach to environmental impact analysis that considers the full range of environmental impacts associated with products, services, or activities throughout their complete life cycles. The integration of LCA with machine learning approaches offers enhanced capabilities for carbon footprint analysis through improved data processing, impact quantification, and uncertainty assessment across complex supply chains and production systems.

Machine learning approaches for LCA typically employ graph neural networks or other structured models that can represent the complex network relationships between different life cycle stages, processes, and impact pathways. These models can learn relationships between process characteristics and environmental impacts while accounting for the interconnected nature of industrial systems and supply chains. The incorporation of uncertainty quantification enables the propagation of uncertainties through LCA calculations, providing more robust assessments of environmental impacts.

Automated LCA approaches employ machine learning models that can process diverse data sources, including process databases, supplier information, and activity monitoring data, to construct and analyze life cycle models without requiring extensive manual data collection and analysis. These approaches can identify data gaps, recommend data collection strategies, and provide impact estimates even when complete life cycle data are not available. Transfer learning techniques enable models trained on comprehensive LCA datasets to be applied to new products or processes with limited data availability.

Supply chain carbon footprint analysis represents a particular focus area for LCA integration, as the tracking of emissions across complex global supply chains requires sophisticated approaches that can handle data limitations, supply chain complexity, and dynamic supplier relationships. Machine learning models can learn relationships between supplier characteristics, product specifications, and associated carbon footprints, enabling the estimation of supply chain emissions even when direct supplier data are not available.

Personal carbon footprint tracking represents an emerging application area that leverages machine learning approaches to provide individuals and households with detailed information about their carbon emissions and actionable guidance for emission reduction. These applications typically employ smartphone-based data collection systems that can automatically monitor transportation patterns, energy consumption, and consumption behaviors while providing personalized feedback and recommendations for emission reduction.

Activity recognition algorithms employ machine learning models that can process smartphone sensor data, location information, and other digital traces to automatically identify carbon-relevant activities such as transportation mode choice, energy consumption patterns, and consumption behaviors. These models must balance the need for accurate activity recognition with privacy protection requirements, often employing federated learning approaches that enable model training without requiring the sharing of personal data.

Behavioral intervention systems employ machine learning models that can identify effective strategies for encouraging emission reduction behaviors based on individual characteristics, preferences, and response patterns. These models learn relationships between different intervention strategies and behavioral outcomes, enabling the personalization of carbon reduction recommendations and feedback systems. The incorporation of behavioral science principles ensures that intervention strategies remain grounded in the established understanding of behavior change processes.

Gamification and social comparison features employ machine learning models that can identify engaging and motivating elements for different user types while providing meaningful comparisons with peer groups or community benchmarks. These systems must balance the motivational benefits of social comparison with privacy protection requirements and the need to provide fair comparisons across different demographic groups and living situations.

Organizational carbon management platforms employ machine learning approaches to provide comprehensive carbon footprint analysis and management capabilities for businesses, institutions, and other organizations. These platforms typically integrate multiple data sources, including energy management systems, transportation records, supply chain information, and facility monitoring data, to provide comprehensive carbon footprint assessments with detailed attribution to different emission sources and activities.

Automated data integration systems employ machine learning models that can process diverse organizational data sources and extract emission-relevant information while handling data quality issues, missing values, and inconsistent data formats. These systems learn relationships between different data types and organizational activities, enabling the automatic categorization and analysis of emission sources without requiring extensive manual data processing.

Predictive analytics capabilities enable organizations to forecast future carbon emissions based on planned activities, operational changes, and external factors such as energy grid carbon intensity variations. Machine learning models for carbon forecasting can identify the factors that most strongly influence organizational carbon footprints and provide scenario analysis capabilities that support strategic planning and goal setting. The incorporation of uncertainty quantification enables organizations to understand the reliability of carbon forecasting and plan for different potential outcomes.

Carbon reduction optimization systems employ machine learning approaches that can identify the most effective strategies for reducing organizational carbon footprints while accounting for cost constraints, operational requirements, and other organizational priorities. These systems can analyze historical data to identify successful emission reduction interventions and recommend similar strategies for new situations. Multi-objective optimization approaches enable the balancing of carbon reduction goals against other organizational objectives, such as cost minimization or operational efficiency.

Supply chain carbon assessment represents one of the most complex challenges in carbon footprint analysis, requiring approaches that can map complex networks of suppliers, manufacturers, distributors, and service providers while attributing emissions to specific products, services, and activities. Modern supply chains often involve hundreds or thousands of suppliers across multiple tiers, with dynamic relationships and limited transparency regarding environmental performance. Machine learning approaches offer enhanced capabilities for supply chain carbon assessment through their ability to process diverse data sources, identify patterns in supply chain relationships, and provide emission estimates even when complete data are not available.

Graph neural networks provide particularly powerful frameworks for supply chain carbon assessment by explicitly representing the network structure of supply chain relationships and the flow of materials, products, and associated emissions through these networks. These models treat suppliers, facilities, and products as nodes in a graph, with edges representing supply relationships and material flows. The message-passing mechanisms in graph neural networks enable information about emissions to propagate through supply chain networks, providing comprehensive assessments of product and service carbon footprints that account for multi-tier supplier relationships.

Supply chain emission attribution requires models that can allocate emissions from suppliers and processes to specific products or services while accounting for shared infrastructure, multi-product facilities, and complex allocation rules. Machine learning approaches can learn allocation relationships from historical data and supplier reporting while accounting for the uncertainties inherent in allocation processes. These models can identify the most appropriate allocation methodologies for different types of suppliers and products, ensuring consistent and accurate emission attribution across complex supply chains.

Data fusion approaches enable the integration of multiple information sources for supply chain carbon assessment, including supplier self-reporting, third-party databases, satellite observations, and indirect indicators of environmental performance. Machine learning models can learn relationships between different data types and supply chain emission characteristics, enabling the validation and enhancement of supplier-reported data while identifying potential data quality issues or reporting inconsistencies.

The assessment of supplier environmental performance represents a critical component of supply chain carbon management, enabling organizations to identify high-emission suppliers, evaluate emission reduction opportunities, and make informed procurement decisions. Traditional approaches to supplier assessment often rely on self-reporting and periodic auditing processes that may provide limited coverage and temporal resolution. Machine learning approaches offer enhanced capabilities for supplier assessment through their ability to continuously monitor supplier performance indicators and provide predictive assessments of environmental performance.

Multi-modal assessment systems employ machine learning models that can integrate diverse information sources about supplier performance, including financial data, operational characteristics, environmental management system information, and third-party ratings. These models learn relationships between different supplier characteristics and environmental performance outcomes, enabling comprehensive assessments that account for multiple dimensions of supplier capability and performance.

Predictive models for supplier environmental performance can identify suppliers that are likely to experience emission increases or decreases based on business developments, operational changes, or external factors. These models provide early warning capabilities that enable proactive supplier engagement and support for emission reduction efforts. The incorporation of uncertainty quantification enables procurement decisions that account for the reliability of supplier performance predictions.

Benchmarking and peer comparison capabilities employ machine learning models that can identify appropriate peer groups for supplier comparison while accounting for differences in supplier characteristics, operational contexts, and reporting methodologies. These models provide fair and meaningful performance comparisons that support supplier development efforts and procurement decision-making. The identification of best-practice suppliers enables the sharing of successful emission reduction strategies across supplier networks.

Product carbon footprint optimization requires sophisticated approaches that can identify emission reduction opportunities across all stages of product life cycles while accounting for trade-offs between different environmental impacts, cost considerations, and performance requirements. Machine learning approaches enable comprehensive optimization that can consider multiple design variables, supply chain options, and operational parameters while providing solutions that balance carbon reduction against other organizational objectives.

Design optimization systems employ machine learning models that can predict the carbon footprint implications of different product design choices while accounting for manufacturing processes, material selection, and end-of-life considerations. These models learn relationships between product characteristics and life cycle carbon emissions, enabling design teams to evaluate emission implications of different design alternatives early in product development processes.

Supply chain optimization for carbon reduction employs models that can evaluate alternative supplier configurations, transportation modes, and logistics strategies while accounting for emission implications, cost impacts, and operational constraints. These optimization systems can identify supply chain modifications that provide significant emission reductions while maintaining acceptable cost and performance levels. Multi-objective optimization approaches enable the exploration of trade-offs between carbon reduction and other supply chain objectives.

Circular economy integration represents an emerging application area where machine learning models can identify opportunities for incorporating circular economy principles into product and supply chain design. These models can evaluate options such as material recovery, remanufacturing, and sharing economy approaches while quantifying their carbon footprint implications. The optimization of circular economy interventions requires models that can handle complex material flow networks and account for the temporal dynamics of circular economy systems.

Climate-related risks to supply chains are increasing as extreme weather events become more frequent and severe, potentially disrupting supply chain operations and affecting carbon footprint performance. Machine learning approaches for supply chain risk assessment offer enhanced capabilities for identifying vulnerable suppliers and supply chain nodes, predicting disruption risks, and developing resilience strategies that maintain carbon performance while ensuring operational continuity.

Climate risk assessment models employ machine learning approaches that can process climate projections, extreme weather forecasts, and supplier location information to identify supply chain components that face elevated climate risks. These models can quantify the probability and potential impact of climate-related disruptions while accounting for supplier adaptive capacity and risk management capabilities. The integration of real-time monitoring enables dynamic risk assessment that updates as climate conditions and supplier circumstances change.

Alternative supplier identification systems employ machine learning models that can identify potential backup suppliers with acceptable environmental performance characteristics while accounting for operational requirements, cost constraints, and risk diversification objectives. These models can continuously monitor supplier markets to identify emerging suppliers with strong environmental performance and evaluate the carbon footprint implications of supply chain diversification strategies.

Resilience optimization approaches employ machine learning models that can evaluate supply chain design alternatives based on their ability to maintain acceptable carbon performance under different disruption scenarios. These models can identify supply chain configurations that provide robust carbon performance across a range of potential future conditions while maintaining acceptable cost and operational performance levels.

Satellite-based emission monitoring has been revolutionized by advances in sensor technologies and data processing capabilities that enable increasingly precise and comprehensive monitoring of greenhouse gas concentrations from space. Modern satellite platforms employ a variety of sensor types, including hyperspectral imaging spectrometers, interferometers, and lidar systems, each with unique capabilities for detecting and quantifying different greenhouse gases under various atmospheric and surface conditions. Machine learning approaches play critical roles in processing the vast quantities of data generated by these sensors and extracting actionable information about emission sources and atmospheric concentrations.

Hyperspectral imaging sensors measure atmospheric absorption across hundreds or thousands of narrow spectral bands, enabling the detection and quantification of multiple greenhouse gases simultaneously. Machine learning models for hyperspectral data processing must address several technical challenges, including atmospheric correction, spectral unmixing, and the separation of gas absorption signals from various interference sources. Deep learning approaches, particularly convolutional neural networks adapted for spectral data, can learn complex relationships between spectral signatures and atmospheric gas concentrations while accounting for atmospheric and surface variability that affects spectral measurements.

Atmospheric correction represents a critical preprocessing step for satellite-based emission monitoring, as atmospheric scattering and absorption by water vapor, aerosols, and other constituents can significantly affect measured spectral signatures. Machine learning approaches to atmospheric correction employ models that can learn relationships between measured spectral data and atmospheric conditions while providing corrected spectral signatures that accurately represent greenhouse gas concentrations. These models typically integrate information from multiple spectral bands and auxiliary data sources to provide robust atmospheric correction across different atmospheric conditions.

Real-time data processing capabilities enable satellite-based emission monitoring systems to provide near-instantaneous information about atmospheric concentrations and emission sources. These capabilities require efficient algorithms that can process high-volume data streams from multiple satellite platforms while maintaining the accuracy required for emission monitoring applications. Machine learning approaches enable the development of computationally efficient processing algorithms that can operate within the constraints of satellite-based computing systems while providing accurate emission detection and quantification.

Satellite-based emission monitoring provides unprecedented capabilities for validating and improving global emission inventories that serve as the foundation for climate policy, carbon markets, and emission reduction efforts. Traditional emission inventories rely primarily on bottom-up approaches that combine activity data with emission factors, often resulting in significant uncertainties and potential biases. Satellite observations provide independent, top-down constraints on emission estimates that can identify discrepancies between reported emissions and actual atmospheric observations.

Machine learning approaches for inventory validation typically employ inverse modeling techniques that use atmospheric observations to estimate surface emission patterns while accounting for atmospheric transport uncertainties and measurement errors. These models can identify regions or sectors where inventory estimates differ significantly from satellite-derived emission estimates, providing valuable feedback for inventory improvement efforts. The integration of multiple satellite platforms and sensor types enables more comprehensive validation that covers different greenhouse gases, spatial scales, and temporal periods.

Bias detection algorithms employ machine learning models that can identify systematic differences between inventory estimates and satellite observations while accounting for uncertainties in both data sources. These models can distinguish between random uncertainties and systematic biases, providing information that helps inventory developers identify and correct specific problems in emission estimation methodologies. The temporal analysis of inventory-satellite differences can reveal trends in inventory accuracy and help identify changing emission patterns that traditional inventory approaches may not capture.

Uncertainty quantification for inventory validation requires sophisticated approaches that can properly account for uncertainties in satellite observations, atmospheric transport modeling, and inventory estimates while providing reliable assessments of agreement between different emission estimation methods. Bayesian approaches provide principled frameworks for uncertainty propagation and combination that enable robust validation assessments even when individual data sources have significant uncertainties.

High-resolution emission source detection represents a frontier application for satellite-based monitoring that enables the identification and characterization of individual emission sources such as power plants, industrial facilities, and urban areas. These applications require satellite sensors with high spatial resolution and sophisticated analysis techniques that can separate emission signals from background concentrations while attributing observed concentrations to specific sources.

Point source detection algorithms employ computer vision techniques adapted for atmospheric applications to identify individual emission sources from satellite imagery and concentration data. These algorithms must distinguish between emission plumes and various background features while accounting for atmospheric transport effects that can displace observed concentration enhancements from their source locations. Machine learning approaches can learn to recognize the characteristic spatial patterns associated with different types of emission sources while filtering out false detections caused by atmospheric variability or surface features.

Emission quantification for point sources requires models that can relate observed atmospheric concentrations to source emission rates while accounting for meteorological conditions, atmospheric transport processes, and measurement uncertainties. Machine learning approaches typically employ physics-informed models that combine understanding of atmospheric dispersion with data-driven approaches that can learn from observational data. These models must account for the complex, time-varying nature of atmospheric transport while providing emission rate estimates with appropriate uncertainty bounds.

Multi-temporal analysis enables the monitoring of emission source behavior over time, including the detection of operational changes, emission control effectiveness, and long-term emission trends. Machine learning models for temporal analysis can identify periodic patterns associated with operational cycles, detect anomalous emission events, and quantify changes in emission rates over different time scales. These capabilities are particularly valuable for regulatory compliance monitoring and the verification of emission reduction measures.

The integration of satellite-based emission monitoring with ground-based measurement networks provides enhanced capabilities for emission detection, quantification, and source attribution through the combination of high spatial coverage from satellites with high temporal resolution and accuracy from ground-based measurements. This integration requires sophisticated data fusion approaches that can optimally combine information from different measurement types while accounting for their different characteristics, uncertainties, and limitations.

Multi-platform data fusion employs machine learning models that can learn optimal combination strategies for different types of measurements while accounting for their complementary strengths and limitations. Satellite observations provide broad spatial coverage and the ability to detect emission sources across large areas, while ground-based measurements provide high accuracy and temporal resolution at specific locations. Machine learning approaches can learn relationships between these different measurement types and develop fusion strategies that maximize the information content of combined datasets.

Observation system optimization uses machine learning models to identify optimal deployment strategies for ground-based measurement networks that complement satellite observations while maximizing overall system performance. These models can evaluate different network configurations and identify measurement locations that provide maximum information gain for emission monitoring applications. The integration of cost considerations enables the optimization of measurement networks within realistic budget constraints.

Quality assurance and validation approaches employ machine learning models that can identify measurement inconsistencies, detect instrument problems, and provide bias corrections that ensure data quality across integrated measurement networks. These models can learn relationships between different measurement types and identify situations where measurements may be compromised by instrument issues, atmospheric interference, or other factors that affect data quality.

The application of artificial intelligence and machine learning to extreme weather event detection and emissions monitoring represents a transformative development in climate science with profound implications for both scientific understanding and societal response to climate change. The comprehensive exploration of these applications in this chapter demonstrates the remarkable breadth and depth of AI contributions to climate science, from the detection and prediction of individual extreme events to the global monitoring of greenhouse gas emissions and the detailed analysis of carbon footprints across complex supply chains.

The success of machine learning approaches in extreme event applications stems from their ability to identify complex patterns in large datasets, handle the inherent rarity and statistical challenges of extreme events, and provide rapid automated detection capabilities that are essential for effective early warning systems. The integration of diverse data sources, from satellite observations to social media feeds, enables comprehensive situational awareness that surpasses traditional monitoring approaches. Similarly, the application of AI to emissions monitoring has revolutionized our ability to track greenhouse gas sources with unprecedented precision and coverage, providing essential capabilities for climate policy verification, carbon market integrity, and emission reduction planning.

The evolution from single-hazard to multi-hazard early warning systems represents a critical advancement that reflects the increasing complexity of climate-related risks. The compound and cascading nature of many extreme events requires sophisticated modeling approaches that can capture the interactions between different hazard types and their cumulative impacts on vulnerable systems. Machine learning architectures, particularly graph neural networks and multi-modal approaches, provide powerful frameworks for modeling these complex interactions while maintaining computational efficiency and providing actionable information for decision-makers.

The development of impact-based forecasting represents another significant advancement that moves beyond traditional hazard-focused approaches to provide information about expected consequences for specific sectors and communities. This evolution requires sophisticated models that can integrate hazard predictions with vulnerability assessments, infrastructure characteristics, and socioeconomic factors to provide comprehensive risk assessments. The personalization of risk communication through machine learning approaches enables more effective public engagement and supports improved decision-making across diverse user communities.

In the realm of emissions monitoring, the integration of satellite-based observations with machine learning analysis has created unprecedented capabilities for tracking global greenhouse gas sources with spatial and temporal resolution that was previously impossible. The ability to detect and quantify emissions from individual facilities, validate national emission inventories, and provide near real-time monitoring of emission changes represents a fundamental shift in our capacity to understand and manage atmospheric greenhouse gas concentrations. These capabilities are essential for supporting international climate agreements, carbon market mechanisms, and national emission reduction policies.

The application of AI to supply chain carbon assessment addresses one of the most challenging aspects of organizational carbon management by enabling comprehensive analysis of complex supply network emissions. The development of automated carbon accounting systems, integrated life cycle assessment approaches, and predictive carbon optimization tools provides organizations with unprecedented capabilities for understanding and managing their full carbon footprints. These advances are essential for achieving the deep emission reductions required to meet global climate goals while maintaining economic competitiveness and operational efficiency.

The future development of these applications will likely focus on several key areas that address current limitations and emerging needs. Enhanced uncertainty quantification remains a priority across all applications, as decision-makers require reliable assessments of prediction confidence to support risk-based planning and resource allocation. The integration of physical constraints and climate knowledge into machine learning models represents an ongoing challenge that is essential for ensuring physically realistic predictions and maintaining scientific credibility.

The scalability of AI approaches to global applications presents both opportunities and challenges, as the computational requirements of sophisticated models may limit their deployment in resource-constrained environments where climate risks are often highest. Edge computing approaches and efficient model architectures offer potential solutions, but continued research is needed to develop AI systems that can operate effectively across diverse technological and institutional contexts.

Privacy and data sharing considerations become increasingly important as AI applications require access to detailed activity data, location information, and other sensitive information types. Federated learning approaches and privacy-preserving techniques offer promising solutions that can enable collaborative model development while protecting sensitive information, but these approaches require continued development and validation for climate applications.

The integration of AI approaches with existing climate monitoring and prediction systems represents both a technical challenge and an institutional one, requiring coordination between research communities, operational agencies, and technology providers. The development of standardized interfaces, data formats, and validation procedures will be essential for enabling widespread adoption of AI approaches while maintaining system reliability and interoperability.

Climate change adaptation and mitigation applications will continue to drive innovation in AI approaches as the urgency of climate action increases and the stakes of accurate prediction and monitoring continue to rise. The development of AI systems that can support both short-term operational decisions and long-term strategic planning will require advances in multi-scale modeling, scenario analysis, and decision support systems that can operate effectively across diverse temporal and spatial scales.

The democratization of AI capabilities for climate applications represents both an opportunity and a responsibility for the research community. Making sophisticated AI tools accessible to smaller organizations, developing countries, and community-based organizations will be essential for ensuring that the benefits of AI advances are widely shared and that local knowledge and priorities are incorporated into climate risk management approaches.

Education and training programs will play critical roles in developing the human capacity needed to effectively deploy and maintain AI systems for climate applications. The interdisciplinary nature of these applications requires professionals who understand both climate science and artificial intelligence, creating new educational challenges and opportunities for universities and training institutions.

The ethical implications of AI deployment in climate applications deserve continued attention, particularly regarding equity, accessibility, and the potential for algorithmic bias in systems that influence resource allocation and risk management decisions. The development of ethical frameworks and evaluation procedures for climate AI systems will be essential for ensuring that these powerful technologies serve the public interest and support just and effective climate action.

In conclusion, the integration of artificial intelligence with extreme event detection and emissions monitoring represents a fundamental advancement in climate science capabilities with far-reaching implications for scientific understanding, policy development, and societal response to climate change. The continued development and deployment of these approaches will play essential roles in supporting global efforts to understand, predict, and respond to climate change while building more resilient and sustainable societies. The success of these efforts will depend on continued collaboration between climate scientists, AI researchers, policy makers, and the communities that must live with the consequences of climate change, ensuring that technological advances are effectively translated into improved climate outcomes and reduced climate risks.

SEVEN

Physics-Informed ML

The convergence of physics-based understanding and machine learning capabilities represents one of the most promising frontiers in computational climate science. This chapter explores the development and application of physics-informed machine learning approaches and hybrid modeling systems that combine the interpretability and physical consistency of traditional climate models with the pattern recognition capabilities and computational efficiency of artificial intelligence. These approaches address fundamental limitations of purely data-driven machine learning methods while enhancing the capabilities of physics-based models through intelligent parameterizations and computational optimizations.

Traditional climate modeling approaches rely on the numerical solution of partial differential equations that govern atmospheric, oceanic, and terrestrial processes. While these physics-based models provide interpretable results and maintain conservation principles, they face significant computational constraints when attempting to resolve all relevant scales of motion and process interactions. Subgrid-scale processes must be parameterized using simplified representations that introduce uncertainties and biases, while computational limitations restrict the spatial and temporal resolution achievable in practical applications.

Conversely, purely data-driven machine learning approaches excel at pattern recognition and can achieve remarkable accuracy for specific prediction tasks, but they often lack physical interpretability and may violate fundamental conservation principles. These models can perform poorly when applied to conditions outside their training data range and may learn spurious correlations that do not reflect underlying physical processes. The integration of physical principles with machine learning offers pathways to overcome these limitations while leveraging the complementary strengths of both approaches.

Physics-informed machine learning represents a paradigm shift that embeds physical knowledge directly into machine learning architectures through modified loss functions, constrained optimization procedures, and hybrid network designs. These approaches ensure that learned solutions remain consistent with known physical laws while benefiting from the flexibility and efficiency of neural network approximations. The resulting models can extrapolate more reliably to new conditions, require less training data to achieve acceptable accuracy, and provide physically meaningful insights into the processes they represent.

Hybrid modeling systems take this integration further by combining physics-based model components with machine learning elements in unified frameworks that leverage the strengths of both approaches. These systems typically employ physics-based models for large-scale, well-understood processes while using machine learning components for complex parameterizations, bias correction, and computational acceleration. The seamless integration of these components enables the development of climate models that maintain physical realism while achieving enhanced accuracy and computational efficiency.

The applications of physics-informed and hybrid approaches span the full spectrum of climate modeling challenges, from improved parameterizations of cloud processes and boundary layer dynamics to enhanced seasonal prediction systems and climate projection capabilities. These approaches are particularly valuable for addressing the multi-scale nature of climate systems, where processes operating on vastly different temporal and spatial scales interact through complex feedback mechanisms that are difficult to represent using traditional modeling approaches.

Physics-Informed Neural Networks represent a revolutionary approach to solving differential equations by embedding physical laws directly into neural network training procedures. The fundamental innovation of PINNs lies in their ability to approximate solutions to partial differential equations while simultaneously satisfying physical constraints, boundary conditions, and conservation principles through specially designed loss functions. This approach transforms the traditional numerical solution of differential equations into an optimization problem where neural networks learn to satisfy both data constraints and physical laws.

The mathematical foundation of PINNs rests on the principle of automatic differentiation, which enables the efficient computation of derivatives required for evaluating differential equation residuals. Architecture Design for Climate Applications

The application of PINNs to climate science requires specialized architectural considerations that account for the unique characteristics of atmospheric and oceanic systems. Climate variables often exhibit multiple time scales, from rapid turbulent fluctuations to slow seasonal and inter-annual variations, requiring network architectures that can capture these multi-scale dependencies effectively. Additionally, climate systems are characterized by conserved quantities such as mass, momentum, and energy, which any physically consistent solution must preserve.

Multi-scale architectures for climate PINNs typically employ hierarchical network designs that process different temporal and spatial scales through separate subnetworks that are then combined through learned mixing functions. These architectures might include fast-scale networks that capture high-frequency variability and slow-scale networks that represent longer-term evolution, with interaction terms that couple the different scales according to known physical principles.

Conservation-aware architectures explicitly enforce conservation laws through network design choices and constraint formulations. This constraint can be enforced by parameterizing velocity fields through a vector potential or by including strong penalty terms in the loss function that penalize violations of conservation laws.

Boundary condition handling represents a critical aspect of PINN architecture design for climate applications. Atmospheric and oceanic systems involve complex boundary interactions, including surface energy and moisture exchange, topographic effects, and lateral boundary conditions for regional models. PINNs can handle these boundary conditions through hard constraints built into the network architecture or through soft constraints incorporated into the loss function.

The incorporation of uncertainty quantification into PINN architectures enables the development of probabilistic solutions that provide confidence estimates for predictions. Bayesian PINNs employ stochastic networks with uncertainty in network weights, while ensemble approaches use multiple PINNs with different initializations to quantify solution uncertainty. These probabilistic extensions are particularly valuable for climate applications where quantifying uncertainty is essential for decision-making.

The training of Physics-Informed Neural Networks for climate applications presents several unique optimization challenges that require specialized training strategies and algorithmic innovations. The multi-objective nature of PINN loss functions, which must simultaneously satisfy data constraints and physics constraints, can lead to optimization difficulties where different loss components may conflict or have vastly different scales. Additionally, the evaluation of differential equation residuals through automatic differentiation can lead to high-order derivative computations that may suffer from numerical instability or computational inefficiency.

Adaptive weighting strategies address the challenge of balancing different components of the physics-informed loss function. Simple fixed weighting schemes often perform poorly because data and physics terms may have different magnitudes or optimization landscapes. Advanced approaches include learning-based weighting schemes that automatically adjust constraint weights based on training progress, and dynamic balancing methods that modify weights to ensure all constraints receive appropriate attention during optimization.

Multi-stage training procedures often prove more effective than single-stage optimization for complex climate applications. These approaches might begin with pre-training on data constraints to establish reasonable initial solutions, followed by the gradual introduction of physics constraints as the network learns to satisfy increasingly sophisticated physical requirements. Alternatively, curriculum learning approaches can start with simplified physics constraints and progressively incorporate more complex physical relationships as training proceeds.

Residual-based sampling strategies address the challenge of efficiently selecting training points for physics constraint evaluation. Rather than using uniform sampling over the computational domain, adaptive sampling can concentrate training points in regions where physics residuals are largest, leading to more efficient training and better solution quality. Self-adaptive sampling methods automatically adjust the distribution of training points based on local solution quality and constraint violation levels.

The optimization landscape of PINNs often exhibits multiple local minima and saddle points that can trap traditional gradient-based optimizers. Advanced optimization strategies for climate PINNs include second-order methods that can navigate complex loss surfaces more effectively, stochastic optimization approaches that can escape local minima, and hybrid methods that combine different optimization strategies for different training phases.

Physics-Informed Neural Networks provide powerful frameworks for both forward and inverse problems in climate science. Forward problems involve solving known differential equations with specified parameters and boundary conditions to predict system behavior, while inverse problems involve inferring unknown parameters, boundary conditions, or even governing equations from observational data. The flexibility of PINN formulations enables seamless integration of forward and inverse problems within unified frameworks.

Forward problem applications in climate science typically focus on solving known governing equations for atmospheric and oceanic flows with enhanced computational efficiency or improved representation of multi-scale processes. For example, PINNs can solve the primitive equations governing atmospheric motion while automatically satisfying conservation laws and boundary conditions, potentially achieving accuracy comparable to traditional numerical methods with reduced computational cost. The meshless nature of PINNs provides advantages for problems with complex geometries or moving boundaries that are challenging for traditional grid-based methods.

Inverse problem formulations enable the discovery of unknown parameters or governing equations from climate observations. Parameter estimation applications can infer values of poorly known model parameters, such as turbulent diffusion coefficients or cloud microphysical parameters, by training PINNs to match observational data while satisfying known physical constraints. These approaches can provide parameter estimates with quantified uncertainties and can identify parameters that vary in space or time rather than assuming constant values.

System identification applications represent the most ambitious inverse problem formulations, where PINNs attempt to discover unknown governing equations from data. These approaches can identify previously unknown processes or improve existing parameterizations by learning functional forms that best explain observational data while remaining consistent with known physical principles. The interpretability of discovered equations depends on network architecture choices and regularization strategies that encourage simple, physically meaningful functional forms.

Joint forward-inverse formulations enable the simultaneous solution of prediction problems and parameter estimation problems within unified PINN frameworks. These approaches are particularly valuable for data assimilation applications, where observations must be combined with model predictions to provide optimal estimates of system states and parameters. The seamless integration of forward and inverse components enables more sophisticated data assimilation schemes that can adapt model parameters based on observational evidence while maintaining physical consistency.

Climate systems involve complex interactions between atmospheric, oceanic, terrestrial, and cryospheric components that operate on different temporal and spatial scales with distinct governing equations and coupling mechanisms. The application of PINNs to these multi-physics systems requires sophisticated formulations that can handle coupled differential equations, interface conditions, and multi-scale interactions within unified frameworks.

Atmospheric-oceanic coupling represents a fundamental challenge for climate modeling that PINNs can address through coupled network architectures that simultaneously solve atmospheric and oceanic equations while satisfying interface conditions for heat, momentum, and moisture exchange. These coupled PINNs must handle the disparate time scales of atmospheric and oceanic processes, with atmospheric variables evolving on time scales of hours to days while oceanic variables may evolve on time scales of months to years.

Land-atmosphere interactions entail intricate exchanges of energy, water, and carbon, necessitating coupled representations of atmospheric boundary layer processes and terrestrial ecosystem dynamics. PINN formulations for these systems must incorporate biogeochemical processes, vegetation dynamics, and soil physics while maintaining consistent coupling with atmospheric processes. The multi-scale nature of these interactions, ranging from leaf-level processes to regional-scale patterns, necessitates hierarchical PINN architectures that can effectively bridge different scales.

Interface condition handling presents a critical technical challenge for multi-physics PINNs, as different system components may have distinct governing equations that must be coupled through boundary conditions or interface relationships. These conditions can be enforced through penalty methods that introduce interface constraint violations to the loss function, or through hard constraints embedded within network architectures that ensure interface conditions are satisfied by design.

Conservation across interfaces demands special attention in multi-physics PINN formulations to ensure the proper transfer of conserved quantities such as mass, energy, and momentum between different system components. This may necessitate global conservation constraints that guarantee total system conservation even when individual components may exhibit minor conservation violations, or specialized network architectures that guarantee conservation through their mathematical structure.

The integration of data-driven methods with physical principles represents a sophisticated approach that leverages the complementary strengths of empirical observations and theoretical understanding. Unlike purely physics-informed approaches that embed known equations into neural networks, hybrid frameworks combine data-driven discovery with physics constraints to learn relationships that are both empirically supported and physically consistent. These frameworks are particularly valuable for climate applications where some processes are well-understood while others remain poorly characterized or involve complex interactions that are difficult to represent analytically.

Constrained optimization frameworks provide mathematical foundations for hybrid data-physics learning by formulating machine learning problems as optimization procedures subject to physical constraints. These formulations typically employ Lagrangian methods that incorporate constraint violations as penalty terms in objective functions, enabling models to learn from data while satisfying physical requirements. The resulting optimization problems often involve complex non-convex landscapes that require sophisticated solution strategies.

Multi-objective learning approaches treat data fitting and physics consistency as separate objectives that must be balanced during training. These methods employ Pareto optimization concepts to identify solutions that achieve acceptable trade-offs between empirical accuracy and physical consistency. The resulting Pareto frontiers provide insights into the inherent tensions between data fitting and physics satisfaction, helping identify situations where improved data collection or modified physical understanding may be necessary.

Regularization-based approaches incorporate physical knowledge through specialized regularization terms that encourage solutions to exhibit physically reasonable behavior even when not explicitly constrained by known equations. These regularization terms might promote smoothness, energy minimization, or other physical principles that are expected to govern system behavior. The strength of physics regularization can be adapted during training to balance data fitting against physical plausibility.

Hierarchical learning frameworks employ multi-stage procedures that first learn data-driven relationships and subsequently refine these relationships to ensure physical consistency. These approaches recognize that data-driven learning may provide good initial approximations that can be improved through physics-based refinement. Alternatively, hierarchical methods might begin with physics-based approximations that are subsequently calibrated or corrected using observational data.

Incorporating Physical Priors and Domain Knowledge

The effective incorporation of physical priors and domain knowledge represents a critical aspect of hybrid data-physics learning that can significantly improve model performance while reducing data requirements. Physical priors provide information about expected solution characteristics based on theoretical understanding, observational experience, or analogous systems. The challenge lies in representing this prior knowledge in forms that can be effectively incorporated into machine learning frameworks while maintaining sufficient flexibility to discover new relationships.

Bayesian approaches provide principled frameworks for incorporating physical priors through prior distributions that encode expected parameter ranges, functional forms, or solution characteristics. These priors can be based on physical understanding, previous empirical studies, or expert knowledge, and are combined with data likelihood functions to produce posterior distributions that reflect both prior expectations and observational evidence. The strength of physical priors can be adjusted based on confidence levels and data availability.

Structural priors encode knowledge about expected functional forms or mathematical relationships that govern system behavior. For example, physical understanding might suggest that certain relationships should be monotonic, periodic, or exhibit specific symmetries. These structural constraints can be incorporated through specialized network architectures, custom activation functions, or constraint terms in loss functions that penalize solutions violating expected structural properties.

Symmetry-preserving architectures explicitly incorporate known symmetries of physical systems into neural network designs, ensuring that learned solutions respect fundamental symmetries such as rotational invariance, translational invariance, or scaling relationships. These architectures often employ specialized layer types or weight-sharing schemes that guarantee symmetry preservation while maintaining sufficient expressiveness for learning complex relationships.

Energy-based priors incorporate thermodynamic principles or energy minimization concepts into machine learning frameworks. Many physical systems evolve toward energy-minimizing states or exhibit relationships governed by energy balance requirements. Neural networks can incorporate these principles through energy-based loss functions, Hamiltonian neural network architectures, or constraint terms that enforce energy conservation or minimization principles.

Scale-separation techniques acknowledge that many physical systems exhibit behaviors on multiple time or space scales that can be treated separately or through different mathematical approaches. Machine learning frameworks can incorporate scale separation through multi-scale network architectures, hierarchical learning procedures, or explicit fast-slow decompositions that handle different scales through specialized computational approaches.

Residual learning approaches represent sophisticated strategies for combining physics-based models with data-driven corrections that address systematic biases, unresolved processes, or approximation errors in traditional modeling approaches. Rather than replacing physics-based models entirely, residual learning treats machine learning components as correction terms that improve upon physics-based baseline solutions. This approach maintains the interpretability and physical consistency of traditional models while benefiting from the pattern recognition capabilities of machine learning.

Additive correction models employ neural networks to learn residual functions that are added to physics-based model output to improve accuracy. These residual functions typically focus on correcting systematic biases or representing unresolved processes that are not adequately captured by physics-based formulations. The additive nature of these corrections ensures that the overall solution retains the physical characteristics of the baseline model while incorporating data-driven improvements.

Multiplicative correction approaches apply neural network-based scaling factors to physics-based model components, enabling corrections that depend on local conditions or system states. These multiplicative corrections can address parameter uncertainties, improve parameterization schemes, or account for processes that modify the effectiveness of physical mechanisms under different conditions. Multiplicative corrections often prove more stable than additive approaches and can provide more physically meaningful adjustments.

State-dependent corrections employ machine learning models that adapt their correction strategies based on current system conditions, recognizing that optimal correction approaches may vary depending on atmospheric state, seasonal cycle, or other environmental factors. These adaptive approaches can learn when different types of corrections are most needed and can avoid applying corrections in situations where physics-based models are already performing well.

Multi-level correction strategies apply residual learning at different levels of model hierarchy, from individual process parameterizations to overall model output. These hierarchical approaches can address errors at their sources while also providing final output corrections that account for error interactions and accumulation effects. The multi-level nature enables targeted improvements while maintaining overall model consistency.

Uncertainty-aware corrections incorporate uncertainty quantification into residual learning frameworks, providing correction estimates with associated confidence levels. These probabilistic corrections can adapt their magnitude based on local data availability, model confidence, or prediction accuracy, enabling more conservative corrections in situations with high uncertainty and more aggressive corrections where confidence levels are high.

Transfer learning approaches enable the application of models trained on one climate system or geographical region to different systems or regions while maintaining physical consistency. These approaches are particularly valuable for climate applications where data availability varies significantly across different regions, time periods, or system configurations. Physical constraints play a crucial role in ensuring that transferred knowledge remains meaningful and applicable across different domains.

Domain adaptation methods address the challenge of applying models across different climate regimes while maintaining physical realism. These approaches typically employ adversarial training or distribution matching techniques to learn representations that are invariant to domain differences while preserving physically meaningful relationships. Physical constraints can guide the domain adaptation process by ensuring that invariant features correspond to fundamental physical processes rather than dataset artifacts.

Few-shot learning approaches enable rapid model adaptation to new domains with limited training data by leveraging physical constraints to guide learning processes. These methods are particularly valuable for data-sparse regions or novel climate conditions where traditional machine learning approaches would require extensive training datasets. Physical priors provide essential guidance for few-shot learning by constraining the space of possible solutions and enabling more efficient parameter estimation.

Meta-learning frameworks learn adaptation strategies that can be rapidly applied to new domains while respecting physical constraints. These approaches train models to learn how to learn, developing optimization procedures and architectural adaptations that can be quickly applied to new situations. Physical constraints inform the meta-learning process by providing consistent objectives across different domains and ensuring that adaptation strategies maintain physical realism.

Cross-scale transfer enables the application of models developed at one spatial or temporal scale to different scales while maintaining appropriate physical scaling relationships. These approaches must account for scale-dependent processes and ensure that transferred relationships remain valid across different resolution regimes. Physical scaling laws provide essential guidance for cross-scale transfer by constraining how relationships should change with scale.

Multi-task transfer approaches simultaneously learn relationships for multiple related climate prediction tasks while sharing physically meaningful representations across tasks. These approaches can leverage commonalities in physical processes while allowing task-specific adaptations that account for different variables, regions, or prediction horizons. Physical constraints help identify appropriate shared representations and ensure that task-specific adaptations remain physically meaningful.

Constraint-based learning approaches provide systematic frameworks for incorporating physical knowledge and domain expertise into machine learning models through mathematical constraints that restrict the solution space to physically meaningful regions. These approaches distinguish between hard constraints that must be satisfied exactly and soft constraints that are encouraged but may be violated to some degree. The choice between hard and soft constraint implementation depends on the confidence level in physical knowledge, computational considerations, and the trade-offs between constraint satisfaction and other learning objectives.

Hard constraint implementation ensures exact satisfaction of physical principles through mathematical formulations that eliminate constraint violations by construction. These approaches modify neural network architectures or parameterizations to guarantee that outputs automatically satisfy specified constraints regardless of network parameters. For example, incompressible flow constraints can be enforced by parameterizing velocity fields through stream functions that automatically satisfy continuity equations, or conservation laws can be enforced through specialized layer designs that preserve conserved quantities.

Projection-based methods provide alternative approaches to hard constraint enforcement by projecting network outputs onto constraint manifolds after each forward pass. These methods allow networks to learn unconstrained representations internally while ensuring that final outputs satisfy required constraints. Projection approaches are particularly useful when constraints have complex geometric structures that are difficult to incorporate directly into network architectures.

Soft constraint implementation treats physical constraints as regularization terms in loss functions, allowing constraint violations while penalizing deviations from physically expected behavior. The strength of constraint penalties can be adjusted to balance constraint satisfaction against data fitting objectives, enabling exploration of trade-offs between physical consistency and empirical accuracy. Soft constraints are particularly useful when physical knowledge is uncertain or when exact constraint satisfaction would severely limit model expressiveness.

Lagrangian multiplier methods provide principled approaches to soft constraint implementation by introducing auxiliary variables that adaptively adjust constraint penalty weights during training. These methods automatically balance constraint satisfaction against other learning objectives by learning optimal penalty strengths rather than requiring manual tuning of constraint weights. The resulting optimization problems often exhibit improved convergence properties compared to fixed-penalty approaches.

Barrier function approaches prevent constraint violations by introducing penalty terms that become infinite as constraints are approached, effectively creating hard boundaries in parameter space. These methods provide strong constraint enforcement while maintaining the differentiability required for gradient-based optimization. Barrier functions are particularly useful for inequality constraints or when constraint violations would lead to physically meaningless solutions.

Conservation Law Enforcement

Conservation laws represent fundamental physical principles that any realistic climate model must respect. These laws, including conservation of mass, momentum, energy, and chemical species, provide strong constraints on allowable solution behavior and can significantly improve model reliability and physical interpretability. The enforcement of conservation laws in machine learning frameworks requires sophisticated approaches that can handle the global nature of conservation principles while maintaining computational efficiency.

Mass conservation represents a fundamental constraint for atmospheric and oceanic flow systems that must be carefully enforced in machine learning models. For incompressible flows, mass conservation requires that velocity fields satisfy the continuity equation with zero divergence. Neural network approaches can enforce this constraint through stream function parameterizations, divergence-free basis functions, or projection methods that ensure mass conservation at each time step.

Momentum conservation involves both linear momentum and angular momentum conservation principles that constrain the evolution of flow fields in climate systems. These constraints couple velocity components through complex nonlinear relationships that machine learning models must preserve. Hamiltonian neural networks provide architectures specifically designed to preserve momentum conservation through symplectic integration schemes and energy-preserving transformations.

Energy conservation encompasses multiple forms of energy, including kinetic energy, potential energy, and internal energy, as well as the transformation processes between different energy types. Machine learning models for climate applications must preserve total energy while allowing realistic energy transfers between different system components. Energy-conserving architectures employ specialized layer designs and activation functions that preserve energy throughout forward passes.

Chemical species conservation applies to atmospheric chemistry and biogeochemical cycle modeling, where chemical concentrations must satisfy mass balance relationships and reaction stoichiometry. These applications require models that preserve total elemental masses while allowing chemical transformations according to known reaction mechanisms. Constraint-based learning can enforce these conservation principles through specialized network architectures or loss function terms.

Multi-scale conservation challenges arise when different system components operate on different spatial or temporal scales but must satisfy global conservation principles. These situations require hierarchical approaches that ensure conservation at multiple scales while allowing realistic scale interactions. Homogenization techniques and multi-scale analysis provide mathematical frameworks for addressing these challenges within machine learning contexts.

Boundary and initial conditions represent critical components of well-posed climate modeling problems that must be appropriately handled in machine learning frameworks. These conditions provide essential information about system state and evolution while constraining solution behavior at domain boundaries and initial times. The accurate representation of boundary and initial conditions often determines solution quality and physical realism for climate applications.

Dirichlet boundary conditions specify fixed values of solution variables at domain boundaries and can be enforced through hard constraint methods that parameterize boundary behavior explicitly. Neural networks can satisfy Dirichlet conditions by construction through modified architectures that automatically produce specified boundary values, or through soft constraint approaches that penalize boundary condition violations in loss functions.

Neumann boundary conditions specify normal derivatives or flux values at boundaries and require more sophisticated enforcement methods that account for derivative constraints. These conditions are particularly important for climate applications involving energy and moisture fluxes at surface boundaries or lateral boundaries in regional models. Automatic differentiation enables efficient computation of boundary derivatives required for Neumann condition enforcement.

Robin boundary conditions combine value and derivative constraints, representing complex boundary relationships such as surface energy balance equations that couple atmospheric and land surface processes. These conditions often involve nonlinear relationships between different variables and may require iterative solution procedures or specialized network architectures that can handle coupled boundary constraints.

Periodic boundary conditions apply to global climate models or regional models with periodic lateral boundaries, requiring that solution values and derivatives match at opposite boundaries. These conditions can be enforced through specialized network architectures that guarantee periodicity or through constraint terms that penalize violations of periodicity.

Initial condition specification provides starting values for time-dependent problems and must be consistent with any static constraints, such as conservation laws or diagnostic relationships. Machine learning approaches can learn optimal initial conditions from data or can incorporate known initial states as hard constraints that must be satisfied at initial times.

Moving boundary problems involve boundaries whose locations change over time, such as ice-water interfaces or cloud boundaries, and require specialized approaches that can handle boundary evolution while maintaining appropriate boundary conditions. These problems often require level-set methods or other advanced techniques that can track boundary movement while enforcing evolving boundary constraints.

Inequality constraints represent bounds on solution behavior that reflect physical limitations such as non-negative concentrations, bounded temperatures, or stability conditions that must be satisfied for realistic solutions. These constraints often define feasible regions for climate variables and can significantly improve model reliability by preventing physically impossible solutions. The enforcement of inequality constraints in neural networks requires specialized techniques that can handle bounded solution spaces while maintaining differentiability.

Box constraints specify simple upper and lower bounds on individual variables and represent the most common type of inequality constraint in climate applications. These constraints can enforce physically meaningful ranges for temperature, humidity, concentration, or other climate variables. Sigmoid activation functions provide natural approaches to box constraint enforcement by mapping unbounded network outputs to bounded ranges.

Non-negativity constraints ensure that variables representing physical quantities such as concentrations, densities, or energy remain positive throughout solution domains. These constraints are essential for maintaining physical realism in many climate applications. Exponential activation functions, rectified linear units, or specialized parameterizations can enforce non-negativity constraints while maintaining network expressiveness.

Monotonicity constraints require that relationships between variables exhibit monotonic behavior when physical understanding suggests increasing or decreasing relationships. These constraints are particularly important for parameterization development, where physical insight suggests the direction of variable relationships even when exact functional forms are unknown. Monotonic networks employ specialized architectures that guarantee monotonic relationships through weight sign constraints or special layer designs.

Convexity constraints ensure that learned relationships exhibit convex or concave behavior when physical principles suggest such properties. These constraints can improve extrapolation behavior and ensure that optimization problems involving learned relationships remain well-posed. Convex neural networks employ specialized architectures that guarantee convex relationships through network structure.

Stability constraints ensure that dynamic systems represented by neural networks exhibit appropriate stability properties such as bounded growth, convergence to equilibrium states, or preservation of stability conditions. These constraints are crucial for time-dependent climate applications where unstable solutions would lead to unrealistic behavior. Lyapunov-based approaches provide mathematical frameworks for stability constraint enforcement.

Multi-objective optimization constraints arise when multiple physical principles must be balanced simultaneously, such as energy minimization subject to conservation constraints. These problems require sophisticated optimization approaches that can identify Pareto-optimal solutions or that employ hierarchical objective structures to prioritize different physical principles appropriately.

Climate systems exhibit dynamics across an enormous range of temporal scales, from turbulent fluctuations occurring on the scale of seconds to climate variations spanning centuries or millennia. Traditional climate models handle this multi-scale nature through parameterizations and scale separation techniques, but these approaches often introduce approximations that may not be valid under all conditions. Machine learning approaches to multi-scale temporal integration offer enhanced capabilities for bridging different time scales while maintaining computational efficiency and physical consistency.

Fast-slow decomposition techniques separate climate system variables into fast-evolving components that respond quickly to forcing and slow-evolving components that provide long-term memory and boundary conditions. Machine learning models can learn these decompositions automatically from data while ensuring that fast and slow components interact appropriately. These decompositions enable efficient numerical integration schemes that use different time steps for different components while maintaining overall accuracy.

Hierarchical temporal modeling employs neural network architectures with multiple temporal pathways that process information at different time scales before combining results through learned mixing functions. These architectures might include fast pathways that capture high-frequency variability, intermediate pathways that represent synoptic-scale variations, and slow pathways that account for seasonal and longer-term changes. The hierarchical structure enables efficient processing of multi-scale temporal information while maintaining interpretability of scale-specific contributions.

Temporal attention mechanisms enable neural networks to adaptively focus on relevant time periods when making predictions, automatically identifying which past time periods are most informative for current predictions. These mechanisms are particularly valuable for climate applications where the relevant temporal context may vary depending on the predicted variable, season, or dynamical regime. Temporal attention can span multiple scales simultaneously, identifying both recent conditions and longer-term patterns that influence current behavior.

Recurrent architectures with multi-scale memory provide frameworks for modeling temporal dependencies across multiple scales through specialized memory mechanisms that operate at different time scales. These architectures might employ fast memory components that capture short-term dependencies and slow memory components that maintain information about longer-term conditions. Gated mechanisms enable adaptive control of information flow between different memory components.

Continuous-time approaches employ neural ordinary differential equations and related techniques to represent climate system evolution as continuous processes rather than discrete time steps. These approaches can naturally handle irregular time sampling and can adapt their temporal resolution based on local dynamics. Continuous-time models are particularly valuable for multi-scale applications where appropriate time stepping may vary significantly across the solution domain.

Adaptive time stepping strategies use machine learning models to predict optimal time step sizes based on local solution characteristics and dynamics. These approaches can significantly improve computational efficiency by using large time steps during slowly varying periods and small time steps during rapidly changing conditions. The adaptive strategies must ensure numerical stability while maintaining accuracy across all represented time scales.

Climate systems involve interactions across spatial scales ranging from molecular processes to planetary-scale circulation patterns. Traditional approaches handle this scale separation through sub-grid-scale parameterizations, but these parameterizations often struggle to capture the complex relationships between scales and may not adapt appropriately to changing conditions. Machine learning approaches to spatial scale bridging offer enhanced capabilities for representing multi-scale interactions while maintaining computational tractability.

Upscaling techniques aggregate information from fine spatial scales to coarse scales in ways that preserve essential physical relationships and maintain consistency with coarse-scale dynamics. Machine learning models can learn optimal upscaling relationships from high-resolution simulations or observations, automatically identifying which fine-scale features are most important for coarse-scale behavior. These learned upscaling operators can adapt to local conditions and may perform better than traditional averaging or filtering approaches.

Downscaling applications generate fine-scale information from coarse-scale conditions while maintaining physical consistency and realistic small-scale variability. Super-resolution neural networks adapted for climate applications can generate high-resolution fields from coarse-resolution input while preserving important statistical properties and physical relationships. Conditional downscaling models can generate multiple realizations of fine-scale fields that are consistent with coarse-scale constraints.

Multi-resolution architectures process climate data at multiple spatial resolutions simultaneously, enabling efficient representation of multi-scale phenomena without requiring uniform high resolution across entire domains. These architectures typically employ pyramid structures or multi-grid approaches that exchange information between different resolution levels through learned interpolation and restriction operators.

Adaptive mesh refinement strategies use machine learning models to identify regions requiring high spatial resolution based on local dynamics, gradients, or other solution characteristics. These approaches can significantly reduce computational requirements by concentrating high resolution only where needed while maintaining coarse resolution in slowly varying regions. The refinement criteria can be learned from training data rather than specified a priori.

Scale-aware parameterizations employ machine learning models that adapt their behavior based on the spatial resolution of the host model, recognizing that appropriate parameterizations may depend on the resolved scales. These approaches can learn how parameterization relationships should change with resolution and can provide smooth transitions between different resolution regimes.

Homogenization approaches derive effective coarse-scale models that capture the statistical effects of fine-scale processes without resolving those processes explicitly. Machine learning can enhance homogenization techniques by learning complex averaging procedures and by identifying the most important fine-scale statistics that must be preserved in coarse-scale representations.

Traditional parameterizations in climate models are often designed for specific spatial and temporal resolutions. They may not perform well when applied at different scales or when resolution changes during model development. Scale-aware parameterizations represent sophisticated approaches that adapt their behavior based on the resolved scales in the host model, providing more robust and flexible representations of subgrid-scale processes.

Resolution-dependent parameterization schemes employ machine learning models that adjust their parameters and functional forms based on model resolution, recognizing that appropriate representations of unresolved processes depend on what scales are explicitly resolved. These schemes can learn how parameterization relationships should change with resolution and can provide smooth transitions between different resolution regimes.

Gray-zone parameterizations address the challenging intermediate regime where some scales of motion are partially resolved rather than being clearly resolved or unresolved. Machine learning approaches can learn appropriate treatments for these partially resolved scales by analyzing high-resolution simulations and identifying optimal blending strategies between explicit resolution and parameterized representation.

Multi-scale interaction terms capture the effects of cross-scale interactions that traditional scale-separated approaches may miss. Machine learning models can identify important interaction pathways and learn functional forms that represent how processes at different scales influence each other. These interaction terms can significantly improve model performance by accounting for scale coupling that is often neglected in traditional parameterizations.

Stochastic parameterizations incorporate random variability that represents the effects of unresolved scales on resolved scales, acknowledging that deterministic parameterizations may not capture the full range of subgrid-scale behavior. Machine learning approaches can learn appropriate stochastic formulations by analyzing the residual variability in high-resolution simulations and developing noise models that reproduce the statistical characteristics of unresolved processes.

Conditional parameterizations adapt their behavior based on large-scale atmospheric or oceanic conditions, recognizing that optimal subgrid-scale representations may depend on the dynamical regime. Machine learning models can identify relevant conditioning variables and learn how parameterization behavior should change under different large-scale conditions. These conditional approaches can significantly improve parameterization performance across diverse climate regimes.

Ensemble parameterizations employ multiple parameterization schemes simultaneously and use machine learning to determine optimal mixing weights based on current conditions. These approaches can adapt to situations where different parameterization schemes perform better and can provide uncertainty quantification through the diversity of parameterization responses. The mixing weights can be learned from validation data or updated online based on model performance.

Turbulence represents one of the most challenging multi-scale phenomena in climate modeling, involving nonlinear interactions across a continuous range of scales from millimeters to kilometers. Traditional turbulence parameterizations employ closure schemes that relate unresolved turbulent fluxes to resolved variables through algebraic or differential equations. Machine learning approaches offer enhanced capabilities for turbulence modeling through their ability to learn complex nonlinear relationships from high-resolution simulation data while maintaining computational efficiency in coarse-resolution models.

Reynolds-Averaged Navier-Stokes (RANS) approaches employ machine learning models to improve closure relationships for turbulent Reynolds stresses. These models can learn more sophisticated relationships between mean flow variables and turbulent fluxes than traditional algebraic closures, potentially improving accuracy while maintaining computational efficiency. Data-driven RANS closures can be trained on high-resolution simulation data and can adapt to different flow configurations and stability conditions.

Large Eddy Simulation (LES) applications use machine learning to improve sub-grid-scale models that represent the effects of turbulent scales smaller than the LES grid resolution. Neural network-based sub-grid-scale models can learn complex relationships between resolved-scale variables and sub-grid-scale fluxes while maintaining the conservation properties and numerical stability required for LES applications. These learned models can potentially achieve accuracy similar to dynamic sub-grid-scale models with reduced computational cost.

Boundary layer parameterizations represent critical components of climate models that determine surface-atmosphere exchanges and vertical mixing processes. Machine learning approaches can improve these parameterizations by learning from high-resolution boundary layer simulations and incorporating more sophisticated representations of stability effects, surface heterogeneity, and boundary layer structure. Neural network boundary layer schemes can adapt to different surface types and atmospheric conditions while maintaining physical consistency.

Convection parameterizations address the representation of cumulus convection that occurs on scales smaller than typical climate model grid resolution but has profound impacts on larger-scale circulation and energy balance. Machine learning approaches can learn convection triggering, intensity, and organization relationships from high-resolution convection-resolving simulations, potentially improving upon traditional convection schemes that rely on simplified assumptions about convective behavior.

Mixed-layer ocean models employ machine learning to improve representations of upper ocean turbulence and mixing processes that are crucial for air-sea interaction and ocean heat content evolution. These models can learn relationships between surface forcing, stratification, and mixing rates while maintaining conservation properties and physical consistency required for climate applications.

Non-local transport processes involve turbulent transport that cannot be represented through local gradient relationships, requiring more sophisticated approaches that account for counter-gradient fluxes and non-local mixing effects. Machine learning models can learn these non-local relationships from high-resolution data while providing computationally efficient representations suitable for climate models.

Cloud Microphysics and Radiation Interactions

Cloud processes represent some of the most complex and uncertain components of the climate system, involving multi-scale interactions between microphysical processes, radiation, and dynamics that span orders of magnitude in spatial and temporal scales. Traditional cloud parameterizations employ bulk microphysical schemes that represent cloud particle populations through moment-based approaches or bin-based methods. Machine learning offers enhanced capabilities for cloud process representation through its ability to learn complex relationships between environmental conditions and cloud properties while maintaining computational efficiency.

Microphysical process modeling employs machine learning to improve representations of cloud particle formation, growth, and interaction processes. Neural networks can learn relationships between environmental conditions and microphysical rates that are more sophisticated than traditional parameterizations while maintaining the computational efficiency required for climate model applications. These learned microphysical schemes can adapt to different cloud types and environmental conditions.

Cloud-radiation interactions involve complex relationships between cloud properties and radiative fluxes that are crucial for climate sensitivity and energy balance. Machine learning approaches can learn these relationships from detailed radiative transfer calculations while providing fast approximations suitable for climate model applications. Neural network radiation schemes can account for cloud heterogeneity and three-dimensional effects that are often neglected in traditional approaches.

Aerosol-cloud interactions represent particularly challenging multi-scale processes that involve relationships between aerosol properties, cloud condensation nuclei, and cloud microphysical properties. Machine learning models can learn these complex relationships from detailed process-level simulations while providing parameterizations that can adapt to different aerosol regimes and environmental conditions.

Cloud morphology and organization involve spatial patterns and structures that evolve through complex interactions between dynamics, microphysics, and radiation. Convolutional neural networks can learn to recognize and predict cloud organization patterns while providing statistical parameterizations that represent the effects of organization on radiative properties and precipitation efficiency.

Multi-phase processes in clouds involve interactions between water vapor, liquid water, and ice that occur through complex phase transition processes. Machine learning approaches can learn representations of these phase transitions that account for supercooling, ice nucleation, and mixed-phase processes while maintaining mass and energy conservation requirements.

Precipitation formation processes involve complex interactions between collision-coalescence, ice processes, and evaporation that determine precipitation efficiency and surface precipitation characteristics. Neural network approaches can learn these relationships from high-resolution microphysical simulations while providing efficient parameterizations for climate model applications.

Integration Strategies for Physics and AI Components

The development of effective hybrid modeling systems requires sophisticated integration strategies that seamlessly combine physics-based model components with artificial intelligence elements while maintaining the strengths of both approaches. These integration strategies must address challenges related to temporal and spatial scale matching, data flow between components, conservation property maintenance, and computational efficiency optimization. The choice of integration strategy significantly influences system performance, interpretability, and applicability to different climate modeling challenges.

Sequential integration approaches employ physics-based and AI components in a temporal sequence, with outputs from one component providing inputs to subsequent components. These approaches are particularly suitable for applications where different processes operate on clearly separated time scales or where preprocessing and postprocessing stages can benefit from AI enhancement. Sequential integration maintains clear separation between physics and AI components while enabling sophisticated processing chains.

Parallel integration strategies employ physics-based and AI components simultaneously, with both components processing the same input data and producing outputs that are combined through learned or prescribed mixing functions. These approaches are valuable when physics-based models provide baseline capabilities that can be enhanced through AI-based corrections or when ensemble methods combine multiple modeling approaches to improve accuracy and reliability.

Nested integration employs AI components within physics-based model frameworks, replacing specific parameterization schemes or computational modules with neural network-based alternatives. This approach maintains the overall structure and conservation properties of physics-based models while benefiting from improved process representations. Nested integration is particularly valuable for replacing computationally expensive components or improving uncertain parameterizations.

Bidirectional coupling strategies enable information exchange between physics and AI components throughout simulation execution, allowing both components to adapt their behavior based on feedback from other system elements. These approaches are particularly powerful for tightly coupled systems where physics and AI components must interact dynamically to achieve optimal performance.

Multi-level integration employs different integration strategies at different levels of model hierarchy, recognizing that optimal integration approaches may vary depending on the specific processes and scales involved. These hierarchical approaches can employ nested integration for individual parameterizations while using sequential integration for broader processing chains.

Adaptive integration strategies employ machine learning to determine optimal integration approaches based on current system conditions, data availability, or performance requirements. These approaches can dynamically adjust the relative contributions of physics and AI components or modify integration strategies based on evolving system characteristics.

Physics-based climate models provide robust frameworks for representing atmospheric, oceanic, and terrestrial processes through numerical solutions of fundamental governing equations. However, these models face limitations related to computational constraints, parameterization uncertainties, and resolution restrictions that can affect their accuracy and applicability. Machine learning approaches offer multiple pathways for enhancing physics-based models while maintaining their interpretability and physical consistency.

Bias correction applications employ machine learning models to identify and correct systematic biases in physics-based model output. These approaches can learn complex relationships between model errors and environmental conditions while providing corrections that improve model accuracy without modifying underlying physics representations. Bias correction models can be applied to different variables, regions, or time scales as needed.

Parameterization improvement employs machine learning to enhance or replace existing parameterization schemes with more sophisticated representations that better capture the relationships between resolved and unresolved processes. Neural network-based parameterizations can learn complex nonlinear relationships from high-resolution simulation data while maintaining the conservation properties and stability characteristics required for climate model applications.

Resolution enhancement techniques employ machine learning to generate high-resolution information from coarse-resolution model output, enabling detailed regional analysis without the computational cost of high-resolution global simulations. Super-resolution neural networks adapted for climate applications can generate realistic fine-scale features while maintaining consistency with coarse-scale dynamics and conservation properties.

Computational acceleration applications employ machine learning to approximate computationally expensive model components with fast neural network surrogates. These approaches can significantly reduce computational requirements for radiation schemes, chemistry modules, or other expensive components while maintaining acceptable accuracy for most applications. Surrogate models can be trained offline and deployed within operational model frameworks.

Data assimilation enhancement employs machine learning to improve the integration of observational data with model predictions. Neural network-based data assimilation schemes can learn complex relationships between observations and model states while providing more sophisticated error modeling and bias correction capabilities than traditional approaches.

Uncertainty quantification applications employ machine learning to provide enhanced estimates of model uncertainty that account for parametric uncertainties, structural uncertainties, and input uncertainties. Probabilistic neural networks can learn uncertainty relationships from ensemble simulations while providing fast uncertainty estimates for individual model runs.

Hybrid modeling systems must balance the competing demands of accuracy, physical consistency, and computational efficiency to remain practical for operational applications and long-term climate simulations. Machine learning components often require significant computational resources during training, but can provide substantial efficiency gains during operational deployment. Optimization strategies must consider both training costs and operational performance while maintaining acceptable accuracy levels.

Model compression techniques reduce the computational requirements of trained neural network components through methods such as pruning, quantization, and knowledge distillation. Pruned networks remove unnecessary connections or neurons while maintaining performance, quantization reduces numerical precision requirements, and knowledge distillation trains smaller student networks to approximate larger teacher networks. These techniques can significantly reduce computational and memory requirements for deployment.

Hardware acceleration strategies optimize machine learning components for specific computational architectures such as graphics processing units (GPUs), tensor processing units (TPUs), or field-programmable gate arrays (FPGAs). These optimizations can provide orders of magnitude improvement in computational performance while maintaining accuracy. Hardware-specific optimization often requires specialized implementations and deployment procedures.

Algorithmic optimization employs more efficient algorithms and numerical methods to reduce computational requirements without sacrificing accuracy. These optimizations might include more efficient training procedures, improved numerical solvers, or specialized algorithms designed for climate applications. Algorithmic improvements can provide benefits across different hardware platforms and deployment scenarios.

Memory optimization strategies reduce memory requirements through techniques such as gradient checkpointing, mixed precision training, and efficient data structures. Memory optimization is particularly important for large-scale climate applications where memory constraints may limit model size or require distributed computing approaches.

Load balancing and parallelization strategies distribute computational work across multiple processors or computational nodes while maintaining efficiency and minimizing communication overhead. Effective parallelization requires careful consideration of data dependencies, communication patterns, and load distribution to achieve optimal performance.

Online learning and adaptation techniques enable hybrid models to update their behavior based on new data or changing conditions without requiring complete retraining. These approaches can maintain model performance as conditions evolve while minimizing computational overhead associated with model updates.

The deployment of hybrid modeling systems in operational environments presents unique challenges related to computational constraints, reliability requirements, data integration, and decision support needs. Operational systems must maintain performance standards while operating under real-time constraints and varying data availability conditions. The integration of machine learning components introduces additional considerations related to model updating, uncertainty quantification, and failure handling.

Real-time data processing systems must efficiently integrate observational data streams from multiple sources while maintaining data quality and timeliness requirements. Machine learning components can enhance data processing through quality control algorithms, gap-filling procedures, and bias correction schemes that improve data consistency and completeness. These processing systems must operate reliably under varying data availability conditions.

Nowcasting applications employ hybrid models to provide short-term forecasts with lead times from minutes to hours, typically focusing on high-impact weather events such as severe thunderstorms, flash floods, or air quality episodes. These applications require rapid model execution and continuous updating as new observations become available. Machine learning components can significantly improve nowcasting accuracy through pattern recognition and rapid extrapolation capabilities.

Early warning systems integrate hybrid models with risk assessment and communication frameworks to provide timely warnings of hazardous conditions. These systems must balance the competing objectives of providing adequate lead time while minimizing false alarms. Machine learning components can improve warning accuracy through sophisticated pattern recognition and probabilistic risk assessment capabilities.

Decision support applications employ hybrid models to provide information that supports operational decisions in sectors such as agriculture, energy, transportation, and emergency management. These applications must translate model output into actionable information while accounting for user needs and decision contexts. Machine learning can enhance decision support through user modeling, optimization, and adaptive information presentation.

Model monitoring and validation systems continuously assess hybrid model performance and identify situations where model accuracy may be degraded. These systems employ automated performance metrics, comparison with observations, and anomaly detection to maintain model quality. Machine learning approaches can enhance monitoring systems through sophisticated performance assessment and automated quality control procedures.

Fallback and redundancy systems ensure continued operation when primary model components fail or produce unreliable results. These systems must identify failure conditions and switch to alternative modeling approaches while maintaining acceptable performance levels. Ensemble approaches and multi-model frameworks provide natural redundancy, while machine learning can enhance failure detection and recovery procedures.

Parameterization Enhancement through AI

Traditional parameterization schemes in climate models represent sub-grid-scale processes through simplified mathematical relationships that capture the essential physics while remaining computationally tractable. These schemes typically employ empirical relationships, scaling arguments, or simplified physical models that approximate complex process interactions. While traditional parameterizations have enabled significant advances in climate modeling capabilities, they face fundamental limitations that artificial intelligence approaches can help address.

Scale dependence represents a fundamental limitation of many traditional parameterizations that were developed for specific spatial and temporal resolutions and may not perform well when applied at different scales. As model resolution increases or varies spatially through adaptive mesh approaches, parameterizations may require adjustment or complete reformulation to maintain accuracy. Traditional approaches often lack systematic methods for handling scale dependence beyond simple scaling relationships.

Parameter uncertainty affects virtually all parameterization schemes through uncertain values of empirical coefficients, physical constants, or relationship parameters. Traditional approaches typically employ fixed parameter values that may not be optimal across different climate regimes, geographical regions, or temporal periods. The lack of systematic parameter optimization and uncertainty quantification limits parameterization performance and reliability.

Process coupling limitations arise when traditional parameterizations treat individual processes in isolation without adequately accounting for interactions and feedback between different physical processes. Many climate phenomena result from complex interactions between multiple processes that independent parameterization schemes may not capture. Traditional coupling approaches often employ simple linear superposition that may miss important nonlinear interaction effects.

Environmental state dependence is often inadequately represented in traditional parameterizations that may not adapt appropriately to different atmospheric or oceanic conditions. Many physical processes exhibit strongly nonlinear dependencies on environmental variables such as stability, moisture content, or wind shear that are difficult to capture through simple functional forms. Traditional parameterizations may perform well under typical conditions but fail under extreme or unusual environmental states.

Temporal memory effects are often neglected in traditional instantaneous parameterizations that assume process rates depend only on current environmental conditions. Many physical processes exhibit memory effects where current behavior depends on previous conditions or where process rates evolve over time scales longer than model time steps. Traditional approaches may miss important hysteresis effects or temporal accumulation processes.

Spatial heterogeneity and non-local effects are often inadequately represented in traditional parameterizations that assume spatial homogeneity over grid cells and employ purely local relationships. Many processes exhibit significant subgrid-scale variability or involve non-local transport and interaction effects that cannot be captured through simple area-averaged approaches.

Neural network-based parameterizations represent sophisticated approaches that employ artificial intelligence to learn complex relationships between environmental conditions and process rates from high-resolution simulation data or observational datasets. These approaches can potentially overcome many limitations of traditional parameterizations by learning nonlinear relationships, adapting to different environmental conditions, and accounting for complex process interactions automatically.

Architecture design for parameterization applications requires careful consideration of the specific characteristics of climate processes and the constraints imposed by host climate models. Parameterization networks must be computationally efficient enough for operational use while maintaining sufficient capacity to represent complex physical relationships. Multi-layer perceptrons provide flexibility for learning arbitrary nonlinear relationships, while specialized architectures can incorporate domain-specific knowledge or constraints.

Training data preparation represents a critical aspect of neural network parameterization development that requires high-quality datasets representative of the full range of environmental conditions and process behaviors. Training data are often derived from high-resolution simulations, field campaign observations, or laboratory measurements that must be carefully processed and quality-controlled. Data preprocessing may involve normalization, feature engineering, or dimensionality reduction to improve network training.

Physics constraints can be incorporated into neural network parameterizations through specialized loss functions, architectural choices, or output post-processing procedures that ensure physical consistency. Conservation constraints, monotonicity requirements, or dimensional consistency can be enforced through various techniques that maintain physical realism while benefiting from neural network flexibility.

Multi-variable parameterizations can handle complex process interactions by learning joint relationships between multiple input and output variables simultaneously. These approaches can capture process coupling effects that are difficult to represent through separate single-variable parameterizations. Multi-output networks can ensure consistency between related variables while maintaining computational efficiency.

Uncertainty quantification for neural network parameterizations employs ensemble methods, Bayesian approaches, or other techniques that provide estimates of parameterization uncertainty for use in ensemble forecasting or uncertainty propagation applications. Uncertainty estimates are crucial for maintaining appropriate confidence levels in model predictions that employ neural network parameterizations.

Online adaptation mechanisms enable neural network parameterizations to update their behavior based on new data or changing conditions without requiring complete retraining. These mechanisms can help parameterizations adapt to climate change, model resolution changes, or other evolving conditions while maintaining performance.

Traditional parameter tuning for climate model parameterizations often involves manual adjustment based on expert knowledge and limited sensitivity studies that may not explore the full parameter space or account for parameter interactions. Automated parameter tuning approaches employ systematic optimization techniques that can efficiently explore high-dimensional parameter spaces while accounting for multiple objectives and uncertainties.

Objective function design represents a critical aspect of automated parameter tuning that must balance multiple performance metrics while accounting for the specific goals of parameterization improvement. Objective functions might combine accuracy measures, physical consistency metrics, computational efficiency requirements, and uncertainty considerations. Multi-objective optimization approaches can explore trade-offs between competing objectives rather than requiring a priori weighting schemes.

Gradient-based optimization methods employ derivative information to efficiently navigate parameter spaces and identify optimal parameter configurations. These methods can be particularly effective when objective functions are smooth and gradients can be computed efficiently through automatic differentiation or finite difference approximations. Gradient-based methods often converge rapidly but may become trapped in local optima.

Evolutionary and genetic algorithms provide alternative optimization approaches that can handle discontinuous objective functions, multiple optima, and discrete parameter spaces that are challenging for gradient-based methods. These population-based methods explore parameter spaces through mechanisms inspired by biological evolution, providing good global optimization performance at the cost of increased computational requirements.

Bayesian optimization approaches employ probabilistic models of objective functions to guide parameter exploration efficiently, particularly when objective function evaluations are expensive or noisy. These methods build surrogate models of parameter-performance relationships and use acquisition functions to select promising parameter configurations for evaluation. Bayesian optimization can be particularly effective for tuning computationally expensive parameterizations.

Multi-scale optimization strategies recognize that optimal parameter values may depend on model resolution, domain size, or other modeling choices that affect the role of parameterizations. These approaches can simultaneously optimize parameters across multiple scales or can develop scale-aware parameter relationships that adapt automatically to different modeling configurations.

Ensemble-based optimization employs multiple parameter configurations simultaneously and uses ensemble performance metrics to guide parameter selection. These approaches can provide robust parameter estimates that perform well across diverse conditions while providing uncertainty quantification through ensemble diversity.

Stochastic and Probabilistic Approaches

Traditional deterministic parameterizations may inadequately represent the inherent variability and uncertainty associated with subgrid-scale processes, leading to systematic biases or unrealistic behavior in climate model simulations. Stochastic and probabilistic parameterizations address these limitations by explicitly incorporating randomness and uncertainty into process representations while maintaining computational efficiency and physical consistency.

Stochastic parameterization design involves adding random components to deterministic process representations to account for unresolved variability and uncertainty. The random components must be carefully designed to reproduce appropriate statistical characteristics while maintaining physical consistency and numerical stability. Stochastic parameterizations can improve ensemble spread, reduce systematic biases, and provide more realistic representations of natural variability.

Noise model development requires careful analysis of high-resolution simulation data or observational datasets to characterize the statistical properties of unresolved variability. Machine learning approaches can learn appropriate noise models that capture complex statistical relationships, including non-Gaussian distributions, spatial and temporal correlations, and state-dependent variability characteristics.

Conditional probability distributions represent sophisticated approaches that characterize the full probability distribution of process rates conditioned on environmental variables rather than providing only mean values. These distributions enable sampling of process rates that reflect appropriate uncertainty while maintaining consistency with environmental conditions. Neural networks can learn complex conditional probability relationships from training data.

State-dependent stochasticity acknowledges that the magnitude and characteristics of unresolved variability often depend on environmental conditions such as stability, moisture content, or wind speed. Machine learning approaches can learn relationships between environmental conditions and stochastic parameterization characteristics, enabling adaptive stochastic behavior that responds appropriately to changing conditions.

Temporal correlation modeling addresses the fact that stochastic perturbations often exhibit temporal memory rather than being independent from time step to time step. Autoregressive models, Markov processes, or more sophisticated time series models can represent temporal correlation structure while maintaining computational efficiency. Machine learning approaches can learn appropriate temporal correlation models from high-resolution data.

Spatial correlation considerations account for the fact that stochastic perturbations often exhibit spatial coherence that reflects the underlying physical processes generating the variability. Spatial correlation models must balance realism against computational efficiency while ensuring that spatial patterns are appropriate for the represented processes.

Multivariate stochastic approaches handle situations where multiple process rates exhibit correlated random variations that must be represented consistently. These approaches employ joint probability distributions or copula-based methods that maintain appropriate cross-variable relationships while providing stochastic variability for individual variables.

The implementation of physics-informed machine learning and hybrid modeling systems in operational climate applications requires sophisticated approaches to computational resource management that can balance the competing demands of accuracy, speed, and resource utilization. These systems often involve complex computational workflows that combine traditional numerical methods with machine learning inference, requiring careful optimization to achieve acceptable performance within available computational budgets.

Memory optimization strategies address the significant memory requirements of deep learning models while maintaining performance for large-scale climate applications. These strategies include gradient checkpointing techniques that trade computation for memory by recomputing intermediate values during backpropagation, model parallelism approaches that distribute large models across multiple devices, and data parallelism methods that process large datasets efficiently across distributed systems.

GPU acceleration techniques leverage the parallel computing capabilities of graphics processing units to accelerate both training and inference phases of machine learning components. Climate applications require specialized implementations that can efficiently handle irregular data structures, varying batch sizes, and the specific computational patterns characteristic of atmospheric and oceanic simulations. Mixed precision approaches using both 16-bit and 32-bit arithmetic can provide significant speedups while maintaining numerical accuracy.

Distributed computing frameworks enable the deployment of hybrid modeling systems across multiple computational nodes while maintaining efficient communication and load balancing. These frameworks must handle the complex data dependencies inherent in climate simulations while minimizing communication overhead between distributed components. Asynchronous execution patterns can overlap computation and communication to improve overall system efficiency.

Dynamic resource allocation strategies adapt computational resource usage based on current system state, forecast requirements, and available resources. These approaches can automatically adjust model complexity, batch sizes, or computational precision based on performance requirements and resource constraints. Machine learning meta-models can learn optimal resource allocation strategies based on historical performance data.

Cloud computing integration enables flexible deployment of hybrid modeling systems across different computational infrastructures while providing scalability and cost optimization capabilities. These deployments require careful consideration of data transfer costs, latency requirements, and security constraints while maintaining performance standards. Hybrid cloud-edge architectures can balance computational efficiency with data locality requirements.

Energy efficiency considerations become increasingly important as computational demands grow and environmental sustainability concerns influence computational infrastructure decisions. Energy-efficient algorithms, hardware-aware optimizations, and intelligent workload scheduling can significantly reduce energy consumption while maintaining performance. Green computing approaches consider both computational efficiency and environmental impact in system design decisions.

The deployment of physics-informed machine learning systems at the scales required for global climate modeling presents numerous technical challenges that must be addressed through careful system design and implementation strategies. These challenges span multiple dimensions, including computational scalability, numerical stability, data management, and system reliability under operational constraints.

Numerical stability challenges arise when machine learning components interact with traditional numerical solvers in ways that may introduce instabilities or conservation violations. Hybrid systems must carefully manage time stepping, variable coupling, and numerical precision to maintain stability while benefiting from machine learning enhancements. Stability analysis techniques adapted from traditional numerical methods provide frameworks for assessing and ensuring hybrid system stability.

Data management requirements for large-scale climate applications involve processing and storing massive datasets while maintaining acceptable performance for data access and manipulation. These systems must handle distributed data storage, efficient data loading pipelines, and data preprocessing workflows that can operate at scale without becoming computational bottlenecks. Modern data engineering approaches, including data lakes, streaming architectures, and caching strategies, provide solutions for large-scale data management.

Model versioning and reproducibility become critical concerns when deploying machine learning components in operational climate systems where model updates may affect long-term climate records or ensemble consistency. Version control systems must track not only model architectures and parameters but also training data, preprocessing procedures, and deployment configurations. Containerization technologies provide platforms for ensuring reproducible deployments across different computational environments.

Quality assurance and testing procedures must validate hybrid system performance across diverse conditions while ensuring that machine learning components maintain acceptable performance as conditions evolve. Continuous integration approaches can automate testing procedures, while monitoring systems can detect performance degradation or anomalous behavior in operational deployments. A/B testing strategies can evaluate new model components against established baselines.

Fault tolerance and error recovery mechanisms ensure continued operation when individual system components fail or produce anomalous results. These mechanisms must detect failures rapidly while providing graceful degradation of system performance rather than complete system failure. Redundancy strategies, checkpoint-restart capabilities, and automatic failover mechanisms provide resilience for operational climate systems.

Monitoring and diagnostics systems provide real-time visibility into hybrid system performance while identifying optimization opportunities and potential issues before they affect operational performance. These systems must track not only computational performance metrics but also physical consistency measures, prediction accuracy statistics, and resource utilization patterns. Machine learning approaches can enhance monitoring systems through anomaly detection and predictive maintenance capabilities.

The optimization of physics-informed machine learning systems for climate applications requires sophisticated approaches that address the unique characteristics of climate simulations, including irregular data patterns, multi-scale temporal dynamics, and complex physical constraints. Performance optimization must balance multiple competing objectives, including computational speed, memory usage, numerical accuracy, and physical consistency.

Algorithm optimization focuses on improving the fundamental algorithms employed in machine learning training and inference to achieve better performance for climate applications. These optimizations might include specialized solvers for physics-informed loss functions, improved automatic differentiation implementations for complex constraint handling, or custom algorithms designed specifically for multi-scale temporal integration. Domain-specific algorithms can often achieve significant performance improvements over general-purpose implementations.

Compilation and just-in-time optimization techniques can significantly improve performance by optimizing code at runtime based on actual data characteristics and hardware capabilities. These approaches are particularly valuable for hybrid systems where computational patterns may vary significantly depending on atmospheric conditions, season, or model configuration. Modern compiler frameworks provide sophisticated optimization capabilities, including vectorization, loop optimization, and hardware-specific code generation.

Caching and memoization strategies can eliminate redundant computations by storing and reusing results from expensive operations such as neural network inference, physical parameterizations, or diagnostic calculations. These approaches must carefully balance memory usage against computational savings while ensuring that cached results remain valid as system state evolves. Intelligent cache replacement policies can maximize cache effectiveness for climate simulation access patterns.

Batch processing optimization enables efficient processing of multiple related computations simultaneously, taking advantage of vectorization capabilities and reducing overhead costs associated with individual operations. Climate applications often involve processing multiple grid points, ensemble members, or time steps that can benefit from batch processing approaches. Dynamic batching strategies can adapt batch sizes based on available computational resources and current workload characteristics.

Precision optimization techniques balance numerical accuracy against computational performance by employing different numerical precisions for different computations based on accuracy requirements and sensitivity analysis. Mixed precision approaches can use reduced precision for less sensitive computations while maintaining full precision for critical calculations. Adaptive precision strategies can adjust numerical precision dynamically based on solution characteristics and accuracy requirements.

Profiling and performance analysis tools provide detailed insights into system performance bottlenecks and optimization opportunities. These tools must handle the complex computational patterns characteristic of hybrid climate systems while providing actionable insights for performance improvement. Performance modeling approaches can predict the impact of various optimization strategies before implementation.

Climate modeling applications are inherently well-suited to parallel computing approaches due to the spatial and temporal decomposition possibilities inherent in atmospheric and oceanic simulations. The integration of machine learning components introduces new parallelization challenges and opportunities that require sophisticated approaches to achieve optimal performance across diverse computational architectures.

Domain decomposition strategies divide spatial simulation domains across multiple computational processes while minimizing communication requirements between processes. These approaches must carefully handle boundary conditions, load balancing, and data dependencies introduced by machine learning components. Hybrid decomposition approaches can employ different strategies for physics-based and machine learning components to optimize overall system performance.

Temporal parallelization techniques enable parallel processing across time dimensions through approaches such as parallel-in-time methods that solve multiple time steps simultaneously or pipeline approaches that overlap different computational phases. These methods are particularly valuable for climate applications involving multiple time scales or when machine learning components have different temporal characteristics than physics-based components.

Model parallelism strategies distribute large machine learning models across multiple computational devices while maintaining efficient execution and communication patterns. These approaches are essential for very large neural networks that exceed the memory capacity of individual computational devices. Efficient model parallelism requires careful partitioning strategies that minimize communication while balancing computational load.

Data parallelism approaches process different subsets of input data simultaneously while maintaining synchronization for model updates and global reductions. These approaches can scale to very large numbers of computational processes but require efficient communication patterns for parameter updates and gradient synchronization. Asynchronous data parallelism can reduce communication overhead at the cost of some convergence guarantees.

Heterogeneous computing strategies leverage different types of computational hardware, including CPUs, GPUs, and specialized accelerators within unified computing systems. These approaches can optimize different components for their most suitable hardware while maintaining efficient data flow between different device types. Dynamic workload allocation can adapt to changing computational requirements and hardware availability.

Communication optimization techniques minimize the overhead associated with data transfer and synchronization between distributed components. These approaches include communication overlapping strategies that hide communication latency behind computation, data compression techniques that reduce communication volume, and topology-aware algorithms that optimize communication patterns for specific network architectures.

Multi-Model Ensemble Frameworks

Multi-model ensemble approaches combine predictions from multiple different climate models to provide improved accuracy and uncertainty quantification compared to individual models. The integration of physics-informed machine learning and hybrid modeling components into ensemble frameworks requires sophisticated approaches that can account for the different characteristics and uncertainties associated with various modeling approaches while maintaining the benefits of ensemble diversity.

Ensemble member selection strategies determine which models should be included in ensemble frameworks while considering factors such as model diversity, individual model skill, computational requirements, and ensemble size constraints. Traditional approaches often employ all available models or select models based on historical performance metrics. Machine learning approaches can optimize ensemble member selection by learning relationships between model characteristics and ensemble performance while accounting for correlation structures between models.

Weighting schemes determine how individual ensemble member predictions should be combined to produce final ensemble predictions. Equal weighting provides a simple baseline approach, while performance-based weighting can emphasize models with better historical skill. Adaptive weighting approaches employ machine learning to determine optimal weights based on current conditions, recognizing that optimal model combinations may vary depending on season, region, or meteorological regime.

Bias correction and calibration procedures address systematic errors in individual ensemble members while maintaining appropriate ensemble spread and reliability. Multi-model ensembles often exhibit biases and dispersion errors that can be corrected through post-processing procedures. Machine learning approaches can learn complex bias correction relationships that account for model-specific error characteristics and environmental dependencies.

Correlation modeling addresses the fact that ensemble members are often not independent due to shared physics, similar numerical methods, or common observational datasets used in model development. These correlations must be accounted for in ensemble uncertainty quantification and may require sophisticated statistical models that can represent complex correlation structures across multiple models and variables.

Dynamic ensemble configuration enables adaptive ensemble composition based on current conditions, forecast requirements, or computational constraints. Some ensemble members may perform better under specific conditions, and dynamic approaches can emphasize appropriate models automatically. Machine learning can learn optimal ensemble configuration strategies while maintaining ensemble diversity and reliability.

Model output integration requires careful handling of different model formats, variable definitions, grid structures, and temporal sampling to create consistent ensemble datasets. Standardization procedures must preserve important model characteristics while enabling meaningful comparison and combination of model outputs. Interpolation and regridding procedures must maintain conservation properties and avoid introducing artificial biases.

Statistical post-processing techniques improve ensemble predictions by correcting systematic biases, calibrating probabilistic forecasts, and enhancing prediction reliability. These approaches are essential for physics-informed machine learning and hybrid modeling systems that may exhibit different bias characteristics than traditional climate models while potentially requiring specialized post-processing procedures.

Bias correction methodologies address systematic differences between model predictions and observations through statistical transformation procedures. Traditional approaches employ simple mean bias removal or linear scaling, while more sophisticated methods can correct biases in higher-order moments, extreme values, or temporal correlation structure. Machine learning approaches can learn complex bias correction relationships that adapt to different conditions while preserving important statistical properties.

Quantile mapping techniques correct distributional biases by matching model prediction quantiles to observed quantiles across the full range of possible values. These approaches can correct biases in extreme events while preserving long-term mean characteristics. Non-parametric quantile mapping provides flexibility for complex distributional shapes, while parametric approaches may provide more robust corrections for limited data situations.

Temporal bias correction addresses systematic errors in temporal correlation, persistence, or variability characteristics that may not be corrected through simple distributional adjustments. These corrections may involve transformation of temporal covariance structures, adjustment of persistence parameters, or modification of transition probabilities for categorical variables. Spectral correction methods can address biases in specific frequency ranges.

Multivariate bias correction procedures handle situations where multiple variables must be corrected simultaneously while maintaining appropriate cross-variable relationships. These approaches are particularly important for applications involving multiple climate variables with complex interdependencies. Copula-based methods provide flexible frameworks for multivariate bias correction while preserving marginal correction quality.

Spatial bias correction addresses systematic errors that vary across geographical regions while accounting for spatial correlation structure in both biases and corrections. These approaches must balance local correction accuracy with spatial consistency requirements. Machine learning methods can learn spatially varying correction functions while maintaining smooth spatial transitions and physical consistency.

Calibration assessment and reliability evaluation ensure that post-processed ensemble predictions provide appropriate uncertainty quantification with reliable probability estimates. Calibration measures assess whether predicted probabilities match observed frequencies, while reliability diagrams provide a visual assessment of forecast reliability. Proper scoring rules provide a comprehensive evaluation of both accuracy and reliability simultaneously.

Uncertainty quantification in physics-informed machine learning and hybrid modeling systems requires sophisticated approaches that can account for multiple uncertainty sources, including parameter uncertainty, model structural uncertainty, input uncertainty, and approximation uncertainty introduced by machine learning components. The propagation of uncertainties through complex modeling chains presents significant technical challenges that require careful mathematical treatment and computational implementation.

Epistemic uncertainty arises from incomplete knowledge about system behavior, model parameters, or physical processes and can potentially be reduced through additional data collection or improved understanding. Machine learning models exhibit epistemic uncertainty through uncertainty in network weights, architectural choices, or training procedures. Bayesian approaches provide principled frameworks for representing and quantifying epistemic uncertainty through posterior distributions over model parameters.

Aleatoric uncertainty reflects inherent randomness in system behavior that cannot be reduced through additional knowledge or data collection. Climate systems exhibit aleatoric uncertainty through chaotic dynamics, stochastic forcing, and inherent variability at unresolved scales. Machine learning models can learn to represent aleatoric uncertainty through learned noise models or probabilistic output distributions.

Uncertainty propagation methodologies transport uncertainty estimates through modeling chains while accounting for nonlinear relationships and cross-variable correlations. Monte Carlo approaches provide straightforward propagation mechanisms through repeated model evaluations with sampled uncertain inputs. More sophisticated approaches employ polynomial chaos expansions, ensemble methods, or analytical approximation techniques that can provide efficient uncertainty propagation for complex systems.

Sensitivity analysis techniques identify which uncertain inputs contribute most significantly to prediction uncertainty, enabling targeted uncertainty reduction efforts and providing insights into system behavior. Global sensitivity analysis methods account for nonlinear relationships and interaction effects, while local sensitivity analysis provides information about system behavior near specific operating points. Machine learning metamodels can accelerate sensitivity analysis for computationally expensive systems.

Uncertainty decomposition approaches separate total prediction uncertainty into contributions from different uncertainty sources, enabling targeted improvement efforts and providing insights into system behavior. Analysis of variance techniques can quantify uncertainty contributions from different model components, while total effect indices can account for interaction effects between different uncertainty sources.

Multi-level uncertainty quantification addresses situations where uncertainty exists at multiple levels of model hierarchy, from individual parameterizations to overall system behavior. These approaches must consistently propagate uncertainties across different scales while accounting for scale-dependent uncertainty characteristics. Hierarchical Bayesian approaches provide frameworks for multi-level uncertainty quantification with appropriate uncertainty sharing across levels.

Ensemble-based data assimilation approaches combine ensemble forecasting with observational data to provide optimal estimates of system states while accounting for both model and observational uncertainties. The integration of physics-informed machine learning components into ensemble data assimilation systems requires sophisticated approaches that can handle the different uncertainty characteristics and computational requirements of hybrid modeling systems.

Ensemble Kalman filter approaches employ ensemble statistics to estimate background error covariances and to update ensemble states based on observational information. Traditional implementations assume Gaussian error distributions and linear relationships between observations and model states. Extensions to handle non-Gaussian error distributions and nonlinear observation operators are particularly relevant for systems involving machine learning components that may exhibit non-Gaussian behavior.

Particle filter approaches represent probability distributions through collections of discrete particles that can handle arbitrary probability distribution shapes and nonlinear system dynamics. These approaches are particularly suitable for highly nonlinear systems or situations with non-Gaussian uncertainty distributions. Particle filters can naturally accommodate machine learning components with complex uncertainty characteristics, but may require large ensemble sizes for high-dimensional systems.

Localization techniques address the fact that distant observations should have limited influence on local state estimates, particularly in high-dimensional systems where spurious correlations may arise from limited ensemble sizes. Spatial localization restricts the influence of observations based on geographical distance, while model variable localization can restrict cross-variable updates based on physical understanding or learned correlation structures.

Inflation procedures address ensemble underdispersion that commonly occurs in ensemble data assimilation systems due to limited ensemble sizes, model approximations, or inadequate representation of model uncertainty. Multiplicative inflation increases ensemble spread uniformly, while additive inflation can account for model error characteristics. Adaptive inflation approaches automatically adjust inflation parameters based on system performance and innovation statistics.

Hybrid data assimilation approaches combine different assimilation methodologies to leverage their complementary strengths. Hybrid ensemble-variational approaches combine ensemble covariance estimates with variational optimization procedures. Hybrid approaches can be particularly valuable for systems involving both traditional physics-based components and machine learning components with different uncertainty characteristics.

Quality control procedures ensure that observational data are appropriate for assimilation while identifying and handling problematic observations that could degrade analysis quality. Machine learning approaches can enhance quality control through sophisticated outlier detection, bias identification, and observation error characterization. Adaptive quality control can adjust acceptance criteria based on current system conditions and observation characteristics.

Model selection and performance evaluation for physics-informed machine learning and hybrid modeling systems require sophisticated approaches that can assess multiple dimensions of system performance while accounting for the specific characteristics and objectives of climate applications. Traditional evaluation metrics may not adequately capture the performance of systems that combine physics-based and data-driven components.

Cross-validation strategies must carefully handle temporal correlation structure and spatial dependencies inherent in climate data to provide reliable performance estimates. Time series cross-validation approaches respect temporal ordering while providing multiple independent evaluation periods. Spatial cross-validation can assess model transferability across different geographical regions while accounting for spatial correlation structure.

Physics consistency evaluation assesses whether hybrid models maintain appropriate physical behavior, including conservation properties, symmetry relationships, and realistic response to forcing changes. These evaluations may require specialized metrics that compare model behavior against physical expectations rather than just observational accuracy. Energy balance analysis, momentum conservation checks, and thermodynamic consistency evaluations provide physics-based performance assessment.

Multi-scale performance evaluation recognizes that climate models must perform well across multiple spatial and temporal scales simultaneously. Spectral analysis can assess model performance at different frequency ranges, while spatial scale analysis can evaluate performance at different spatial resolutions. Scale-dependent metrics can identify whether models perform consistently across different scales or exhibit scale-dependent biases.

Extreme event evaluation focuses specifically on model performance for rare events that may be underrepresented in standard evaluation datasets. These evaluations require specialized metrics that account for event rarity while providing a meaningful assessment of model capability for high-impact events. Extreme value analysis techniques provide frameworks for evaluating model performance in distributional tails.

Uncertainty evaluation assesses whether model uncertainty estimates are reliable and well-calibrated. Rank histograms evaluate ensemble reliability, while spread-error relationships assess whether ensemble spread appropriately represents forecast uncertainty. Probabilistic evaluation metrics assess both accuracy and reliability of probabilistic forecasts simultaneously.

Computational performance evaluation assesses efficiency, scalability, and resource utilization characteristics that are critical for operational deployment. These evaluations must consider both training costs and operational inference costs while accounting for different hardware architectures and deployment scenarios. Performance profiling can identify computational bottlenecks and optimization opportunities.

Explainable AI for Climate

The development of explainable artificial intelligence techniques for climate applications represents a critical frontier that addresses the need for interpretable and trustworthy AI systems in scientific and policy contexts. Climate applications require not only accurate predictions but also an understanding of the physical processes and relationships that drive model behavior. Explainable AI approaches must bridge the gap between black-box machine learning performance and the interpretability requirements of climate science.

Feature importance analysis techniques identify which input variables most strongly influence model predictions, providing insights into the physical relationships learned by machine learning models. Global feature importance measures assess variable significance across all predictions, while local importance measures can identify how variable significance changes under different conditions. SHAP (SHapley Additive exPlanations) values provide mathematically rigorous feature importance measures that satisfy desirable properties such as efficiency and symmetry.

Attention mechanism visualization reveals how transformer-based and attention-enhanced models focus on different spatial regions or temporal periods when making predictions. These visualizations can provide insights into the spatial patterns and temporal relationships that models consider most important for different prediction tasks. Attention patterns can be interpreted in terms of known physical processes and teleconnection patterns.

Activation analysis examines the internal representations learned by neural networks to understand how climate information is processed and represented within model architectures. Activation patterns can reveal whether networks learn physically meaningful feature representations and can identify layers or neurons that respond to specific climate phenomena. Clustering analysis of activations can identify distinct climate regimes or patterns recognized by models.

Counterfactual analysis explores how model predictions would change under hypothetical modifications to input conditions, providing insights into model sensitivity and causal relationships. These approaches can identify the specific changes in input conditions that would lead to different predictions, helping understand model behavior and potential failure modes. Counterfactual explanations can be particularly valuable for understanding extreme event predictions.

Model distillation approaches train simpler, more interpretable models to approximate the behavior of complex neural networks while maintaining acceptable accuracy. Decision trees, linear models, or other interpretable architectures can serve as surrogate models that provide insights into the relationships learned by complex models. Distillation approaches must balance interpretability against accuracy while ensuring that surrogate models capture essential system behavior.

Physical consistency analysis assesses whether learned relationships are consistent with known physical principles and can identify situations where models may be learning spurious correlations rather than physically meaningful relationships. These analyses can compare learned relationships against theoretical expectations or empirical observations to assess model reliability and trustworthiness.

The integration of physics-informed machine learning approaches with comprehensive Earth System Models represents a transformative opportunity to enhance climate modeling capabilities across multiple components and scales. Earth System Models couple atmospheric, oceanic, terrestrial, and cryospheric components with biogeochemical cycles to provide comprehensive representations of climate system behavior. The integration of machine learning components must carefully preserve coupling relationships and conservation properties while enhancing individual component performance.

Component-wise integration strategies replace or enhance individual Earth System Model components with machine learning alternatives while maintaining coupling interfaces and conservation properties. Atmospheric component enhancement might focus on improved cloud parameterizations, boundary layer representations, or radiation schemes. Oceanic component integration might address mixing parameterizations, biogeochemical process representations, or sea ice models.

Cross-component learning approaches develop machine learning models that can leverage information from multiple Earth System Model components simultaneously, potentially identifying cross-component relationships that are not captured by traditional coupling approaches. These models might learn relationships between atmospheric conditions and terrestrial carbon fluxes, or between oceanic conditions and atmospheric chemistry processes.

Scale bridging applications employ machine learning to connect different spatial and temporal scales within and between Earth System Model components. These approaches might develop upscaling relationships that aggregate fine-scale terrestrial processes to grid-scale representations, or downscaling approaches that provide fine-scale information from coarse-scale model output.

Biogeochemical cycle enhancement employs machine learning to improve representations of carbon, nitrogen, and other biogeochemical cycles that are critical for Earth System Model applications. These enhancements might focus on ecosystem process parameterizations, soil biogeochemistry representations, or atmospheric chemistry mechanisms that are computationally expensive or poorly understood.

Human dimension integration represents an emerging area where machine learning approaches can help incorporate human activities and decision-making into Earth System Models. These approaches might model land use change patterns, emission scenarios, or adaptation responses based on socioeconomic and environmental conditions.

Coupled system optimization employs machine learning to optimize the behavior of coupled Earth System Model components simultaneously rather than optimizing individual components separately. These approaches recognize that optimal parameter values or process representations for individual components may depend on the behavior of coupled components.

Quantum computing represents an emerging computational paradigm that may offer significant advantages for certain aspects of physics-informed machine learning and climate modeling applications. While current quantum computers are limited by noise and scale constraints, the potential for quantum advantage in specific problem types motivates ongoing research into quantum approaches for climate science applications.

Quantum machine learning algorithms leverage quantum computational principles to potentially achieve speedups or capabilities beyond classical machine learning approaches. Variational quantum algorithms can train parameterized quantum circuits to perform classification, regression, or optimization tasks that may be relevant for climate applications. Quantum neural networks employ quantum operations that may provide advantages for certain types of pattern recognition or optimization problems.

Quantum optimization approaches may provide advantages for parameter tuning, ensemble optimization, or other optimization problems that arise in climate modeling applications. Quantum annealing approaches can address combinatorial optimization problems, while quantum approximate optimization algorithms may handle more general optimization landscapes. The potential for quantum speedups depends critically on problem structure and may be most relevant for specific classes of optimization problems.

Quantum simulation techniques may enable the simulation of quantum mechanical processes that affect climate systems, such as molecular-level processes in atmospheric chemistry or quantum effects in radiation transfer. These applications may require fault-tolerant quantum computers that are not yet available but could provide unprecedented accuracy for certain process representations.

Near-term quantum approaches focus on hybrid classical-quantum algorithms that can provide benefits using near-term quantum devices with limited coherence and high noise levels. Variational quantum eigensolvers and quantum approximate optimization algorithms represent examples of near-term approaches that might find applications in climate science optimization problems.

Quantum advantage assessment requires careful analysis of problem characteristics to identify situations where quantum approaches may provide genuine advantages over classical alternatives. The overhead costs of quantum computation must be weighed against potential speedups, and realistic assessments must account for noise and error rates in current quantum devices.

The application of machine learning to climate policy and decision support represents an important frontier that extends beyond traditional climate modeling to address the societal applications of climate information. These applications must translate complex scientific information into actionable guidance while accounting for stakeholder needs, uncertainty quantification, and decision contexts.

Risk assessment and impact modeling employ machine learning to translate climate projections into assessments of risks and impacts for specific sectors, regions, or systems. These applications require integration of climate information with vulnerability and exposure data while accounting for adaptation measures and social factors that influence impact severity. Machine learning approaches can learn complex relationships between climate conditions and impact outcomes while providing uncertainty quantification.

Adaptation planning applications employ machine learning to evaluate the effectiveness of different adaptation strategies under different climate scenarios. These approaches can learn relationships between adaptation measures and outcome metrics while accounting for cost constraints and implementation challenges. Optimization approaches can identify cost-effective adaptation portfolios that perform well across multiple climate scenarios.

Mitigation policy analysis employs machine learning to assess the effectiveness of different emission reduction policies while accounting for economic, social, and technological constraints. These applications may involve integrated assessment modeling that couples climate projections with economic and social system representations. Machine learning can enhance these models through improved representation of technological change, behavioral responses, and policy effectiveness.

Decision support systems integrate climate information with decision-making frameworks to provide actionable guidance for planners, managers, and policy makers. These systems must account for different decision contexts, risk preferences, and information needs while providing accessible interfaces and clear communication of uncertainty. Machine learning can enhance decision support through personalization, optimization, and adaptive information presentation.

Early warning and real-time decision support employ machine learning to provide actionable information for short-term decision-making under evolving climate conditions. These applications require rapid processing of observational data and model output while providing clear communication of risks and recommended actions. Machine learning approaches can enhance early warning systems through improved pattern recognition, impact prediction, and decision optimization.

Multi-stakeholder engagement platforms employ machine learning to facilitate communication and collaboration between different stakeholders with diverse information needs and decision contexts. These platforms can provide customized information presentation, facilitate trade-off analysis, and support collaborative decision-making processes that account for different perspectives and priorities.

Physics-informed machine learning and hybrid modeling systems represent a paradigmatic shift in computational climate science that promises to address fundamental limitations of both traditional physics-based models and purely data-driven approaches. Through the integration of physical principles with machine learning capabilities, these approaches provide pathways to enhanced accuracy, improved computational efficiency, and better representation of complex multi-scale processes that characterize Earth's climate system.

The theoretical foundations explored in this chapter demonstrate that physics-informed neural networks provide mathematically rigorous frameworks for embedding physical constraints into machine learning models while maintaining the flexibility and pattern recognition capabilities that make neural networks powerful for complex problem solving. The automatic differentiation techniques that enable efficient evaluation of differential equation residuals, combined with sophisticated loss function designs that balance data fitting against physics satisfaction, create learning frameworks that can discover solutions that are both empirically accurate and physically consistent.

The development of constraint-based learning approaches provides systematic methods for incorporating domain knowledge and physical principles into machine learning models through both hard and soft constraint implementations. These approaches ensure that learned relationships respect fundamental physical laws such as conservation principles while providing sufficient flexibility to discover new relationships and adapt to different environmental conditions. The integration of uncertainty quantification techniques enables these approaches to provide reliable confidence estimates that are essential for climate science applications.

Multi-scale modeling capabilities represent one of the most significant advantages of physics-informed machine learning approaches, enabling the representation of interactions across the vast range of spatial and temporal scales that characterize climate systems. The hierarchical architectures and scale-aware parameterizations discussed in this chapter provide frameworks for bridging scales that are computationally prohibitive to resolve explicitly while maintaining physical consistency across scale interactions.

Hybrid modeling systems extend these capabilities by combining physics-based model components with machine learning elements in unified frameworks that leverage the complementary strengths of both approaches. The integration strategies and parameterization enhancement techniques enable the development of climate models that maintain the interpretability and physical realism of traditional approaches while benefiting from improved accuracy and computational efficiency provided by artificial intelligence.

The scalability and efficiency considerations addressed in this chapter are crucial for the practical deployment of these approaches in operational climate applications. The computational resource management techniques, performance optimization strategies, and parallel computing approaches provide pathways for achieving the computational performance required for large-scale climate simulations while maintaining the sophisticated capabilities enabled by machine learning integration.

Ensemble methods and model averaging approaches provide frameworks for uncertainty quantification and improved prediction reliability that are essential for climate science applications. The statistical post-processing techniques and bias correction approaches enable the integration of physics-informed machine learning components into ensemble forecasting systems while maintaining appropriate uncertainty characterization and prediction reliability.

The advanced topics and future directions explored in this chapter highlight the tremendous potential for continued development in this field. Explainable AI techniques are essential for maintaining the scientific interpretability that is crucial for climate science applications. Integrating these techniques with comprehensive Earth System Models provides opportunities to enhance climate modeling capabilities across multiple components and scales simultaneously.

Looking toward the future, several key research priorities emerge from this analysis. The development of more sophisticated physics constraints that can handle complex multi-physics interactions while maintaining computational efficiency represents an ongoing challenge that will benefit from continued mathematical and computational innovation. The integration of machine learning approaches with high-performance computing architectures optimized for climate applications will be essential for achieving the computational performance required for next-generation climate models.

The democratization of these approaches through user-friendly software frameworks and educational resources will be crucial for widespread adoption across the climate science community. This includes the development of standardized interfaces, validation procedures, and best practices that can ensure consistent and reliable application of physics-informed machine learning techniques across different institutions and applications.

Climate change adaptation and mitigation applications represent important frontiers where physics-informed machine learning can provide enhanced capabilities for translating climate science into actionable information for decision-makers. The development of integrated assessment frameworks that combine climate projections with impact models and decision support systems will require continued collaboration between climate scientists, machine learning researchers, and policy experts.

The ethical and societal implications of deploying artificial intelligence (AI) in climate applications warrant sustained attention, particularly concerning equity, accessibility, and the potential for algorithmic bias in systems that influence resource allocation and risk management decisions. The development of ethical frameworks and governance structures for climate AI applications will be crucial in ensuring that these powerful technologies serve the public interest and support just and effective climate action.

In conclusion, physics-informed machine learning and hybrid modeling systems represent transformative approaches that are reshaping computational climate science and providing enhanced capabilities for understanding, predicting, and responding to climate change. The continued development and deployment of these approaches will play essential roles in advancing climate science while supporting society's urgent need for reliable climate information and effective climate solutions. Success in this endeavor will necessitate continued collaboration across disciplinary boundaries, sustained investment in research and development, and careful consideration of the societal implications of these powerful new technologies.

EIGHT

Explainable AI

Spatial consistency evaluation assesses whether AI models generate spatially coherent predictions that adhere to geographical relationships and physical constraints. Climate applications necessitate spatial consistency validation across various scales, from localized weather patterns to global circulation systems. Inconsistent spatial predictions may indicate model issues or unsuitable application conditions.

Uncertainty quantification validation examines whether AI models provide reliable uncertainty estimates that accurately reflect prediction confidence and error characteristics. Climate science applications require well-calibrated uncertainty estimates that neither underestimate nor overestimate prediction reliability. Calibration analysis, reliability assessment, and probabilistic validation provide methods for uncertainty validation.

Long-term stability analysis evaluates whether AI model performance remains consistent over extended time periods and whether the models adapt appropriately to changing conditions. Climate applications may involve decades-long prediction horizons that require sustained model reliability. Stability analysis helps identify potential degradation in model performance and the need for model updates or retraining.

Effective communication of AI model limitations represents a critical component of building appropriate trust and confidence in climate AI systems. Transparent communication of limitations helps stakeholders develop realistic expectations, make appropriate decisions about model applications, and avoid over-reliance on model predictions in situations where limitations may compromise reliability.

Scope and applicability boundaries define the conditions, variables, and applications for which AI models are designed and validated. Clear communication of these boundaries helps stakeholders understand when models are appropriate for their specific needs and when alternative approaches might be more suitable. Boundary documentation should include temporal scales, spatial scales, climate variables, and geographical regions covered by model validation.

Performance limitations across different conditions provide stakeholders with realistic expectations about model accuracy and reliability under various circumstances. Climate AI models may perform differently across seasons, regions, extreme events, or climate regimes, and these performance variations must be clearly communicated. Performance documentation should include accuracy metrics, confidence intervals, and known failure modes.

Data dependency limitations describe how model performance depends on data availability, quality, and characteristics. Climate AI models trained on specific datasets may not perform well when applied to regions or time periods with different data characteristics. Data dependency communication helps stakeholders assess whether models are appropriate for their specific data contexts and applications.

Extrapolation risks arise when AI models are applied to conditions outside their training data range, potentially leading to unreliable or physically unrealistic predictions. Climate change applications often require extrapolation to future conditions that may differ significantly from historical training data. Clear communication of extrapolation risks helps stakeholders understand the uncertainty associated with climate change projections.

Update and maintenance requirements describe the ongoing efforts needed to maintain AI model performance and relevance as conditions change over time. Climate AI models may require periodic retraining, recalibration, or architectural updates to maintain performance. Maintenance communication helps stakeholders plan for long-term model use and budget for necessary updates.

Alternative model recommendations provide guidance on complementary or alternative modeling approaches that might be more appropriate for specific applications or that can provide validation and comparison perspectives. Climate science benefits from diverse modeling approaches, and communication should help stakeholders understand how AI models fit within broader modeling ecosystems.

Known biases and systematic errors provide transparent acknowledgment of model limitations that might affect specific populations, regions, or applications. Climate AI models may exhibit biases due to training data limitations, architectural choices, or optimization procedures. Bias communication enables stakeholders to make informed decisions about model use and to develop mitigation strategies where necessary.

Quality assurance frameworks provide systematic approaches for maintaining and verifying AI model quality throughout their development, deployment, and operational use. Climate science applications require comprehensive quality assurance that addresses technical performance, scientific validity, and ethical considerations while supporting continuous improvement and stakeholder confidence.

Continuous monitoring systems track AI model performance in operational applications, detecting degradation, drift, or anomalous behavior that might indicate quality problems. Climate science monitoring might track prediction accuracy, bias patterns, uncertainty calibration, and consistency with physical constraints. Automated monitoring enables rapid identification of quality issues and triggers for corrective action.

Periodic review and assessment processes systematically evaluate AI model performance, relevance, and alignment with stakeholder needs. Regular assessments might evaluate model performance against new validation data, assess consistency with updated scientific understanding, and gather stakeholder feedback about model utility and limitations. Periodic reviews support evidence-based decisions about model updates, replacement, or discontinuation.

Version control and change management procedures ensure that AI model modifications are systematically tracked, tested, and documented to maintain quality and reproducibility. Climate science applications may involve complex model evolution over time, and robust change management helps maintain consistency and enables rollback to previous versions if problems arise. Version control supports reproducibility and quality assurance across model generations.

Independent audit and certification processes provide external validation of AI model quality through evaluation by qualified third-party assessors. Independent audits can assess technical performance, scientific validity, ethical compliance, and alignment with quality standards. Certification processes provide stakeholder assurance that models meet established quality criteria.

Documentation and transparency standards ensure that AI model development, validation, and operational characteristics are comprehensively documented and accessible to relevant stakeholders. Quality documentation includes technical specifications, validation results, known limitations, and operational guidance. Standardized documentation formats support comparison and evaluation across different models and applications.

Incident response and corrective action procedures provide systematic approaches for addressing quality issues, errors, or failures in AI model performance. Climate science incident response might address prediction failures, bias discoveries, or ethical concerns through root cause analysis, corrective measures, and prevention strategies. Robust incident response maintains stakeholder confidence through transparent problem resolution.

Stakeholder feedback integration ensures that user experiences, concerns, and suggestions are systematically collected and incorporated into quality assurance processes. Stakeholder feedback provides valuable insights into model performance in real applications and helps identify quality issues that might not be apparent through technical testing alone. Feedback integration supports continuous improvement and stakeholder satisfaction.

Gradient-based attribution methods represent fundamental approaches for understanding AI model behavior through analysis of gradients that describe how model outputs change in response to input perturbations. In climate science applications, gradient-based methods provide insights into which climate variables most strongly influence predictions and how sensitive predictions are to changes in atmospheric, oceanic, or terrestrial conditions.

Vanilla gradient attribution computes the partial derivatives of model outputs with respect to input variables, providing direct measures of local sensitivity around specific input points. For climate AI applications, vanilla gradients might reveal that temperature predictions are most sensitive to changes in atmospheric pressure at certain altitudes, or that precipitation predictions are most influenced by specific humidity variables. While computationally efficient, vanilla gradients may suffer from saturation problems in deep networks where gradients become very small.

Integrated gradients address limitations of vanilla gradient methods by integrating gradients along paths from baseline inputs to actual inputs, providing more stable and comprehensive attribution measures. Climate science applications benefit from integrated gradients that can handle the complex, multi-scale nature of climate data while providing meaningful attribution measures that satisfy mathematical properties such as sensitivity and implementation invariance.

Guided back-propagation and deconvolution methods modify gradient computation procedures to enhance attribution quality by focusing on positive contributions and reducing noise from negative gradients. These methods can provide cleaner attribution visualizations for climate data, highlighting the most important patterns and features that drive model predictions while suppressing less relevant details.

SmoothGrad approaches reduce noise in gradient-based attribution by averaging gradients computed over multiple samples drawn from noise distributions around target inputs. Climate data applications benefit from SmoothGrad approaches that can provide more stable attribution measures despite the inherent variability and noise in climate observations. The averaging procedure helps identify robust attribution patterns that persist across small data perturbations.

Gradient times input attribution combines gradient magnitudes with input values to provide attribution measures that account for both sensitivity and input magnitude. This approach can be particularly valuable for climate applications where both the sensitivity to variables and their actual magnitudes contribute to prediction importance. Variables with high gradients but small magnitudes may be less important than variables with moderate gradients but large magnitudes.

Layer-wise relevance propagation extends gradient-based approaches by propagating relevance scores backward through network layers according to conservation principles that maintain total relevance across the network. Climate AI applications can use LRP to understand how different network layers contribute to predictions and how climate information is transformed through different processing stages.

Expected gradients provide probabilistic extensions of gradient-based attribution by computing expected gradients over distributions of baseline inputs rather than using single baseline values. Climate science applications can benefit from expected gradients that account for natural climate variability when establishing baseline conditions for attribution analysis.

Ranking Methods

Feature importance and ranking methods provide systematic approaches for identifying and ordering the climate variables that contribute most significantly to AI model predictions. These methods are essential for climate science applications where understanding the relative importance of different atmospheric, oceanic, and terrestrial variables can inform scientific understanding, model validation, and decision-making processes.

Permutation importance measures feature importance by evaluating how much model performance decreases when specific features are randomly permuted or shuffled. Climate science applications can use permutation importance to assess which climate variables are most critical for maintaining prediction accuracy. This model-agnostic approach works with any AI architecture and provides intuitive importance measures, though it may be computationally expensive for large climate datasets.

Drop-column importance evaluates feature importance by measuring performance changes when specific features are completely removed from the input data. This approach provides insights into which climate variables are essential for model function and which variables are redundant or less important. Drop-column analysis can help identify optimal feature sets for climate AI applications and reduce computational requirements.

Mean decrease impurity and mean decrease accuracy methods, commonly used with tree-based models, measure feature importance based on how much each feature contributes to decreasing impurity or increasing accuracy across all decision trees. While these methods are specific to tree-based approaches, they provide valuable insights for ensemble methods and can serve as benchmarks for feature importance in climate applications.

Recursive feature elimination systematically removes features from models, evaluating performance changes to identify optimal feature subsets and rank feature importance. Climate science applications can utilize RFE to identify the minimal sets of climate variables required for accurate predictions, thereby supporting model simplification and computational efficiency while maintaining performance.

Principal component analysis and factor analysis approaches identify combinations of climate variables that explain the most variance in predictions, providing insights into the underlying patterns and relationships that drive model behavior. These dimensionality reduction techniques can reveal which combinations of climate variables are most informative and how different variables interact to influence predictions.

Mutual information and correlation-based feature selection methods evaluate feature importance based on statistical relationships between input variables and predictions. Climate science applications can use these methods to identify variables with the strongest statistical associations with predicted outcomes while accounting for nonlinear relationships that may not be captured by simple correlation analysis.

Forward and backward feature selection approaches iteratively add or remove features to identify optimal feature sets that maximize performance while minimizing complexity. These methods can help climate scientists understand which combinations of variables provide the most predictive power and identify redundant measurements that do not contribute additional information.

Perturbation-based analysis methods evaluate AI model behavior by systematically modifying input data and observing resulting changes in predictions. These approaches are particularly valuable for climate science applications because they can simulate realistic variations in climate conditions and assess model sensitivity to different types of changes that might occur in nature or under different scenarios.

Input perturbation experiments modify individual climate variables or combinations of variables to assess their impact on model predictions. Climate science applications might perturb temperature fields, precipitation patterns, or atmospheric circulation indices to understand how sensitive predictions are to changes in these variables. Perturbation experiments can simulate measurement uncertainties, climate variability, or potential climate change impacts.

Ablation studies systematically remove or mask different components of input data to assess their contribution to model predictions. Climate AI applications might use ablation studies to understand the importance of different spatial regions, time periods, or atmospheric levels for specific predictions. Spatial ablation can reveal which geographical areas are most important for predicting conditions in target regions.

Occlusion analysis evaluates model predictions when different parts of input data are replaced with neutral or average values, providing insights into which data components are most critical for accurate predictions. Climate science applications might use occlusion analysis to understand which parts of weather maps or time series are most important for extreme event predictions or seasonal forecasts.

Noise injection experiments add controlled amounts of random noise to input data to assess model robustness and identify which components of predictions are most sensitive to data quality issues. Climate AI applications can use noise injection to simulate measurement uncertainties, data transmission errors, or incomplete observations that commonly occur in operational settings.

Adversarial perturbation analysis examines model behavior when inputs are modified in ways specifically designed to cause prediction changes, helping identify model vulnerabilities and robustness limitations. While adversarial examples may not be directly relevant to natural climate variations, they can reveal model instabilities and help improve robustness to unexpected input conditions.

Counterfactual perturbation methods identify minimal changes to input conditions required to achieve specific changes in predictions, providing insights into the decision boundaries and critical thresholds in AI models. Climate science applications might use counterfactual analysis to understand the minimum atmospheric changes needed to shift drought predictions or to trigger extreme weather warnings.

Scenario-based perturbation experiments evaluate model behavior under realistic alternative conditions such as different emission scenarios, land use changes, or natural variability patterns. These experiments help assess model behavior under conditions that may occur in the future but are not well-represented in historical training data.

Causal Inference in Climate Models

Causal inference represents an advanced frontier in explainable AI that attempts to identify genuine causal relationships rather than merely correlational associations in AI model behavior. Climate science applications particularly benefit from causal inference approaches because understanding causal mechanisms is essential for scientific interpretation, policy development, and intervention design in climate systems.

Causal discovery algorithms attempt to infer causal graph structures from observational data, identifying potential causal relationships between different climate variables and model predictions. These approaches can help climate scientists understand whether AI models have learned physically meaningful causal relationships or whether they rely on spurious correlations that might not hold under different conditions.

Instrumental variable approaches use external variables that affect predictors but not outcomes directly to identify causal effects in situations where confounding variables make causal identification challenging. Climate science applications might use natural experiments such as volcanic eruptions or El Niño events as instrumental variables to identify causal relationships in AI models.

Counterfactual reasoning frameworks provide formal approaches for reasoning about causal effects by comparing observed outcomes with hypothetical outcomes under alternative conditions. Climate AI applications can use counterfactual frameworks to assess how predictions would change under different intervention scenarios or alternative climate conditions.

Mediation analysis examines causal pathways by identifying intermediate variables that mediate relationships between predictors and outcomes. Climate science applications might use mediation analysis to understand whether temperature effects on ecosystem productivity are mediated through soil moisture changes or whether precipitation effects on flooding are mediated through soil saturation conditions.

Natural experiment identification leverages quasi-experimental situations in climate data where natural variations approximate controlled experiments. Volcanic eruptions, major climate oscillations, or land use changes can provide natural experiments that help identify causal relationships in AI model behavior.

Granger causality and temporal causal analysis examine whether past values of certain variables help predict future values of other variables beyond what can be predicted from the target variable's own history. Climate AI applications can use Granger causality to assess whether models have learned appropriate temporal causal relationships between different climate variables.

Structural causal modeling provides comprehensive frameworks for representing and reasoning about causal relationships using directed acyclic graphs and structural equation models. These approaches can help climate scientists understand the causal assumptions embedded in AI models and assess whether those assumptions are consistent with a physical understanding of climate processes.

SHAP (SHapley Additive exPlanations) values represent a unified framework for model explanation, providing theoretically grounded attribution measures based on cooperative game theory principles. The mathematical foundation of SHAP ensures that attributions satisfy desirable properties, including efficiency, symmetry, dummy feature, and additivity, making SHAP particularly valuable for climate science applications where rigorous mathematical guarantees are important for scientific credibility and reproducibility.

The Shapley value concept originates from cooperative game theory, where it provides a method for fairly distributing payoffs among players in a coalition based on their marginal contributions. In the context of explainable AI, features are treated as players, and the prediction is treated as the payoff that must be fairly attributed among contributing features. This game-theoretic foundation ensures that SHAP attributions satisfy mathematical properties that make them reliable and interpretable.

The symmetry property ensures that features with identical contributions to model predictions receive identical SHAP values, regardless of their ordering or labeling. Climate science applications benefit from this property because it ensures that equivalent climate variables or measurements receive appropriate attribution without bias from arbitrary feature ordering or naming conventions.

The dummy feature property ensures that features that do not contribute to model predictions receive zero SHAP values. This property helps climate scientists identify which variables are genuinely important for specific predictions and which variables may be included in models but do not actually influence outcomes.

The additivity property ensures that SHAP values for combined models equal the sum of SHAP values from individual component models. This property is valuable for climate science applications involving ensemble models or hybrid approaches where understanding the contributions of different model components is important for validation and interpretation.

The computation of SHAP values for climate AI applications presents unique challenges due to the high dimensionality, multi-scale temporal and spatial structure, and complex correlation patterns characteristic of climate data. Efficient computation methods and appropriate approximation techniques are essential for making SHAP analysis practical for large-scale climate applications while maintaining accuracy and interpretability.

Exact SHAP computation requires evaluating model predictions for all possible feature subsets, leading to exponential computational complexity that is prohibitive for high-dimensional climate datasets. The exact approach may be feasible for small climate models or when focusing on limited sets of key variables, but approximation methods are generally necessary for practical climate applications.

Sampling-based approximation methods estimate SHAP values by randomly sampling feature subsets rather than exhaustively evaluating all possible combinations. These methods can provide reasonable SHAP estimates with manageable computational requirements, though the accuracy depends on sampling strategies and sample sizes. Climate applications may benefit from importance sampling approaches that focus computational effort on the most relevant feature combinations.

TreeSHAP provides efficient exact computation of SHAP values for tree-based models, including random forests and gradient boosting machines. Many climate science applications employ tree-based models due to their interpretability and robustness, making TreeSHAP a valuable tool for efficient SHAP computation. TreeSHAP can handle high-dimensional climate data efficiently while providing exact rather than approximate SHAP values.

DeepSHAP extends SHAP computation to deep neural networks by combining SHAP with gradient-based attribution methods. Climate science applications using deep learning models can benefit from DeepSHAP approaches that provide efficient approximations of SHAP values while leveraging gradient information available in neural networks. DeepSHAP can handle the complex architectures commonly used in climate AI applications.

KernelSHAP provides model-agnostic SHAP computation that can be applied to any machine learning model regardless of its internal architecture. This approach treats models as black boxes and estimates SHAP values through systematic sampling and local linear approximation. Climate science applications can use KernelSHAP to provide consistent SHAP analysis across different model types and architectures.

Interventional SHAP modifies standard SHAP computation to account for feature dependencies and correlations that are particularly important in climate data. Traditional SHAP computation assumes feature independence, which may not be appropriate for climate variables that exhibit strong spatial and temporal correlations. Interventional approaches provide more realistic SHAP estimates for correlated climate data.

Conditional SHAP computation accounts for feature dependencies by conditioning SHAP calculations on observed feature relationships. Climate applications can benefit from conditional SHAP that maintains realistic relationships between climate variables while computing attribution measures. Conditional approaches may provide more interpretable results for climate scientists familiar with physical relationships between variables.

Case Studies

SHAP values provide powerful tools for understanding AI model behavior in diverse climate science applications, from weather prediction and climate projection to extreme event analysis and impact assessment. The theoretical guarantees and intuitive interpretation of SHAP values make them particularly suitable for climate applications where scientific rigor and stakeholder communication are essential.

Seasonal prediction applications can use SHAP analysis to understand which climate variables contribute most significantly to seasonal forecasts for different regions and seasons. SHAP analysis might reveal that Pacific sea surface temperatures are most important for winter precipitation predictions over North America, while Atlantic conditions are more important for European seasonal forecasts. These insights support validation against known teleconnection patterns and help identify potential model improvements.

Extreme event prediction applications employ SHAP analysis to understand the factors driving predictions of hurricanes, droughts, floods, heat waves, and other high-impact events. SHAP values can identify which atmospheric conditions are most critical for the development of extreme events and help validate model reasoning against meteorological understanding. For hurricane intensity prediction, SHAP analysis might reveal the relative importance of sea surface temperatures, wind shear, atmospheric instability, and other environmental factors.

Climate change attribution studies use SHAP analysis to understand how AI models distinguish between natural climate variability and anthropogenic climate change signals. SHAP values can identify which variables and patterns are most important for attribution decisions and help validate model reasoning against the established understanding of climate change fingerprints. These applications support confidence in AI-based attribution methods and help communicate attribution results to stakeholders.

Regional climate analysis employs SHAP values to understand how AI models adapt their behavior to different geographical regions and climate regimes. SHAP analysis can reveal which climate variables are most important in different regions and how model behavior changes across spatial gradients. These insights support validation of AI models for regional applications and help identify potential biases or limitations in regional coverage.

Agricultural impact assessment applications use SHAP analysis to understand how AI models predict crop yields, pest outbreaks, or other agricultural impacts based on climate conditions. SHAP values can identify which climate variables are most critical for agricultural predictions and help validate model reasoning against agronomic knowledge. These applications support precision agriculture and climate adaptation planning for agricultural systems.

Urban climate applications employ SHAP analysis to understand how AI models predict urban heat islands, air quality, or other urban climate phenomena. SHAP values can reveal the relative importance of meteorological conditions, urban morphology, and anthropogenic activities for urban climate predictions. These insights support urban planning and climate adaptation strategies for cities.

Ecosystem response modeling uses SHAP analysis to understand how AI models predict vegetation dynamics, carbon fluxes, or biodiversity responses to climate conditions. SHAP values can identify which climate variables are most important for ecosystem predictions and help validate model reasoning against ecological understanding. These applications support ecosystem management and conservation planning under climate change.

The effective interpretation of SHAP values in climate science applications requires understanding both the mathematical properties of SHAP and the domain-specific considerations that arise in climate data analysis. Guidelines for SHAP interpretation help climate scientists extract meaningful insights while avoiding common pitfalls and misinterpretations that can lead to incorrect conclusions.

Baseline selection represents a critical consideration for SHAP interpretation in climate applications. The baseline or expected value used in SHAP computation affects the magnitude and interpretation of SHAP values, and appropriate baseline selection depends on the specific application and scientific questions. Climate applications might use climatological means, seasonal averages, or specific reference conditions as baselines, depending on the analysis objectives.

Feature correlation effects must be carefully considered when interpreting SHAP values for climate data, which often exhibit strong spatial and temporal correlations. High correlations between features can make SHAP interpretation challenging because attribution may be distributed among correlated features in ways that do not reflect clear causal relationships. Climate scientists should consider the feature correlation structure when interpreting SHAP results.

Temporal interpretation challenges arise when applying SHAP analysis to time series climate data, where the same variables at different time points are treated as separate features. SHAP values for different time points must be interpreted carefully to understand temporal patterns and avoid over-interpretation of specific time point contributions. Temporal aggregation or smoothing may help identify robust temporal patterns.

Spatial interpretation considerations apply when SHAP analysis is used to understand the importance of different geographical regions or spatial patterns for climate predictions. SHAP values for different spatial locations must be interpreted in the context of physical processes and teleconnection patterns that govern climate system behavior. Spatial visualization and aggregation approaches can help identify meaningful spatial patterns in SHAP values.

Statistical significance and confidence intervals for SHAP values help climate scientists assess the reliability of attribution measures and avoid overinterpretation of small or unstable SHAP values. Bootstrap sampling or other statistical techniques can provide confidence estimates for SHAP values, supporting more robust interpretation and comparison of attribution measures.

Comparison and benchmarking of SHAP values across different models, conditions, or time periods requires careful consideration of baseline consistency, feature definitions, and computational methods. Meaningful comparisons require standardized approaches to SHAP computation and interpretation that account for differences in model architecture, data preprocessing, and analysis contexts.

Physical consistency validation involves comparing SHAP-based insights with established physical understanding of climate processes to identify potential model problems or discover new relationships. SHAP values that contradict well-established physical principles may indicate model limitations, while SHAP values that reveal previously unknown patterns may suggest opportunities for scientific discovery that require further investigation.

Local Interpretable Model-agnostic Explanations

Local Interpretable Model-agnostic Explanations (LIME) represents a powerful approach for understanding individual AI predictions by learning simple, interpretable models that locally approximate complex model behavior around specific instances. LIME is particularly valuable for climate science applications because it provides intuitive explanations for individual predictions while remaining agnostic to the underlying model architecture, enabling consistent explanation approaches across different climate AI systems.

The fundamental principle underlying LIME involves the assumption that complex AI models can be locally approximated by simpler, interpretable models such as linear regression or decision trees. While global AI model behavior may be highly nonlinear and complex, local behavior around specific instances may be approximated reasonably well by simpler models that can be easily understood and interpreted. This local approximation assumption is particularly reasonable for climate applications where smooth physical processes often dominate local behavior.

The LIME algorithm proceeds through several systematic steps for generating explanations of individual predictions. First, LIME generates a dataset of perturbed instances around the target instance by randomly modifying feature values according to specified sampling strategies. Second, LIME obtains predictions for all perturbed instances using the original complex model. Third, LIME weights the perturbed instances based on their proximity to the target instance, giving higher weights to instances that are more similar to the target. Fourth, LIME trains an interpretable model on the weighted dataset to approximate local model behavior. Finally, LIME extracts explanations from the interpretable model coefficients or structure.

Perturbation strategies for climate applications must account for the specific characteristics of climate data, including physical constraints, variable correlations, and realistic variation ranges. Simple random perturbation may generate physically unrealistic instances that do not represent meaningful climate conditions. Climate-specific perturbation approaches might sample from historical variability distributions, maintain physical consistency constraints, or use domain knowledge to generate realistic perturbations.

Distance metrics for weighting perturbed instances must be appropriate for climate data characteristics, including multi-dimensional continuous variables, mixed data types, and different variable scales and units. Euclidean distance may be inappropriate for climate data due to different variable scales and correlations. Climate applications might benefit from specialized distance metrics that account for physical relationships, normalize for variable scales, or weight variables according to their climate relevance.

Interpretable model selection affects both the quality of local approximations and the interpretability of resulting explanations. Linear models provide highly interpretable explanations but may not capture important nonlinear relationships in local model behavior. Decision trees provide rule-based explanations that may be more intuitive for some users but may oversimplify complex relationships.

The choice of an interpretable model should balance explanation quality against interpretability requirements for specific climate applications.

Regularization and feature selection in the interpretable model help focus explanations on the most important features while avoiding overfitting to the local dataset. Climate applications often involve high-dimensional data where regularization becomes essential for identifying the most important contributing factors. Lasso regularization can provide automatic feature selection that identifies the most relevant climate variables for specific predictions.

Neighborhood size and locality definition critically affect the quality of LIME approximations and the relevance of resulting explanations. Small neighborhoods provide very local approximations that may be highly accurate but may not generalize beyond the immediate vicinity of target instances. Large neighborhoods provide more generalizable approximations but may not accurately capture local model behavior. Climate applications require careful tuning of neighborhood parameters to balance approximation quality against explanation relevance.

Climate data presents unique challenges for LIME application due to its multi-dimensional structure, physical constraints, temporal and spatial dependencies, and domain-specific interpretation requirements. Adapting LIME for climate applications requires specialized approaches that maintain the core LIME principles while addressing these climate-specific considerations.

Spatiotemporal perturbation strategies must generate realistic variations in climate data that respect physical constraints and natural variability patterns. Simple independent perturbation of individual variables may create physically impossible combinations, such as extremely high temperatures with ice precipitation or unrealistic pressure-temperature relationships. Climate-adapted perturbation might use historical variability patterns, maintain thermodynamic consistency, or employ conditional sampling approaches.

Multi-scale data handling addresses the challenge of applying LIME to climate datasets that span multiple temporal and spatial scales simultaneously. Climate AI models may use inputs ranging from local weather observations to global circulation patterns, requiring LIME approaches that can handle these scale differences appropriately. Hierarchical perturbation strategies might modify variables at appropriate scales while maintaining cross-scale consistency.

Physical constraint preservation ensures that LIME perturbations generate climate conditions that could plausibly occur in nature, avoiding explanations based on physically impossible scenarios. Constraint preservation might involve thermodynamic consistency checks, energy balance requirements, or conservation law enforcement. Constrained perturbation approaches help ensure that LIME explanations are scientifically meaningful and relevant for climate interpretation.

Correlated feature handling addresses the strong correlations among climate variables that can complicate LIME perturbation and interpretation. Independent perturbation of highly correlated variables may generate unrealistic combinations that bias LIME explanations. Correlation-aware perturbation approaches might use principal component analysis, maintain observed correlation structures, or employ conditional sampling methods.

Temporal coherence preservation ensures that LIME perturbations of time series climate data maintain realistic temporal patterns and

EXPLAINABLE AI • 291

evolution characteristics. Independent perturbation of individual time points may create unrealistic temporal sequences that do not represent plausible climate evolution. Temporal coherence approaches might modify time series through smooth perturbations, maintain autocorrelation structures, or use realistic temporal variability patterns.

Domain knowledge integration enables the incorporation of climate science expertise into LIME perturbation and interpretation processes. Expert knowledge about reasonable variable ranges, typical relationships, and physically plausible scenarios can guide perturbation strategies and help validate explanation quality. Knowledge integration helps ensure that LIME explanations are consistent with established climate science understanding.

Multi-variable explanation handling addresses situations where climate predictions depend on complex interactions among multiple variables that must be explained simultaneously. Single-variable LIME explanations may miss important interaction effects or provide an incomplete understanding of climate model behavior. Multi-variable approaches might group related variables, explain variable combinations, or provide interaction-aware explanations.

Use Cases

LIME provides valuable explanation capabilities for diverse climate science applications where understanding individual predictions is essential for validation, decision-making, or scientific insight. The model-agnostic nature of LIME enables consistent explanation approaches across different AI architectures while providing intuitive explanations that can be communicated to various stakeholders.

Weather forecast explanation applications use LIME to understand individual weather predictions and identify the atmospheric conditions that contribute most significantly to specific forecasts. LIME analysis might reveal that advection patterns primarily drive a particular temperature forecast, while a precipitation forecast depends more on atmospheric instability and moisture content. These explanations support forecast validation and help meteorologists understand AI model reasoning.

Extreme event prediction applications employ LIME to explain individual predictions of hurricanes, tornadoes, floods, droughts, or other high-impact events. LIME explanations can identify which atmospheric or oceanic conditions are most critical for specific extreme event predictions, supporting validation against meteorological knowledge and helping emergency managers understand the basis for warnings. For hurricane intensity predictions, LIME might reveal the relative importance of sea surface temperatures, wind shear, and atmospheric moisture for specific storms.

Climate change impact assessment uses LIME to explain predictions of how climate change will affect specific regions, ecosystems, or sectors. LIME analysis can identify which climate variables are most important for impact predictions and how different emission scenarios or adaptation measures might affect outcomes. Agricultural impact assessments might use LIME to understand which climate factors are most critical for crop yield predictions in specific locations and growing seasons.

Seasonal prediction applications employ LIME to explain individual seasonal forecasts and identify the climate patterns that provide predictive skill for specific seasons and regions. LIME analysis might reveal that winter precipitation forecasts for a particular region depend primarily on Pacific Ocean conditions, while Atlantic patterns more influence summer temperature forecasts. These explanations support validation against known teleconnection relationships.

Air quality prediction applications use LIME to explain individual air quality forecasts and identify the meteorological and emission factors that contribute to pollution episodes. LIME explanations can help air quality managers understand why specific pollution events are predicted and which factors are most amenable to intervention. Urban applications might reveal how local meteorology, regional transport, and emission patterns combine to produce air quality conditions.

Ecosystem response modeling employs LIME to explain predictions of how ecosystems will respond to climate variability and change. LIME analysis can identify which climate variables are most important for ecosystem predictions and how different species or ecosystem components respond to climate forcing. Carbon cycle applications might use LIME to understand which environmental factors drive predictions of forest carbon uptake or soil carbon loss.

Renewable energy applications use LIME to explain predictions of wind, solar, or hydroelectric power generation potential based on weather and climate conditions. LIME explanations can help energy planners understand which meteorological factors are most critical for renewable energy predictions and how climate variability affects energy system reliability. Wind power applications might reveal how atmospheric stability, wind speed profiles, and synoptic patterns combine to determine turbine performance.

While LIME provides valuable explanation capabilities for climate AI applications, it also has important limitations and considerations that must be understood to avoid misinterpretation and ensure appropriate application. These limitations are particularly relevant for climate science applications where explanation quality and scientific validity are critical.

Local approximation quality represents a fundamental limitation of LIME that depends on the assumption that complex AI models can be accurately approximated by simple interpretable models in local neighborhoods. This assumption may not hold for highly nonlinear climate AI models or in regions of input space where model behavior changes rapidly. Poor local approximation quality can lead to misleading explanations that do not accurately reflect AI model reasoning.

Perturbation realism affects the quality and relevance of LIME explanations for climate applications. If perturbations generate climate conditions that are unrealistic or implausible, LIME explanations may be based on model behavior that is not relevant for actual climate situations. Ensuring perturbation realism requires domain expertise and careful validation against climate observations and physical understanding.

Neighborhood definition sensitivity means that LIME explanations can vary significantly depending on choices about neighborhood size, distance metrics, and weighting functions. Different neighborhood definitions may produce different explanations for the same prediction, creating interpretation challenges and uncertainty about explanation reliability. Climate applications require careful sensitivity analysis to understand how neighborhood choices affect explanation quality.

Instability and inconsistency issues arise when LIME explanations for similar instances provide different or contradictory insights about AI model behavior. Explanation instability can result from stochastic perturbation procedures, local model fitting challenges, or inherent limitations in the quality of local approximations. Climate applications require robust explanation, validation, and consistency checking to identify unreliable explanations.

Computational scalability becomes challenging for high-dimensional climate datasets, where LIME requires generating and evaluating large numbers of perturbed instances. The computational cost of LIME scales with neighborhood size, feature dimensionality, and model complexity, potentially making real-time explanation infeasible for operational climate applications. Efficiency improvements and approximation methods may be necessary for large-scale climate applications.

Interpretable model limitations affect the quality and completeness of LIME explanations. Linear models may miss important nonlinear relationships in local model behavior, while decision trees may oversimplify complex decision boundaries. The choice of an interpretable model involves trade-offs between explanation simplicity and accuracy that must be carefully considered for climate applications.

Feature correlation challenges complicate LIME interpretation when climate variables are highly correlated. Correlated features may receive unstable or inconsistent attribution in LIME explanations, making it difficult to identify the true drivers of model predictions. Correlation-aware interpretation techniques or feature preprocessing may be necessary for climate applications with strong variable correlations.

Extrapolation risks arise when LIME perturbations explore regions of input space that are not well-represented in AI model training data. AI models may exhibit unrealistic or unstable behavior in these extrapolation regions, leading to LIME explanations that are not representative of model behavior under realistic conditions. Climate applications require careful validation of perturbation ranges against training data coverage.

Gradient-based explanation methods leverage the computational machinery of neural network training to provide insights into model behavior through analysis of gradients that describe how model outputs respond to input perturbations. These methods are particularly well-suited for climate AI applications using deep learning architectures, where gradient information is readily available and can provide efficient explanation computation for high-dimensional climate datasets.

Vanilla gradient computation represents the most direct approach to gradient-based explanation, computing partial derivatives of model outputs with respect to input features to identify sensitivity patterns. For climate AI applications, vanilla gradients can reveal which atmospheric variables, oceanic conditions, or terrestrial features contribute most strongly to predictions at specific locations and times.

Gradient saturation problems commonly affect vanilla gradient methods in deep neural networks, where gradients may become very small due to activation function characteristics or network depth. Saturated gradients provide little information about feature importance and may lead to misleading explanations. Climate AI applications using deep networks may require specialized gradient computation methods that address saturation issues while maintaining explanation quality.

Input times gradient methods combine gradient magnitudes with input values to provide attribution measures that account for both model sensitivity and actual input magnitudes. This approach recognizes that features with high gradients but small values may be less important than features with moderate gradients but large values. Climate applications can benefit from input-gradient products that provide more intuitive attribution measures.

Gradient normalization techniques address issues related to different scales and units among climate variables by normalizing gradients according to input ranges, standard deviations, or other scaling factors. Normalized gradients enable meaningful comparison of importance across different types of climate variables, such as temperature, pressure, humidity, and wind speed, that have different natural scales and variability ranges.

Layer-wise gradient analysis examines how gradients propagate through different layers of deep neural networks, providing insights into how climate information is processed and transformed at different network levels. Layer-wise analysis can reveal which network layers are most sensitive to specific climate variables and how feature representations evolve through the network processing pipeline.

Temporal gradient analysis for time series climate data examines how gradients vary across different time points in sequential input data, providing insights into temporal dependencies and the relative importance of different time periods for predictions. Temporal gradient patterns can reveal whether models rely primarily on recent conditions, historical patterns, or specific temporal relationships for climate predictions.

Spatial gradient analysis for gridded climate data examines gradient patterns across geographical locations to understand spatial dependencies and identify regions that contribute most significantly to predictions. Spatial gradient visualization can reveal teleconnection patterns, identify critical climate regions, and validate model behavior against known physical relationships.

Advanced gradient-based explanation methods address limitations of vanilla gradient approaches while providing enhanced explanation capabilities for complex climate AI applications. These techniques employ sophisticated computational approaches to extract more reliable and informative explanations from gradient information while maintaining computational efficiency suitable for operational climate applications.

Integrated gradients address gradient saturation and baseline dependence issues by integrating gradients along paths from baseline inputs to target inputs. Climate applications benefit from integrated gradients that provide more stable and comprehensive attribution measures while satisfying mathematical properties such as sensitivity and implementation invariance.

Baseline selection for integrated gradients requires careful consideration in climate applications where appropriate reference conditions may not be obvious. Baselines might represent climatological means, neutral conditions, or specific reference scenarios depending on the application context. Climate-specific baselines should reflect physically meaningful reference states rather than arbitrary values such as zeros that may not represent realistic climate conditions.

SmoothGrad approaches reduce noise in gradient-based explanations by averaging gradients computed over multiple samples drawn from noise distributions around target inputs. Climate applications benefit from SmoothGrad averaging that provides more stable explanations despite inherent noise in climate observations and model predictions.

Guided back-propagation modifies gradient computation procedures to focus on positive contributions while suppressing negative gradients that may provide less interpretable explanations. Modified ReLU operations during back-propagation ensure that only positive gradients are propagated, potentially providing a cleaner visualization of important features. Climate applications might benefit from guided back-propagation for highlighting the most relevant atmospheric patterns or oceanic conditions.

Deconvolution approaches provide alternative gradient computation methods that aim to reverse the network forward pass to identify input patterns that most strongly activate specific network components. DeconvNet and similar approaches can help climate scientists understand which input patterns are most important for different types of predictions while providing visualization-friendly explanation formats.

GradCAM (Gradient-weighted Class Activation Mapping) combines gradient information with activation maps to provide spatially-aware explanations for convolutional neural networks commonly used in climate applications. GradCAM can highlight specific regions of weather maps, satellite imagery, or other gridded climate data that contribute most significantly to predictions.

Expected gradients provide probabilistic extensions of gradient-based attribution by computing expected gradients over distributions of baseline inputs rather than using single baseline values. This approach can provide more robust attribution measures for climate applications where baseline selection is challenging or where multiple reference conditions might be appropriate.

Path-integrated gradients explore alternative integration paths between baselines and target inputs to provide a more comprehensive understanding of gradient-based attribution. Different integration paths may reveal different aspects of model behavior and provide insights into model stability and consistency across different explanation approaches.

The implementation of gradient-based explanation methods for climate AI applications requires specialized approaches that account for the unique characteristics of climate data, the physical constraints governing Earth system behavior, and the specific interpretation needs of climate science applications. These implementations must balance computational efficiency with explanation quality while maintaining scientific validity and practical utility.

Multi-scale gradient analysis addresses the challenge of explaining AI models that process climate data at multiple temporal and spatial scales simultaneously. Climate AI systems often employ hierarchical architectures that handle everything from local turbulent processes to global circulation patterns. Multi-scale gradient methods must provide explanations that are appropriate for different scales while maintaining consistency across scale interactions.

Physical constraint integration ensures that gradient-based explanations respect known physical relationships and conservation laws in climate systems. Unconstrained gradient analysis might suggest importance patterns that violate thermodynamic principles or energy conservation. Physics-informed gradient methods can incorporate conservation constraints, thermodynamic consistency, or other physical principles to ensure scientifically meaningful explanations.

Ensemble gradient analysis provides explanation approaches for ensemble-based climate prediction systems that employ multiple models or multiple realizations of the same model. Ensemble gradients must account for variability across ensemble members while providing robust attribution measures that reflect consensus and uncertainty in ensemble predictions. Statistical approaches can summarize gradient distributions across ensemble members.

Seasonal and regime-aware gradient analysis recognizes that climate AI models may exhibit different behavior during different seasons, weather regimes, or climate states. Gradient patterns during winter may differ significantly from summer patterns, and models may respond differently during El Niño versus La Niña conditions. Conditional gradient analysis can provide regime-specific explanations that account for these behavioral differences.

Teleconnection-aware gradient analysis focuses on identifying remote influences and long-distance relationships that are characteristic of climate systems. Conditions may strongly influence climate predictions for specific regions in distant regions through atmospheric or oceanic teleconnections. Gradient analysis methods can be designed to highlight these remote influences and validate them against known teleconnection patterns.

Extreme event gradient analysis provides specialized approaches for understanding gradient patterns during rare events that may not be well-represented in standard gradient analyses. Extreme events often involve different physical processes and relationships than typical conditions, requiring gradient analysis methods that can identify the unique factors driving extreme event predictions.

Uncertainty-aware gradient analysis incorporates prediction uncertainty information into gradient-based explanations to provide a more complete understanding of model behavior. Gradient patterns may be less reliable when model uncertainty is high, and explanation methods should account for this relationship between gradient reliability and prediction confidence.

The integration of gradient-based explanations with physical understanding of climate processes represents a critical aspect of making gradient methods useful for climate science applications. This integration ensures that explanations are not only mathematically correct but also physically meaningful and scientifically interpretable within the context of Earth system science.

Physical validation of gradient patterns involves comparing gradient-based importance measures with established physical understanding of climate processes and relationships. Gradient patterns that contradict well-established physical principles may indicate model problems, while patterns that reveal previously unknown relationships require careful validation through independent analysis and observational evidence.

Process attribution through gradient analysis can identify which physical processes are most important for specific predictions by analyzing gradient patterns in the context of process representations within AI models. Climate AI systems that explicitly represent different processes can use gradient analysis to understand process importance and validate process representations against observational evidence.

Scale interaction analysis uses gradient methods to understand how different temporal and spatial scales interact within climate AI models. Gradient analysis can reveal whether models appropriately represent upscale and downscale interactions and whether scale coupling relationships are consistent with the physical understanding of climate system behavior.

Conservation law validation employs gradient analysis to assess whether AI models maintain appropriate conservation relationships for energy, mass, momentum, and other conserved quantities. Gradient patterns should be consistent with conservation requirements, and violations may indicate model problems or training data issues that require correction.

Causal relationship identification uses gradient-based methods to identify potential causal relationships within AI models while distinguishing between causal effects and spurious correlations. Climate systems involve complex causal networks, and gradient analysis can help identify whether models have learned physically meaningful causal relationships or whether they rely on correlational patterns that may not hold under different conditions.

Feedback mechanism analysis employs gradient methods to understand how AI models represent feedback processes critical for climate system behavior. Positive and negative feedback mechanisms affect climate sensitivity and system stability, and gradient analysis can reveal whether models appropriately represent these feedback relationships.

Diagnostic relationship validation uses gradient analysis to assess whether AI models maintain appropriate diagnostic relationships between different climate variables. Diagnostic relationships such as hydrostatic balance, geostrophic balance, or thermodynamic relationships should be reflected in gradient patterns, providing validation of model physical consistency.

Advanced XAI Techniques

Attention mechanisms in transformer-based and other neural network architectures provide natural pathways for understanding model focus and decision-making processes in climate AI applications. These mechanisms explicitly learn to weight different parts of input data, offering interpretability advantages over black-box approaches while maintaining the sophisticated pattern recognition capabilities that make modern AI systems effective for complex climate modeling tasks.

Self-attention analysis in transformer models reveals how different spatial locations and temporal periods influence each other within climate AI predictions. Climate applications can visualize attention weights to understand teleconnection patterns, identify remote influences on local climate, and validate model behavior against known atmospheric and oceanic coupling mechanisms. Attention patterns may reveal previously unknown relationships or confirm established climate dynamics.

Multi-head attention decomposition enables understanding of how different attention heads focus on different aspects of climate data, potentially specializing in different types of patterns or relationships. Climate AI models might employ attention heads that focus on seasonal cycles, others that capture extreme events, and still others that identify long-term trends. Analyzing individual attention heads provides insights into model specialization and processing strategies.

Cross-attention analysis for multi-modal climate AI systems reveals how models integrate information from different data sources, such as atmospheric observations, oceanic measurements, and terrestrial monitoring data. Cross-attention patterns can show which combinations of data types are most informative for different types of predictions and how models balance different information sources.

Temporal attention visualization for climate time series applications shows which historical time periods are most important for current predictions. Attention patterns may reveal that seasonal predictions rely primarily on recent conditions, that certain historical periods provide long-term memory, or that specific temporal relationships drive predictive skill. Temporal attention patterns can validate model behavior against climate science understanding.

Spatial attention mapping for gridded climate data identifies geographical regions that contribute most significantly to predictions for specific locations. Spatial attention visualization can reveal atmospheric wave patterns, oceanic influence regions, or terrestrial coupling areas that drive regional climate predictions. These patterns can be validated against known teleconnection relationships and climate dynamics.

Layer-wise attention evolution analysis examines how attention patterns change through different layers of deep networks, providing insights into hierarchical information processing in climate AI systems. Early layers might focus on local patterns while deeper layers capture larger-scale relationships and interactions. Layer-wise analysis helps understand how climate information is progressively integrated and abstracted.

Attention pattern stability analysis assesses whether attention mechanisms provide consistent explanations across similar inputs or time periods. Stable attention patterns suggest reliable model behavior, while unstable patterns may indicate overfitting, noise sensitivity, or model limitations that require attention. Stability analysis supports confidence assessment for attention-based explanations.

Counterfactual explanations provide powerful approaches for understanding AI model behavior by exploring hypothetical scenarios and identifying the minimal changes required to alter predictions. Climate science applications particularly benefit from counterfactual analysis because it naturally aligns with scenario-based thinking and what-if analysis that are central to climate research and policy development.

Counterfactual generation algorithms identify minimal modifications to input conditions that would change model predictions to specified alternative outcomes. Climate applications might explore questions such as: "What is the minimum temperature increase required to shift a drought prediction to normal conditions?" or "How much would sea surface temperatures need to change to alter a hurricane intensity forecast?" These analyses provide insights into model sensitivity and decision boundaries.

Realistic counterfactual constraints ensure that generated scenarios represent plausible climate conditions rather than arbitrary mathematical constructs. Unconstrained counterfactual generation might produce physically impossible combinations of temperature, pressure, and humidity that would not occur in nature. Climate-specific constraints can incorporate thermodynamic relationships, conservation laws, and observed climate variability ranges.

Multi-objective counterfactual analysis explores trade-offs between different types of changes required to achieve specific prediction outcomes. Climate systems involve complex interactions where changing one variable may require compensating changes in other variables. Multi-objective approaches can identify the most efficient or realistic combination of changes needed to achieve desired prediction alterations.

Temporal counterfactual analysis examines how changes at different time points affect prediction outcomes, providing insights into temporal dependencies and memory effects in climate AI models. Climate predictions may be more sensitive to changes at certain time periods, and temporal counterfactual analysis can identify these critical periods and validate them against climate science understanding.

Probabilistic counterfactual approaches generate distributions of counterfactual scenarios rather than single-point alternatives, providing a more comprehensive understanding of the range of changes that could affect predictions. Climate applications benefit from probabilistic approaches that can quantify uncertainty in counterfactual scenarios and provide robust insights into model sensitivity.

Causal counterfactual analysis attempts to identify counterfactual scenarios that represent realistic interventions or causal mechanisms rather than arbitrary data modifications. Climate policy applications particularly benefit from causal counterfactuals that represent feasible interventions such as emission reductions, land use changes, or adaptation measures that could alter climate outcomes.

Interactive counterfactual exploration enables climate scientists and stakeholders to explore counterfactual scenarios dynamically, testing different hypotheses and understanding model behavior through guided experimentation. Interactive tools can support hypothesis testing, scenario analysis, and educational applications that help build understanding of climate system behavior and AI model capabilities.

Concept-based explanation methods aim to understand AI model behavior in terms of high-level concepts that are meaningful to domain experts rather than individual input features. Climate science applications particularly benefit from concept-based approaches because climate scientists think naturally in terms of concepts such as atmospheric blocking, ocean circulation patterns, or vegetation dynamics rather than individual measurements.

Concept Activation Vectors (CAVs) identify directions in neural network activation spaces that correspond to meaningful climate concepts. Climate applications might develop CAVersus for concepts such as El Niño conditions, atmospheric rivers, or drought patterns. CAVersus enables quantification of how much specific concepts contribute to individual predictions and provides intuitive explanations in terms of familiar climate phenomena.

Concept attribution analysis uses CAVersus or similar concept representations to attribute model predictions to different climate concepts rather than individual variables. Climate AI explanations might indicate that a seasonal precipitation forecast is influenced 40% by Pacific Ocean patterns, 30% by atmospheric blocking, and 20% by soil moisture conditions. Concept-based attribution provides higher-level explanations that align with expert thinking.

Automated concept discovery algorithms attempt to identify meaningful concepts directly from data without requiring pre-specification by domain experts. These approaches might discover previously unknown climate patterns or identify novel ways of organizing climate information that improve prediction accuracy. Automated discovery can reveal new scientific insights while providing explanations in terms of learned concepts.

Hierarchical concept organization recognizes that climate concepts exist at multiple levels of abstraction, from specific phenomena such as individual hurricanes to broader patterns such as tropical cyclone activity or climate modes such as ENSO. Hierarchical concept explanations can provide different levels of detail appropriate for different users and applications.

Concept stability and generalization analysis assesses whether learned concepts remain consistent across different datasets, time periods, or model architectures. Stable concepts that generalize across different conditions are more likely to represent meaningful climate phenomena, while unstable concepts may reflect dataset artifacts or model limitations.

Interactive concept refinement enables domain experts to guide concept learning and validation through iterative feedback processes. Climate scientists can provide input about concept relevance, suggest concept modifications, or validate concept representations against physical understanding. Interactive approaches ensure that learned concepts align with domain expertise and scientific knowledge.

Multi-modal concept learning integrates information from different types of climate data to develop richer concept representations that may not be apparent from individual data sources. Concepts might combine atmospheric patterns, oceanic conditions, and terrestrial observations to provide a comprehensive understanding of climate phenomena.

Emerging Directions

The field of explainable AI for climate science continues to evolve rapidly, with emerging directions that promise to address current limitations while opening new possibilities for understanding and applying AI systems in climate research and applications. These emerging directions reflect both advances in XAI methodology and growing understanding of the specific needs and challenges of climate science applications.

Physics-informed explainable AI represents a promising direction that integrates physical constraints and domain knowledge directly into explanation methods. Rather than treating AI models as purely mathematical constructs, physics-informed XAI approaches can provide explanations that respect conservation laws, thermodynamic principles, and causal relationships that govern climate systems. This integration promises more scientifically meaningful and trustworthy explanations.

Causal explanation methods continue to develop sophisticated approaches for identifying genuine causal relationships in AI model behavior rather than mere correlational associations. Climate science particularly benefits from causal explanation approaches because understanding causation is essential for prediction, intervention, and policy development. Advanced causal discovery algorithms and counterfactual reasoning frameworks promise improved causal understanding of AI climate models.

Multi-scale explanation integration addresses the challenge of providing coherent explanations across the multiple temporal and spatial scales that characterize climate systems. Hierarchical explanation frameworks, scale-aware attribution methods, and cross-scale interaction analysis promise improved understanding of how AI models handle scale interactions and dependencies that are central to climate system behavior.

Uncertainty-aware explanation methods increasingly recognize that both predictions and explanations involve uncertainty that must be communicated effectively to support appropriate decision-making. Probabilistic explanation approaches, confidence-aware attribution methods, and uncertainty propagation through explanation chains promise more reliable and informative explanations for climate applications.

Interactive and adaptive explanation systems enable dynamic exploration of AI model behavior through responsive explanation interfaces that adapt to user needs, expertise levels, and inquiry patterns. Machine learning approaches can personalize explanations based on user feedback while maintaining scientific accuracy and consistency. Adaptive systems promise improved accessibility and effectiveness of AI explanations for diverse climate science stakeholders.

Collaborative explanation frameworks facilitate distributed explanation development and validation across multiple institutions, expertise domains, and stakeholder communities. Climate science increasingly relies on collaborative research approaches, and explanation systems must support collaborative validation, peer review, and consensus-building around AI model behavior and interpretation.

Automated explanation validation employs AI methods to assess explanation quality, consistency, and reliability without requiring extensive human evaluation. Automated validation approaches can check explanations against physical consistency requirements, compare explanations across different methods, and identify potential explanation artifacts or biases. Automation promises scalable quality assurance for explanation systems.

The development and application of explainable artificial intelligence in climate science represents a critical frontier that addresses fundamental challenges in the intersection of advanced computational methods and Earth system science. As demonstrated throughout this chapter, the black-box nature of modern AI systems creates significant obstacles for scientific validation, stakeholder trust, and democratic participation in climate-related decision-making processes. However, the diverse array of XAI techniques examined here provides powerful tools for addressing these challenges while maintaining the predictive capabilities that make AI systems valuable for climate applications.

The theoretical foundations of explainable AI provide rigorous mathematical frameworks for understanding AI model behavior while ensuring that explanations satisfy desirable properties such as consistency, stability, and meaningful attribution. The distinction between global and local explanations enables a comprehensive understanding that addresses both systematic model behavior and specific prediction instances, supporting diverse stakeholder needs from scientific validation to operational decision-making.

The specific XAI techniques explored in this chapter—attribution methods, SHAP values, LIME, and gradient-based approaches—each offer unique advantages and capabilities that complement each other in providing a comprehensive understanding of AI climate models. SHAP values provide theoretically grounded attribution measures with mathematical guarantees, while LIME offers intuitive local explanations that can be applied consistently across different model architectures.

Gradient-based methods leverage the computational machinery of deep learning to provide efficient explanation capabilities, while advanced techniques such as attention mechanisms and counterfactual analysis offer sophisticated approaches for understanding complex model behavior.

The climate-specific adaptations and implementations discussed throughout this chapter highlight the importance of domain expertise in developing effective XAI systems. Climate data characteristics, physical constraints, and scientific interpretation requirements necessitate specialized approaches that go beyond generic XAI methods. The integration of physical understanding with explanation techniques ensures that AI insights contribute to rather than compete with scientific knowledge while maintaining the interpretability requirements essential for climate science credibility.

The case studies and applications presented demonstrate the practical value of XAI techniques across diverse climate science contexts, from weather prediction and extreme event analysis to climate change attribution and impact assessment. These applications illustrate how XAI can enhance scientific understanding, support model validation, improve stakeholder communication, and enable more effective decision-making under uncertainty.

Looking toward the future, several key research directions emerge as particularly important for advancing explainable AI in climate science. The integration of physics-informed constraints into explanation methods promises more scientifically meaningful and trustworthy explanations that respect fundamental physical principles while leveraging AI capabilities. Causal explanation approaches offer pathways for identifying genuine causal relationships rather than mere correlational associations, supporting improved understanding of intervention effects and policy implications.

Multi-scale explanation integration represents an ongoing challenge that requires sophisticated approaches for providing coherent explanations across the vast range of temporal and spatial scales characteristic of climate systems. Advanced hierarchical frameworks, scale-aware attribution methods, and cross-scale interaction analysis will be essential for a comprehensive understanding of AI climate model behavior.

The development of uncertainty-aware explanation methods will become increasingly important as climate science grapples with multiple sources of uncertainty while requiring reliable information for high-stakes decisions. Probabilistic explanation approaches, confidence-aware attribution methods, and uncertainty propagation through explanation chains will be essential for appropriate risk assessment and decision-making under uncertainty.

Interactive and adaptive explanation systems represent promising directions for improving accessibility and effectiveness of AI explanations across diverse stakeholder communities. Personalized explanation approaches that adapt to user expertise, needs, and contexts can improve communication while maintaining scientific accuracy and consistency.

The democratization of XAI tools and techniques will be crucial for widespread adoption across the climate science community, requiring user-friendly software frameworks, educational resources, and standardized approaches that enable consistent application across different institutions and contexts. This democratization must be accompanied by appropriate training and capacity building to ensure that XAI techniques are applied effectively and interpreted correctly.

Ethical considerations will continue to require attention as XAI systems are deployed in climate applications that affect vulnerable populations and influence resource allocation decisions. Ensuring fairness, avoiding bias, and supporting democratic participation will require ongoing vigilance and systematic approaches to ethical AI development and deployment.

The integration of XAI approaches with traditional climate science methods and validation procedures will be essential for maintaining scientific rigor while benefiting from AI capabilities. Hybrid approaches that combine AI insights with physics-based understanding and observational validation will likely prove most effective for advancing climate science while maintaining credibility and trust.

In conclusion, explainable artificial intelligence represents both a necessity and an opportunity for climate science as the field increasingly relies on sophisticated AI systems for understanding and predicting Earth system behavior. The techniques and approaches explored in this chapter provide foundations for addressing the transparency and interpretability challenges posed by modern AI systems while enabling the climate science community to harness the full potential of artificial intelligence for addressing one of humanity's most pressing challenges. Success in this endeavor will require continued collaboration between AI researchers, climate scientists, and stakeholders to ensure that powerful AI technologies serve the public interest while maintaining the scientific integrity and democratic accountability essential for effective climate action.

NINE

Explainable AI in Climate Science

The rapid advancement of artificial intelligence and machine learning in climate science has brought unprecedented predictive capabilities and pattern recognition abilities to atmospheric, oceanic, and terrestrial modeling applications. However, this progress has also introduced a fundamental challenge that strikes at the heart of scientific inquiry: the interpretability and explainability of complex AI systems. Climate science, with its deep roots in physical understanding and mechanistic reasoning, demands not only accurate predictions but also comprehensible explanations of how and why those predictions are made. This need for explainable artificial intelligence (XAI) in climate applications represents one of the most critical frontiers in the intersection of AI and Earth system science.

The complexity of modern AI systems, particularly deep learning models, often renders them "black boxes" whose decision-making processes are opaque even to their creators. While these models may achieve remarkable accuracy in predicting climate variables, extreme events, or long-term climate trends, their lack of transparency poses significant challenges for scientific validation, policy development, and public trust. Climate science operates within a framework where physical understanding and mechanistic explanation are as important as predictive accuracy, creating a tension between the power of modern AI systems and the interpretability requirements of scientific and societal applications.

Explainable AI addresses this challenge by developing methods and frameworks that can provide insight into AI model behavior, decision-making processes, and the relationships between input variables and predicted outcomes. These approaches range from global explanation methods that characterize overall model behavior to local explanation techniques that illuminate specific predictions. The application of XAI to climate science requires specialized approaches that account for the unique characteristics of climate data, including multi-scale temporal and spatial dependencies, physical constraints, and the high-stakes nature of climate predictions that inform policy and adaptation decisions.

The importance of explainable AI in climate science extends beyond technical considerations to encompass broader questions of scientific credibility, public trust, and democratic governance of climate policy. As AI systems increasingly influence climate assessments, risk evaluations, and policy recommendations, the ability to understand and explain their reasoning becomes essential for maintaining scientific integrity and public confidence. Furthermore, explainable AI approaches can enhance scientific discovery by revealing previously unknown patterns or relationships in climate data, potentially leading to a new understanding of Earth system processes.

This chapter explores the principles, methods, and applications of explainable AI in climate science, examining both the challenges posed by black-box AI systems and the solutions provided by modern XAI techniques. We begin with an analysis of the black-box problem in climate AI and the fundamental principles of explainable artificial intelligence. We then examine the distinction between global and local explanations and their respective applications in climate science contexts. The latter portion of the chapter provides detailed coverage of specific XAI techniques, including attribution methods, SHAP values, LIME approaches, and gradient-based explanation methods, with particular attention to their implementation and interpretation in climate science applications.

The black-box problem in climate AI emerges from the fundamental architecture and complexity of modern deep learning systems that have proven remarkably effective at climate prediction tasks but remain largely opaque in their internal decision-making processes. Deep neural networks, with their millions or billions of parameters distributed across dozens or hundreds of layers, create computational pathways so complex that traditional analysis methods cannot readily determine how input variables are transformed into output predictions. This opacity becomes particularly problematic in climate science applications where understanding the reasoning behind predictions is as important as the predictions themselves.

The mathematical complexity underlying deep learning models contributes significantly to their opaque nature. Modern climate AI systems employ sophisticated architectures, including convolutional neural networks for spatial pattern recognition, recurrent neural networks for temporal sequence modeling, and transformer architectures for complex relationship modeling across multiple scales. The nonlinear transformations applied at each layer, combined with the high-dimensional parameter spaces and complex optimization landscapes, create models whose behavior cannot be easily characterized through simple mathematical expressions or intuitive reasoning.

Emergent behavior in deep learning systems further compounds the interpretability challenge. Climate AI models often exhibit capabilities that were not explicitly programmed or anticipated during model development, discovering complex patterns and relationships that may not be immediately apparent to human experts. While this emergent behavior can lead to improved predictive performance, it also means that model developers may not fully understand the mechanisms underlying their systems' success, creating challenges for validation, trust, and scientific interpretation.

The interaction effects between different model components create additional layers of complexity that contribute to the black-box problem. Modern climate AI systems often employ ensemble methods, attention mechanisms, and multi-modal architectures that combine information from different sources and scales. The interactions between these components can produce complex behavioral patterns that are difficult to analyze or predict, even when individual components may be relatively well understood.

Scale interactions represent a particular challenge for interpretability in climate AI applications. Climate systems exhibit behavior across multiple temporal scales, from turbulent fluctuations occurring over seconds to climate variations spanning decades or centuries. Deep learning models designed to capture these multi-scale interactions necessarily involve complex temporal processing mechanisms that can obscure the relationships between different time scales and their contributions to final predictions.

The high-dimensional nature of climate data further exacerbates interpretability challenges. Climate datasets often involve hundreds or thousands of variables measured at numerous spatial locations and temporal intervals, creating input spaces with dimensionalities that exceed human comprehension capabilities. Understanding how deep learning models navigate these high-dimensional spaces and identify relevant patterns requires sophisticated analysis techniques that go beyond simple visualization or linear analysis methods.

The opacity of black-box AI systems poses significant challenges for scientific validation processes that are fundamental to climate science research and application. Traditional scientific validation relies on the ability to examine, critique, and replicate research methods and findings. When AI models cannot provide clear explanations for their predictions, the scientific community faces difficulties in evaluating model reliability, identifying potential biases or errors, and ensuring that predictions are based on scientifically sound reasoning rather than spurious correlations.

Peer review processes, which form the backbone of scientific quality assurance, become problematic when AI models cannot be fully examined or understood by reviewers. The complexity of deep learning systems may exceed the technical expertise of many climate scientists, creating situations where important research cannot be adequately evaluated through traditional peer review mechanisms. This challenge is particularly acute when AI systems make predictions that contradict established understanding or when they identify previously unknown patterns that require scientific validation.

Reproducibility concerns arise when black-box AI systems produce results that cannot be easily replicated or verified by independent researchers. The complex initialization procedures, training algorithms, and hyper-parameter choices involved in deep learning can create situations where seemingly identical models produce different results, undermining the reproducibility standards that are essential for scientific credibility. Additionally, the computational resources required for training large AI models may limit the ability of independent researchers to replicate results.

Model validation challenges extend beyond traditional accuracy metrics to encompass questions of physical consistency, causal reasoning, and generalization capability. Black-box AI systems may achieve high accuracy on historical data while failing to maintain physical consistency or exhibiting poor generalization to new conditions. Without a clear understanding of model reasoning processes, it becomes difficult to assess whether high performance reflects genuine understanding of underlying physical processes or memorization of training data patterns.

Scientific discovery applications of AI face particular challenges when models cannot explain their reasoning. While black-box systems may identify novel patterns or relationships in climate data, the inability to understand how these discoveries were made limits their scientific value. The scientific community requires not only the identification of new phenomena but also explanations of the mechanisms underlying these phenomena, creating a need for AI systems that can provide insight into their discovery processes.

Trust and acceptance within the scientific community depend heavily on the ability to understand and validate research methods and findings. Black-box AI systems may face resistance from climate scientists who are uncomfortable relying on predictions they cannot understand or verify. This resistance can slow the adoption of potentially valuable AI technologies and create divisions between traditional climate science approaches and AI-based methods.

Impact on Decision-Making

The black-box problem in climate AI has particularly serious implications for policy and decision-making applications where understanding the basis for recommendations is essential for democratic governance and public accountability. Climate policy decisions often involve significant economic costs, social impacts, and long-term consequences that require transparent and explainable justification. When AI systems contribute to these decisions without providing clear explanations for their recommendations, they can undermine democratic decision-making processes and public trust in climate policies.

Regulatory and legal challenges arise when AI systems are used to support decisions that affect public welfare, resource allocation, or regulatory compliance. Legal systems typically require that decisions affecting individuals or communities be based on clear, understandable reasoning that can be examined and challenged through appropriate legal processes. Black-box AI systems may not provide sufficient transparency to meet these legal requirements, potentially limiting their applicability in regulatory contexts.

Public communication of climate risks and uncertainties becomes problematic when the underlying AI systems cannot provide clear explanations for their assessments. Effective risk communication requires the ability to explain not only what risks are predicted but also why those predictions are made and what factors contribute most significantly to risk levels. Black-box systems may produce accurate risk assessments that cannot be effectively communicated to stakeholders, limiting their utility for public engagement and decision-making.

Accountability and responsibility questions arise when AI systems contribute to decisions that have negative consequences. In traditional decision-making processes, it is possible to trace the reasoning behind decisions and hold responsible parties accountable for their choices. When black-box AI systems influence decisions, it becomes difficult to assign responsibility or to identify where decision-making processes may have gone wrong, creating accountability gaps that can be problematic in policy contexts.

Stakeholder engagement processes require transparency and explainability to enable meaningful participation by affected communities and interest groups. When AI systems influence climate assessments or policy recommendations without providing clear explanations, stakeholders may be unable to evaluate or respond to these inputs effectively, undermining participatory decision-making processes that are essential for democratic governance of climate issues.

Emergency response and adaptation planning applications require a clear understanding of AI-based risk assessments and recommendations to enable effective response strategies. Emergency managers and adaptation planners need to understand not only what actions are recommended but also why those actions are necessary and how different factors contribute to overall risk levels. Black-box systems may provide accurate warnings or recommendations that cannot be effectively acted upon due to a lack of understanding of their underlying reasoning.

The deployment of black-box AI systems in climate science raises significant ethical concerns related to transparency, fairness, and democratic participation in scientific and policy processes. Climate change disproportionately affects vulnerable populations and developing countries, making it essential that AI systems used in climate applications are transparent and accountable to those who are most affected by their predictions and recommendations.

Algorithmic bias represents a major concern when black-box AI systems are trained on historical data that may reflect existing inequalities or biases. Climate datasets often exhibit spatial and temporal biases due to uneven observation coverage, with better data availability in developed countries and regions with extensive monitoring infrastructure. AI systems trained on these biased datasets may perpetuate or amplify existing inequalities, producing predictions that are less accurate for underrepresented regions or populations.

Environmental justice implications arise when black-box AI systems are used to assess climate risks or allocate resources for adaptation and mitigation efforts. If these systems exhibit biases or make decisions based on criteria that are not transparent, they may inadvertently discriminate against vulnerable communities or fail to adequately address environmental justice concerns. Ensuring fairness and equity in AI-based climate applications requires transparency and explainability to identify and correct potential biases.

Democratic participation in climate governance requires that citizens and their representatives be able to understand and evaluate the AI systems that influence climate policies and decisions. Black-box systems that cannot be understood or scrutinized by the public may undermine democratic oversight and accountability, creating situations where important decisions are made by AI systems that are not subject to appropriate democratic control.

International cooperation and technology transfer for climate applications may be hindered when AI systems are not explainable or transparent. Developing countries and international organizations may be reluctant to rely on AI technologies they cannot understand or validate independently, limiting the global deployment of potentially beneficial AI applications for climate adaptation and mitigation.

Trust and legitimacy of climate science may be undermined when the field increasingly relies on AI systems that cannot be understood or explained to the broader public. Public trust in climate science depends on the ability of scientists to explain their methods and findings in ways that can be understood and evaluated by informed citizens. The increasing use of black-box AI systems may erode this trust if the public perceives climate science as relying on incomprehensible technological systems rather than transparent scientific reasoning.

XAI Principles of Explainable AI

Explainable Artificial Intelligence represents a multidisciplinary field that encompasses computer science, cognitive psychology, and domain-specific applications to develop AI systems that can provide human-understandable explanations for their decisions, predictions, and behaviors. In the context of climate science, XAI approaches must address the unique challenges of Earth system complexity while meeting the interpretability requirements of scientific research, policy development, and public communication.

Interpretability, as distinct from explainability, refers to the degree to which a human can understand the cause of a decision made by an AI system. In climate science applications, interpretability often involves understanding how specific atmospheric patterns, oceanic conditions, or terrestrial processes contribute to model predictions. High interpretability systems allow domain experts to trace the logical pathways from input conditions to output predictions, enabling validation against physical understanding and identification of potential model limitations or biases.

Explainability encompasses the broader concept of providing explanations that help users understand, trust, and effectively manage AI systems in practical applications. Climate science explainability requirements extend beyond technical interpretability to include communication with policymakers, stakeholders, and the public who may not have technical expertise but need to understand the basis for climate assessments and recommendations. Effective explainability must translate complex AI reasoning into accessible explanations appropriate for different audiences.

Transparency refers to the degree to which AI system design, training procedures, and operational characteristics are open to inspection and understanding. Transparent climate AI systems provide clear documentation of model architectures, training datasets, validation procedures, and operational limitations, enabling independent evaluation and replication. Transparency supports both interpretability and explainability by providing the foundational information needed for understanding AI system behavior.

Post-hoc explainability approaches develop explanation methods that can be applied to existing AI systems without modifying their architectures or training procedures. These methods are particularly valuable for climate science applications where high-performing AI systems may already be deployed and where modifying model architectures could affect predictive accuracy. Post-hoc methods must reverse-engineer explanations from AI system behavior through analysis of input-output relationships.

Ante-hoc explainability approaches integrate interpretability considerations directly into AI system design and training procedures, creating inherently interpretable models that can provide explanations as part of their normal operation. While these approaches may sometimes sacrifice some predictive accuracy, they can provide more reliable and comprehensive explanations that are integrated into the AI reasoning process rather than being reconstructed after the fact.

Model-agnostic explanation methods can be applied to any AI system regardless of its internal architecture, providing flexibility for climate science applications that may employ diverse modeling approaches. These methods treat AI systems as black boxes and develop explanations based solely on input-output behavior, enabling consistent explanation approaches across different climate modeling contexts. Model-agnostic methods facilitate comparison and integration of explanations from different AI systems.

The development of explainable AI systems for climate science applications must adhere to specialized design principles that account for the unique characteristics of Earth system processes, the multi-scale nature of climate phenomena, and the diverse stakeholder needs in climate science and policy contexts. These principles guide the selection and implementation of explanation methods while ensuring that explanations remain scientifically valid and practically useful.

Physical consistency principles require that explanations provided by climate AI systems align with established physical understanding of Earth system processes. Explanations should not violate conservation laws, thermodynamic principles, or well-established causal relationships unless there is strong evidence for a new physical understanding. This principle helps ensure that AI explanations contribute to rather than undermine scientific understanding of climate processes.

Scale awareness principles recognize that climate phenomena operate across multiple temporal and spatial scales with complex interactions between scales. Explanations must account for these scale interactions and provide appropriate context for understanding how different scales contribute to predictions. Multi-scale explanations help users understand whether local conditions, regional patterns, or global-scale phenomena drive predictions.

Uncertainty characterization principles ensure that explanations include appropriate representation of uncertainty in AI predictions and the reliability of explanation methods themselves. Climate science inherently involves uncertainty from multiple sources, and explanations must help users understand both the confidence levels associated with predictions and the limitations of explanation methods. Probabilistic explanations provide more complete information for decision-making under uncertainty.

Audience appropriateness principles recognize that different stakeholders require different types and levels of explanation detail. Climate scientists may need detailed technical explanations that can be validated against physical understanding, while policymakers may require higher-level explanations focused on decision-relevant information. Adaptive explanation approaches can provide different explanation types based on user expertise and information needs.

Actionability principles ensure that explanations provide information that can support decision-making and action rather than merely satisfying curiosity about AI system behavior. Climate science explanations should identify the key factors driving predictions and provide insight into how different interventions or conditions might affect outcomes. Actionable explanations connect AI insights to practical decision-making needs.

Temporal coherence principles require that explanations maintain consistency over time and account for the temporal evolution of climate phenomena. Climate AI systems often make predictions about future conditions based on current and historical data, and explanations must help users understand how temporal relationships contribute to predictions. Coherent temporal explanations support understanding of climate system memory and predictability sources.

Comparative analysis principles enable explanations to highlight differences between predictions for different scenarios, time periods, or locations. Climate science applications often involve comparing alternative scenarios or understanding how conditions vary across space and time. Comparative explanations help identify the key factors responsible for differences between predictions and support scenario-based decision-making.

The diversity of climate science applications and stakeholder needs requires a comprehensive taxonomy of explanation types that can address different interpretability requirements and decision-making contexts. This taxonomy provides a framework for selecting appropriate explanation methods and designing explanation systems that meet specific user needs while maintaining scientific validity and practical utility.

Feature importance explanations identify which input variables contribute most significantly to AI predictions, helping users understand the relative importance of different climate factors. In climate science applications, feature importance might reveal whether temperature, precipitation, wind patterns, or other variables are most influential for specific predictions. These explanations support validation against expert knowledge and identification of potentially spurious relationships.

Causal explanations attempt to identify causal relationships between input variables and predictions, going beyond correlation to provide insight into the mechanisms underlying AI system behavior. Climate science applications benefit from causal explanations that can distinguish between direct causal effects and indirect effects mediated through other variables. Causal explanations support understanding of intervention effects and scenario analysis.

Counterfactual explanations describe how predictions would change under hypothetical modifications to input conditions, providing insight into AI system sensitivity and the critical factors driving predictions. Climate science applications might use counterfactual explanations to understand how predictions would differ under alternative emission scenarios, different initial conditions, or modified boundary conditions.

Example-based explanations identify specific instances from training data that are most similar to current prediction contexts, helping users understand AI reasoning through analogy to known cases. Climate science applications can use example-based explanations to connect current predictions to historical events or similar conditions, supporting pattern recognition and risk assessment through historical analogies.

Rule-based explanations extract simple logical rules that approximate AI system behavior, providing interpretable summaries of complex decision-making processes. Climate science applications might derive rules that describe conditions leading to extreme events, seasonal prediction accuracy, or regional climate patterns. Rule-based explanations offer high interpretability but may oversimplify complex relationships.

Attention-based explanations reveal which parts of input data AI systems focus on when making specific predictions, providing insight into the spatial and temporal patterns that drive AI reasoning. Climate science applications can use attention explanations to understand which geographic regions, time periods, or atmospheric levels are most relevant for specific predictions.

Hierarchical explanations provide multiple levels of explanation detail, from high-level summaries to detailed technical analyses, enabling different stakeholders to access appropriate explanation levels. Climate science applications benefit from hierarchical explanations that can serve both technical experts and general audiences while maintaining consistency across explanation levels.

The development of effective explainable AI systems for climate science requires careful consideration of human-AI collaboration patterns and how explanations can enhance rather than replace human expertise. This collaboration framework recognizes that the goal of explainable AI is not to make human experts obsolete but rather to augment human capabilities and support more effective decision-making through enhanced understanding of AI system behavior.

Complementary expertise models recognize that human experts and AI systems bring different strengths to climate science applications. Human experts provide domain knowledge, physical understanding, and contextual reasoning, while AI systems offer pattern recognition capabilities, computational efficiency, and the ability to process large datasets. Explanations should facilitate effective integration of these complementary capabilities rather than creating competition between human and AI approaches.

Interactive explanation approaches enable iterative exploration of AI system behavior through dynamic explanation interfaces that respond to user questions and interests. Climate science experts can use interactive systems to probe AI reasoning, test hypotheses about model behavior, and validate explanations against physical understanding. Interactive approaches support active learning and enable users to develop a deeper understanding of AI system capabilities and limitations.

Explanation validation frameworks provide systematic approaches for assessing the quality, accuracy, and utility of AI explanations. Climate science applications require validation methods that can assess whether explanations are consistent with physical understanding, whether they provide actionable insights for decision-making, and whether they enhance rather than confuse user understanding. Validation frameworks must account for the diverse needs of different stakeholders.

Trust calibration mechanisms help users develop appropriate levels of trust in AI systems by providing accurate information about system capabilities, limitations, and reliability. Overconfidence in AI systems can lead to poor decision-making, while underconfidence can prevent effective utilization of AI capabilities. Trust calibration through explanations helps users understand when and how to rely on AI systems effectively.

Collaborative decision-making frameworks integrate AI explanations into decision-making processes that involve multiple stakeholders with different expertise levels and information needs. Climate science decisions often require input from scientists, policymakers, and affected communities, and explanation systems must support collaborative processes that enable effective participation by all stakeholders. Collaborative frameworks ensure that AI insights are appropriately integrated into democratic decision-making processes.

Continuous learning approaches enable both AI systems and human users to learn from their interactions and improve their collaborative effectiveness over time. Climate science applications can benefit from explanation systems that learn from user feedback and adapt their explanation strategies to better meet user needs. Similarly, human users can develop a better understanding of AI capabilities and limitations through experience with explanation systems.

Global explanation methods provide comprehensive characterizations of AI system behavior across the entire input space, offering insights into overall model functionality, general patterns of decision-making, and systematic biases or preferences. In climate science applications, global explanations are particularly valuable for understanding how AI systems respond to different climate regimes, seasonal patterns, and long-term trends, providing insights that can inform model validation, scientific understanding, and policy development.

Model-wide feature importance analysis provides global perspectives on which climate variables are most influential for AI predictions across all possible input conditions. These analyses might reveal that sea surface temperatures are more important than atmospheric pressure for seasonal precipitation predictions, or that wind patterns dominate temperature predictions in certain regions. Global feature importance helps climate scientists understand the overall priorities embedded in AI systems and validate them against physical understanding.

Global sensitivity analysis examines how AI predictions respond to systematic changes in input variables across their entire ranges, providing insights into model behavior under extreme conditions and identifying potential instabilities or unrealistic responses. Climate science applications benefit from global sensitivity analysis that can reveal whether AI systems maintain realistic behavior under climate change scenarios or extreme weather conditions.

Decision boundary analysis characterizes the thresholds and transitions that govern AI system classification or prediction decisions, providing insights into how AI systems distinguish between different climate states or categories. Global decision boundary analysis might reveal the temperature and humidity combinations that lead AI systems to predict drought conditions, or the atmospheric circulation patterns associated with extreme weather classifications.

Systematic bias assessment employs global analysis methods to identify consistent patterns of over-prediction or under-prediction that may affect AI system reliability. Climate science applications require global bias analysis across different seasons, regions, and climate conditions to ensure that AI systems provide consistent performance and do not exhibit systematic errors that could mislead scientific understanding or policy development.

Pattern discovery through global analysis can reveal previously unknown relationships or phenomena that AI systems have learned from climate data. Global explanation methods might identify new teleconnection patterns, previously unrecognized climate modes, or novel relationships between different Earth system components. These discoveries require careful validation against physical understanding but can contribute to scientific advancement.

Regime identification through global explanation analysis can reveal how AI systems adapt their behavior to different climate regimes, seasons, or geographical regions. Understanding these behavioral adaptations helps climate scientists assess whether AI systems appropriately account for regime-dependent processes and whether they maintain consistent performance across different conditions.

Model comparison and benchmarking benefit from global explanation methods that can characterize differences in behavior between different AI systems or between AI systems and traditional climate models. Global comparisons help identify the strengths and weaknesses of different modeling approaches and support model selection and ensemble design decisions.

Local explanation methods focus on understanding AI system behavior for specific predictions or small regions of input space, providing detailed insights into the reasoning behind particular decisions. In climate science applications, local explanations are essential for understanding extreme event predictions, validating individual forecasts, and providing decision-relevant information for specific situations or locations.

Instance-specific feature attribution identifies which climate variables contribute most significantly to individual predictions, helping users understand the specific factors driving particular forecasts or assessments. Local feature attribution might reveal that a hurricane intensity prediction is primarily driven by sea surface temperatures and wind shear conditions, while atmospheric pressure and humidity play secondary roles for that specific case.

Temporal attribution analysis examines how different time periods in historical data contribute to specific predictions, providing insights into the temporal dependencies that influence AI reasoning. Climate science applications benefit from temporal attribution that can identify whether seasonal predictions are primarily based on recent conditions, longer-term trends, or specific historical patterns that provide predictive information.

Spatial attribution methods identify which geographical regions contribute most significantly to predictions for specific locations, revealing the spatial dependencies and teleconnections that AI systems utilize. Local spatial attribution might show that precipitation predictions for a particular region are most strongly influenced by sea surface temperature patterns in distant ocean basins, confirming known teleconnection relationships.

Nearest neighbor analysis identifies the most similar cases from training data that influence specific predictions, providing insights into AI reasoning through historical analogies. Climate science applications can use nearest neighbor explanations to understand which past events or conditions AI systems consider most relevant for current predictions, supporting risk assessment through historical precedents.

Counterfactual analysis for specific predictions explores how individual predictions would change under hypothetical modifications to input conditions, providing insights into prediction sensitivity and the critical factors that determine outcomes. Local counterfactual analysis might reveal the minimum changes in atmospheric conditions required to shift a drought prediction to normal conditions.

Prediction confidence and uncertainty analysis provide local assessments of AI system confidence in specific predictions, helping users understand the reliability of individual forecasts. Local uncertainty analysis is crucial for climate science applications where prediction confidence may vary significantly depending on location, season, or meteorological conditions.

Explanation consistency analysis examines whether local explanations for similar cases provide consistent insights, helping identify potential instabilities or contradictions in AI system reasoning. Consistency analysis supports validation of explanation methods and helps identify situations where AI systems may be unreliable or where additional validation may be needed.

Analysis of Global and Local Approaches

The choice between global and local explanation approaches depends on the specific objectives, stakeholder needs, and decision-making contexts of climate science applications. Each approach offers distinct advantages and limitations that must be considered when designing explanation systems for climate AI applications.

Scope and generalizability represent fundamental differences between global and local explanation approaches. Global explanations provide insights that apply across the entire model domain and can inform general understanding of AI system behavior, while local explanations focus on specific instances and may not generalize to other conditions. Climate science applications often require both perspectives, with global explanations supporting model validation and scientific understanding, while local explanations support specific decisions and forecasts.

Computational requirements differ significantly between global and local explanation methods, with global approaches typically requiring more extensive computation to characterize behavior across entire input spaces. Local explanations can often be computed more efficiently for specific instances, making them more suitable for real-time applications or situations with computational constraints. Climate science operational systems may favor local approaches for routine explanation needs while employing global approaches for periodic model assessment.

Detail and specificity levels vary between global and local explanation approaches, with global methods providing broader perspectives that may miss important details visible in local analysis. Local explanations can reveal subtle relationships and interactions that contribute to specific predictions but may not reflect systematic patterns in model behavior. Climate science applications benefit from the complementary use of both approaches to achieve a comprehensive understanding.

Validation challenges differ between global and local explanation approaches due to differences in scope and available validation data. Global explanations can be validated against broad physical understanding and systematic patterns in climate data, while local explanations may require validation against specific observations or detailed process understanding. Climate science validation requires careful consideration of appropriate validation strategies for different explanation types.

User interpretation requirements vary significantly between global and local explanations, with global approaches requiring users to synthesize broad patterns and relationships while local approaches focus on specific, concrete examples. Climate science stakeholders may find local explanations more intuitive and actionable while struggling to interpret complex global patterns. Explanation system design must account for user capabilities and preferences.

Decision-making support effectiveness depends on alignment between the explanation scope and decision requirements. Strategic decisions about climate policy or long-term adaptation may benefit more from global explanations that characterize systematic patterns, while operational decisions about specific events or locations may require local explanations that address immediate concerns. Climate science explanation systems should provide appropriate explanation types for different decision contexts.

Effective explainable AI systems for climate science applications must integrate global and local explanation approaches to provide a comprehensive understanding that addresses diverse user needs and decision-making requirements. Integration strategies must balance the complementary strengths of different explanation types while maintaining consistency and avoiding confusion from contradictory insights.

Hierarchical explanation systems provide multiple levels of explanation detail, starting with global overviews and enabling users to drill down into local details for specific cases or regions of interest. Climate science applications can benefit from hierarchical systems that allow policymakers to access high-level summaries while enabling scientists to explore detailed technical explanations. Hierarchical approaches support different user expertise levels and information needs.

Multi-perspective explanation frameworks present both global and local insights simultaneously, enabling users to understand how specific instances relate to broader patterns and trends. Climate science applications might display global feature importance alongside local attribution for specific predictions, helping users understand whether individual cases reflect systematic patterns or unusual circumstances.

Consistency validation approaches compare global and local explanations to identify potential contradictions or inconsistencies that might indicate problems with AI systems or explanation methods. Systematic inconsistencies between global and local explanations may reveal model instabilities, explanation method limitations, or situations requiring additional investigation. Consistency validation supports quality assurance for explanation systems.

Interactive exploration tools enable users to navigate fluidly between global and local explanation perspectives, supporting investigation of questions that span multiple scales or levels of detail. Climate science experts can use interactive tools to explore global patterns and then examine specific instances that exemplify or contradict those patterns, supporting hypothesis testing and scientific investigation.

Contextual explanation selection automatically determines whether global or local explanations are most appropriate for specific user queries or decision-making situations. Intelligent explanation systems can recognize when users need a broad understanding versus specific details and provide appropriate explanation types accordingly. Contextual selection reduces cognitive load and improves explanation effectiveness.

Synthetic explanation approaches combine insights from multiple explanation methods to provide a comprehensive understanding that leverages the strengths of different approaches. Climate science applications might combine global sensitivity analysis with local counterfactual analysis to provide a complete understanding of prediction drivers and sensitivities. Synthetic approaches require careful integration to avoid overwhelming users with information.

Confidence and Trust in AI Climate Models

The development of stakeholder confidence in AI climate models represents a critical challenge that extends beyond technical performance to encompass broader questions of transparency, reliability, and alignment with stakeholder values and needs. Climate science operates within a complex ecosystem of stakeholders, including researchers, policymakers, industry leaders, and affected communities, each with different expertise levels, information needs, and trust requirements that must be addressed through comprehensive confidence-building strategies.

Transparency in model development processes provides stakeholders with visibility into how AI climate models are designed, trained, and validated, enabling informed evaluation of model reliability and appropriateness for specific applications. Comprehensive transparency includes documentation of data sources, model architectures, training procedures, validation methodologies, and known limitations or biases. Transparent development processes enable stakeholders to assess whether models meet their quality standards and ethical requirements.

Performance validation through independent testing and comparison provides objective evidence of AI model capabilities and limitations across different conditions and applications. Stakeholder confidence benefits from validation studies conducted by independent organizations using standardized datasets and evaluation protocols. Transparent reporting of validation results, including failures and limitations, builds credibility and helps stakeholders understand appropriate model applications.

Uncertainty communication strategies help stakeholders understand the confidence levels and reliability limitations associated with AI climate model predictions. Effective uncertainty communication avoids both overconfidence and excessive caution while providing stakeholders with the information needed for risk-based decision-making. Probabilistic prediction formats and confidence intervals support informed interpretation of model outputs.

Expert endorsement and peer review processes provide professional validation of AI climate models through evaluation by qualified experts who can assess technical quality and scientific validity. Stakeholder confidence benefits from evidence that models have been reviewed and endorsed by recognized experts in climate science and artificial intelligence. Professional endorsement provides quality assurance that may be particularly valuable for non-technical stakeholders.

Track record demonstration through historical performance analysis provides evidence of AI model reliability based on past performance across diverse conditions and applications. Long-term performance tracking enables stakeholders to assess whether models maintain consistent quality over time and adapt appropriately to changing conditions. Historical performance data provides concrete evidence of model capabilities and limitations.

Stakeholder engagement processes enable meaningful participation by affected communities and interest groups in model evaluation and validation processes. Engaging stakeholders in model assessment helps ensure that AI systems address relevant questions and concerns while providing opportunities for feedback and validation against local knowledge and experience. Participatory approaches build ownership and trust through inclusive decision-making processes.

Ethical compliance and fairness assessment demonstrate that AI climate models adhere to ethical principles and do not exhibit discriminatory biases against vulnerable populations or regions. Stakeholder confidence requires evidence that AI systems promote rather than undermine equity and justice in climate science and policy applications. Bias testing and fairness auditing provide systematic approaches for ethical compliance assessment.

Technical reliability represents the foundation upon which stakeholder trust in AI climate models must be built, encompassing accuracy, consistency, robustness, and appropriate handling of uncertainty across diverse conditions and applications. Climate science applications require particularly stringent reliability standards due to the high-stakes nature of climate predictions and the long-term consequences of climate-related decisions.

Cross-validation methodologies provide systematic approaches for assessing AI model performance using independent datasets that were not involved in model training. Climate science cross-validation must carefully handle temporal correlation and spatial dependencies in climate data to provide realistic performance estimates. Time-series cross-validation, spatial block cross-validation, and leave-one-out validation approaches provide different perspectives on model reliability and generalization capability.

Stress testing and robustness analysis evaluate AI model performance under extreme conditions, data quality issues, and adversarial inputs that may occur in operational applications. Climate science stress testing might involve evaluating model performance during extreme weather events, with corrupted or missing data, or under climate conditions outside the training data range. Robustness analysis helps identify failure modes and operational limitations.

Ensemble validation approaches compare AI model predictions with those from multiple independent models or modeling approaches, providing insights into consistency and reliability across different methodological frameworks. Climate science ensemble validation might compare AI models with traditional physics-based models, other AI approaches, or expert assessments to identify systematic differences and assess relative performance.

Physical consistency validation assesses whether AI model predictions are consistent with established physical principles, conservation laws, and causal relationships. Climate science applications require validation against thermodynamic constraints, energy balance requirements, and known atmospheric and oceanic dynamics. Physical consistency validation helps ensure that AI models produce scientifically reasonable results.

Temporal consistency analysis examines whether AI models maintain appropriate relationships between predictions at different time scales and whether they exhibit realistic temporal evolution patterns. Climate models must maintain consistency between short-term weather patterns and long-term climate trends while appropriately representing seasonal cycles and interannual variability.

Spatial consistency evaluation assesses whether AI models produce spatially coherent predictions that respect geographical relationships and physical constraints. Climate applications require spatial consistency validation.

TEN

Emerging Methods and the Future

As we stand at the threshold of unprecedented technological advancement and escalating climate challenges, the convergence of artificial intelligence, climate science, and emerging intervention technologies presents both extraordinary opportunities and profound responsibilities. This final chapter explores the cutting-edge developments that are reshaping our understanding of climate systems while examining the future pathways that will define the next generation of climate research and action. From the controversial realm of climate geo-engineering to the revolutionary potential of quantum computing, these emerging developments represent transformative possibilities that could fundamentally alter our approach to climate science and planetary stewardship.

The intersection of AI and climate science has already demonstrated remarkable progress in prediction capabilities, pattern recognition, and system understanding. However, the frontier applications explored in this chapter venture into uncharted territories where artificial intelligence must grapple with questions of unprecedented complexity and ethical weight. Climate intervention technologies, particularly geoengineering approaches, present scenarios where AI systems must not only understand natural climate processes but also predict and optimize deliberate human modifications to Earth's climate system. These applications demand levels of precision, reliability, and ethical consideration that push the boundaries of current AI capabilities.

The development of explainable AI frameworks for climate intervention represents a critical necessity rather than merely an academic pursuit. When considering interventions that could affect the entire planet's climate system, the ability to understand, validate, and communicate the reasoning behind AI recommendations becomes paramount. The stakes involved in geoengineering decisions require transparency and interpretability standards that exceed those of traditional climate applications, demanding new approaches to explainable AI that can handle the complexity and uncertainty inherent in planetary-scale interventions.

Simultaneously, the future research directions examined in this chapter point toward a transformation of climate science itself through technologies that promise unprecedented capabilities in observation, computation, and reasoning. Real-time adaptive systems that can continuously learn and respond to changing climate conditions, next-generation climate models that integrate AI capabilities from the ground up, and global monitoring networks enhanced by artificial intelligence represent paradigm shifts that could revolutionize our understanding and management of Earth's climate system.

The emergence of quantum computing approaches for climate science applications introduces computational possibilities that could solve previously intractable problems while opening entirely new research directions. The potential for quantum advantage in optimization, simulation, and machine learning applications relevant to climate science suggests that we may be approaching computational capabilities that could transform our ability to understand and predict climate system behavior at scales and resolutions previously impossible.

This chapter also addresses the critical need for rigorous validation processes and success metrics that can ensure the reliability and effectiveness of these emerging technologies. As AI systems become increasingly central to climate science and potentially to climate intervention decisions, the development of comprehensive validation frameworks becomes essential for maintaining scientific integrity and public trust while enabling innovation and progress.

Climate Intervention Technologies

Climate intervention technologies, commonly referred to as geoengineering, encompass a diverse range of approaches designed to deliberately modify Earth's climate system to counteract or mitigate the effects of anthropogenic climate change. These technologies broadly fall into two categories: carbon dioxide removal (CDR) methods that extract greenhouse gases from the atmosphere, and solar radiation management (SRM) techniques that modify Earth's energy balance by reflecting incoming solar radiation. The integration of artificial intelligence into the development, deployment, and management of these technologies represents a frontier application that combines the complexity of climate system science with the ethical and practical challenges of planetary-scale intervention.

Carbon dioxide removal technologies range from nature-based solutions such as reforestation and soil carbon sequestration to engineered approaches, including direct air capture, enhanced weathering, and ocean alkalinization. Each CDR approach presents unique challenges for AI integration, from optimizing the spatial deployment of natural solutions to managing complex chemical processes in engineered systems. AI applications in CDR must address questions of scalability, permanence, and environmental side effects while optimizing deployment strategies across diverse geographical and ecological contexts.

Solar radiation management technologies aim to modify Earth's radiative balance through approaches such as stratospheric aerosol injection, marine cloud brightening, and cirrus cloud modification. These SRM approaches present particularly complex challenges for AI integration due to their global-scale effects, potential for rapid implementation, and significant governance implications. AI systems designed for SRM applications must model complex atmospheric chemistry and physics while accounting for regional and temporal variability in intervention effects.

The temporal scales of intervention effects present unique challenges for AI system design, ranging from immediate responses in solar radiation management to century-scale carbon cycle perturbations in CDR approaches. AI systems must be capable of reasoning across these diverse temporal scales while maintaining consistency and accuracy in their recommendations. Multi-scale modeling approaches and hierarchical AI architectures become essential for handling the temporal complexity inherent in climate intervention applications.

Intervention cascades and unintended consequences represent critical considerations for AI systems designed to support geoengineering decisions. Climate interventions may trigger complex chains of effects that propagate through the Earth system in ways that are difficult to predict or control. AI systems must be capable of identifying potential cascade effects, assessing their likelihood and magnitude, and incorporating this uncertainty into intervention recommendations and risk assessments.

The reversibility and termination characteristics of different intervention technologies create distinct requirements for AI system design and operation. Solar radiation management technologies that can be rapidly deployed may also require continuous maintenance and face potentially severe consequences if terminated abruptly. AI systems must account for these reversibility characteristics when evaluating intervention options and developing long-term management strategies.

Regional and distributional effects of climate interventions present complex optimization challenges where global benefits must be balanced against local impacts and equity considerations. AI systems must be capable of modeling intervention effects across multiple spatial scales while incorporating justice and equity considerations into their decision-making frameworks. Multi-objective optimization approaches become essential for balancing competing objectives and stakeholder interests.

AI Integration in Geoengineering

The integration of artificial intelligence into geoengineering system design represents a fundamental shift from traditional engineering approaches toward adaptive, intelligent systems capable of managing unprecedented complexity and uncertainty. AI integration spans the entire lifecycle of geoengineering technologies, from initial concept development and feasibility assessment through detailed design optimization and operational management. This integration requires sophisticated AI systems capable of handling multi-physics modeling, uncertainty quantification, and real-time adaptive control across planetary scales.

Design optimization using AI approaches enables systematic exploration of vast parameter spaces that characterize geoengineering systems, identifying optimal configurations that balance effectiveness, cost, environmental impact, and risk considerations. Machine learning algorithms can process complex design trade-offs while accounting for uncertainty in climate models, technology performance, and environmental responses. Evolutionary algorithms and multi-objective optimization techniques prove particularly valuable for geoengineering design problems that involve competing objectives and complex constraint sets.

System-level integration employs AI to coordinate multiple intervention technologies and their interactions with natural climate systems. Large-scale geoengineering deployment may involve combinations of different technologies operating at different scales and time horizons. AI systems must orchestrate these interventions to maximize synergistic effects while minimizing conflicts and unintended interactions. System integration requires sophisticated modeling capabilities that can represent both technological systems and natural processes within unified frameworks.

Adaptive control systems employ AI to continuously adjust geoengineering operations based on observed climate responses and changing conditions. Unlike traditional engineering systems that operate according to fixed parameters, geoengineering systems must adapt to evolving climate conditions, technology performance, and societal objectives. Machine learning approaches enable continuous optimization of intervention strategies based on accumulating data and experience.

Uncertainty propagation and robust design approaches use AI to ensure that geoengineering systems perform acceptably across the range of possible future conditions and system uncertainties. Climate uncertainty, technology performance variability, and model limitations create challenges for traditional deterministic design approaches. AI systems can employ probabilistic methods and robust optimization techniques to ensure reliable performance despite significant uncertainties.

Real-time monitoring and feedback systems integrate AI with observation networks to provide continuous assessment of geoengineering effectiveness and environmental impacts. Satellite observations, ground-based measurements, and numerical models must be integrated to provide comprehensive situational awareness for geoengineering operations. AI systems can process these diverse data streams to identify performance trends, detect anomalies, and recommend operational adjustments.

Failure detection and emergency response capabilities employ AI to identify potential system failures or unintended consequences that require rapid intervention. Geoengineering systems operating at planetary scales could potentially cause significant environmental damage if they malfunction or produce unintended effects. AI systems must continuously monitor for signs of system failure and be prepared to implement emergency response procedures, including intervention termination or modification.

The optimization of geoengineering deployment strategies represents a complex multi-objective problem that requires AI systems capable of balancing effectiveness, cost, environmental impact, and societal considerations across diverse geographical and temporal scales. Deployment optimization must account for spatial and temporal variability in intervention effects, infrastructure constraints, and coordination with other climate policies and interventions. AI approaches provide essential capabilities for managing this complexity while ensuring that deployment strategies achieve their intended climate objectives.

Spatial optimization algorithms determine optimal locations and configurations for geoengineering interventions based on climate effectiveness, environmental constraints, and logistical considerations. Solar radiation management technologies may require global deployment patterns that account for atmospheric transport and mixing processes, while carbon dioxide removal approaches must consider local environmental conditions and infrastructure availability. Machine learning approaches can identify optimal deployment patterns while accounting for complex spatial interactions and constraints.

Temporal sequencing optimization addresses questions of when and how rapidly different interventions should be deployed to achieve climate objectives while managing transition risks and costs. Gradual deployment strategies may provide opportunities for learning and adaptation but may not achieve climate objectives quickly enough, while rapid deployment may increase risks and costs. AI optimization approaches can identify deployment schedules that balance these competing considerations while maintaining flexibility for adaptive management.

Portfolio optimization approaches determine optimal combinations of different geoengineering technologies and their integration with conventional mitigation and adaptation strategies. No single intervention technology is likely to address all aspects of the climate challenge, requiring careful coordination of multiple approaches. AI systems can optimize intervention portfolios to maximize climate benefits while managing costs, risks, and interactions between different interventions.

Risk-informed deployment strategies employ AI to optimize intervention strategies while explicitly accounting for uncertainty and potential adverse consequences. Traditional optimization approaches may fail to adequately address the low-probability, high-impact risks that characterize many geoengineering interventions. AI systems can employ robust optimization methods that explicitly consider worst-case scenarios and risk aversion in their deployment recommendations.

Adaptive deployment frameworks enable continuous modification of deployment strategies based on observed performance and changing conditions. Climate change, technology development, and evolving societal preferences create dynamic environments where fixed deployment strategies may become suboptimal or inappropriate. AI systems can continuously evaluate deployment performance and recommend strategy modifications based on new information and changing objectives.

International coordination for termination governance employs AI to support multilateral decision-making processes about SAI termination while managing the complex diplomatic and technical challenges of coordinating termination decisions across multiple stakeholders and jurisdictions. SAI termination decisions may require international consensus that could be difficult to achieve under crisis conditions. AI systems can support coordination by modeling stakeholder interests, facilitating communication, and identifying mutually acceptable termination strategies.

Legal and institutional continuity planning uses AI to ensure that termination capabilities and governance mechanisms remain effective even if political priorities change, institutions fail, or international cooperation breaks down. Long-term SAI programs may outlast the political coalitions and institutions that initiated them, creating risks for termination governance. AI systems can support contingency planning while identifying institutional arrangements that can maintain termination capabilities under diverse future scenarios.

Risk Assessment

The development of comprehensive risk modeling frameworks for AI-enhanced climate interventions represents one of the most critical challenges in responsible geoengineering research and deployment. Unlike conventional risk assessment applications, climate intervention risks span multiple interconnected systems with complex feedback mechanisms, operate across unprecedented spatial and temporal scales, and involve deep uncertainty about system behavior under intervention scenarios. AI-based risk modeling frameworks must integrate diverse risk sources while maintaining transparency about uncertainty and enabling democratic participation in risk evaluation and management processes.

Systemic risk integration approaches employ AI to model complex interactions between climate intervention technologies, natural Earth system processes, and human social systems that could produce cascading failures or unintended consequences. Climate interventions may trigger chains of effects that propagate through interconnected systems in ways that are difficult to predict using traditional risk assessment methods. AI systems can model these systemic interactions while identifying potential cascade pathways and their associated probabilities and consequences.

Multi-scale risk analysis uses AI to assess risks that operate across different spatial and temporal scales simultaneously, from local environmental impacts to global climate system perturbations and from immediate technological failures to century-scale environmental changes. Traditional risk assessment methods often struggle to integrate risks operating at different scales, potentially missing important cross-scale interactions and feedback mechanisms. AI approaches can provide unified multi-scale risk assessment while maintaining appropriate resolution for different risk types.

Deep uncertainty quantification employs AI to characterize and communicate risks in situations where probability distributions are unknown or disputed, model structures are uncertain, and stakeholder values about acceptable risk levels vary significantly. Climate intervention risks often involve deep uncertainty where traditional probabilistic risk assessment may be inappropriate or misleading. AI systems can employ alternative uncertainty representation methods while supporting decision-making under deep uncertainty conditions.

Dynamic risk assessment approaches use AI to continuously update risk evaluations based on new scientific understanding, operational experience, and changing environmental conditions rather than relying on static risk assessments developed at the time of initial deployment. Climate intervention risks may evolve as systems operate and as understanding improves through research and experience. AI systems can provide adaptive risk assessment that responds to new information while maintaining consistency in evaluation frameworks.

Compound risk evaluation employs AI to assess situations where multiple risk sources interact simultaneously, potentially producing consequences that exceed the sum of individual risks. Climate interventions may create new risks while interacting with existing climate risks, technological risks, and social risks in complex ways. AI systems can model these compound risk scenarios while identifying interaction effects that may not be apparent when considering individual risks separately.

Tail risk identification uses AI to identify low-probability, high-consequence risk scenarios that may not receive adequate attention in conventional risk assessment but could have catastrophic consequences if they occur. Climate intervention systems operating at planetary scales could potentially produce severe consequences despite careful design and operation. AI systems can systematically explore tail risk scenarios while assessing their plausibility and potential consequences.

Risk communication and visualization frameworks employ AI to translate complex risk assessments into accessible formats that enable meaningful stakeholder engagement and democratic decision-making about risk acceptance and management strategies. Technical risk assessments may be incomprehensible to non-expert stakeholders who nonetheless have legitimate interests in risk management decisions. AI systems can provide adaptive risk communication that matches stakeholder information needs while maintaining accuracy and completeness.

Uncertainty Analysis

The analysis of uncertainty across multiple spatial and temporal scales represents a fundamental challenge for climate intervention risk assessment due to the complex propagation of uncertainties through interconnected Earth system processes and technological systems. AI-enhanced uncertainty analysis provides capabilities for tracking uncertainty propagation while maintaining computational tractability for global-scale applications. The integration of uncertainty analysis across scales enables a more comprehensive understanding of intervention risks while supporting appropriate humility about the limits of prediction and control in complex systems.

Parameter uncertainty propagation employs AI to track how uncertainties in model parameters, physical constants, and system characteristics affect intervention predictions and risk assessments across different scales. Climate intervention models involve numerous uncertain parameters whose impacts may compound across scale interactions and feedback loops. AI systems can efficiently propagate parameter uncertainties while identifying which parameter uncertainties contribute most significantly to overall prediction uncertainty.

Structural uncertainty analysis uses AI to assess how uncertainties in model structure, process representations, and causal assumptions affect risk assessment outcomes. Different modeling approaches may produce significantly different risk estimates due to structural differences rather than parameter uncertainties. AI systems can compare multiple modeling approaches while assessing the impact of structural uncertainties on risk evaluation outcomes.

Scale interaction uncertainty focuses on uncertainties in how processes operating at different scales interact and influence each other within climate intervention systems. Cross-scale interactions may be poorly understood or represented in models, creating significant uncertainties about system behavior. AI approaches can characterize scale interaction uncertainties while assessing their implications for intervention planning and risk management.

Temporal uncertainty evolution employs AI to understand how uncertainties change over time as intervention systems operate and as natural and human systems respond to interventions. Early intervention phases may have different uncertainty characteristics than mature operational phases. AI systems can model uncertainty evolution while supporting adaptive management approaches that account for changing uncertainty levels.

Spatial uncertainty propagation uses AI to track how local uncertainties propagate across spatial scales and geographical regions through atmospheric and oceanic transport processes and ecological interactions. Local intervention effects may have regional or global consequences through complex transport and interaction mechanisms. AI systems can model spatial uncertainty propagation while identifying regions where uncertainty levels may be particularly high or consequential.

Scenario uncertainty analysis employs AI to assess how different assumptions about future conditions, policy choices, and technological development affect intervention risks and uncertainty levels. Future scenarios involve fundamental uncertainties about emissions pathways, technological development, and social responses that significantly affect intervention planning. AI systems can analyze scenario uncertainty while identifying robust intervention strategies that perform well across multiple scenarios.

Observational uncertainty integration uses AI to incorporate uncertainties in observational data, measurement systems, and monitoring capabilities into risk assessment frameworks. Intervention monitoring and evaluation depend on observational systems that have their own uncertainties and limitations. AI systems can account for observational uncertainties while assessing their implications for intervention evaluation and adaptive management.

Decision-Making and Deep Uncertainty

Climate intervention decisions must be made in contexts of deep uncertainty where traditional decision-making frameworks based on probabilistic risk assessment may be inappropriate or insufficient. Deep uncertainty characterizes situations where stakeholders disagree about model structures, probability distributions are unknown or disputed, and value systems differ significantly regarding acceptable risk levels and appropriate precautionary measures. AI-enhanced decision-making frameworks for deep uncertainty provide structured approaches for making robust decisions while maintaining transparency about value judgments and uncertainty that influence decision outcomes.

Robust decision-making approaches employ AI to identify intervention strategies that perform acceptably well across a wide range of possible future scenarios rather than optimizing for single best-guess scenarios. Robust approaches explicitly acknowledge that predictions may be wrong while seeking strategies that minimize regret across multiple possible futures. AI systems can evaluate strategy robustness while identifying trade-offs between robustness and performance optimization.

Adaptive management frameworks use AI to support iterative decision-making processes that can modify intervention strategies based on new information and changing conditions while maintaining progress toward overall objectives. Adaptive management acknowledges that initial decisions may need to be revised as understanding improves and conditions change. AI systems can support adaptive management by providing decision triggers, performance monitoring, and strategy modification recommendations.

Multi-stakeholder decision integration employs AI to facilitate decision-making processes that involve multiple stakeholders with different values, preferences, and risk tolerances while seeking solutions that can achieve broad support or consensus. Climate intervention decisions affect diverse stakeholder communities who may have conflicting interests and values. AI systems can support multi-stakeholder processes by identifying areas of agreement, clarifying trade-offs, and exploring compromise solutions.

Precautionary decision frameworks use AI to implement precautionary approaches that err on the side of caution when facing potentially catastrophic risks with high uncertainty. Precautionary principles suggest that the lack of complete scientific certainty should not be used to postpone action to prevent potential environmental harm. AI systems can implement precautionary approaches while balancing caution against other decision criteria and objectives.

Real options analysis employs AI to evaluate intervention strategies that maintain flexibility and preserve options for future decisions rather than committing irrevocably to specific intervention pathways. Real options approaches recognize that uncertainty may decrease over time and that preserving flexibility may be valuable even if it requires accepting lower expected performance. AI systems can evaluate option values while optimizing portfolios of intervention investments.

Participatory decision modeling uses AI to support inclusive decision-making processes that enable meaningful participation by affected communities and stakeholders in intervention planning and evaluation. Participatory approaches recognize that those affected by intervention decisions have legitimate rights to participate in decision-making processes. AI systems can facilitate participation by providing accessible information, supporting dialogue, and integrating diverse perspectives.

Value-focused thinking frameworks employ AI to structure decision-making processes around stakeholder values and objectives rather than available alternatives, ensuring that intervention decisions serve stakeholder values rather than being constrained by existing options. Value-focused approaches can identify creative alternatives and highlight value trade-offs that may not be apparent in alternative-focused decision processes. AI systems can support value elicitation and alternative generation while maintaining transparency about value implications.

The ethical dimensions of AI-enhanced climate interventions represent fundamental considerations that must be integrated throughout research, development, and deployment processes rather than being treated as external constraints or afterthoughts. The planetary scope of potential climate interventions creates ethical challenges of unprecedented scale and complexity that require sophisticated frameworks for ethical analysis and decision-making. These ethical considerations span multiple domains, including justice, rights, democracy, precaution, and intergenerational responsibility, while addressing the unique challenges posed by AI system decision-making in high-stakes contexts.

Intergenerational justice frameworks address the fundamental ethical challenge of making decisions about planetary-scale interventions that will affect future generations who cannot participate in current decision-making processes. Climate interventions may create benefits and risks that persist for centuries while current decision-makers bear none of the long-term consequences. AI systems must incorporate sophisticated temporal discounting and intergenerational equity principles that protect future interests while accounting for uncertainty about future preferences and values.

Environmental justice considerations ensure that AI-enhanced climate interventions do not disproportionately burden vulnerable populations or exacerbate existing environmental inequalities. Climate change and climate interventions may affect different communities differently, with vulnerable populations often bearing disproportionate risks while having limited influence over intervention decisions. AI systems must incorporate equity analysis and distributional assessment capabilities that identify and address potential environmental justice concerns.

Democratic legitimacy requirements ensure that AI systems support rather than undermine democratic decision-making processes about climate intervention deployment and governance. AI recommendations must be developed through processes that enable meaningful democratic participation and oversight rather than technocratic decision-making that excludes affected communities. Democratic frameworks must balance technical expertise against participatory governance principles while ensuring that AI systems remain subject to appropriate democratic control.

Rights-based constraints ensure that AI recommendations respect fundamental human rights, including rights to environmental quality, cultural integrity, and self-determination. Climate interventions may disproportionately affect indigenous communities, small island states, or other groups who have rights to maintain their traditional ways of life and cultural practices. AI systems must incorporate rights-based constraints that prevent recommendations that would violate these fundamental protections.

Precautionary principle implementation employs AI to incorporate precautionary approaches that err on the side of caution when facing potentially catastrophic risks with high uncertainty. Traditional decision theory may inadequately address situations where probability estimates are highly uncertain but potential consequences are severe. AI systems must be capable of reasoning about deep uncertainty while maintaining appropriate precautionary stances toward potentially irreversible interventions.

Consent and participation frameworks address the challenge of obtaining appropriate consent for planetary-scale interventions that affect all human beings and natural ecosystems. Traditional consent models may be inadequate for interventions that affect global populations who cannot meaningfully consent to or opt out of intervention effects. AI systems must support consent and participation processes that are as inclusive and democratic as possible while acknowledging the practical limitations of global consent processes.

Transparency and accountability mechanisms ensure that AI system decision-making processes remain open to scrutiny and that responsibility for intervention decisions can be appropriately assigned. The complexity of AI systems may create opacity that undermines democratic accountability, while the global scale of interventions may complicate traditional responsibility assignment mechanisms. Ethical frameworks must ensure that AI systems enhance rather than undermine accountability for intervention decisions.

Research and Expected Path

The development of real-time adaptive systems represents a transformative frontier in climate science and AI integration, promising unprecedented capabilities for continuous learning, adaptation, and response to evolving climate conditions. These systems move beyond static models and fixed intervention strategies toward dynamic, intelligent systems that can adjust their behavior based on continuous observation and learning. Real-time adaptive capabilities are essential for managing the complexity and uncertainty inherent in climate systems while enabling rapid response to unexpected events or changing conditions.

Continuous learning architectures employ AI systems that can incorporate new observational data, scientific understanding, and operational experience without requiring complete system retraining or replacement. Traditional AI systems often become outdated as conditions change or as new data becomes available, requiring expensive and time-consuming retraining processes. Continuous learning approaches enable systems to adapt incrementally while maintaining performance and reliability standards appropriate for climate applications.

Edge computing and distributed intelligence frameworks deploy AI capabilities across distributed sensor networks and monitoring systems, enabling rapid local processing and decision-making without requiring constant communication with centralized systems. Climate monitoring systems often operate in remote locations with limited communication capabilities while requiring rapid response to changing conditions. Edge AI can provide local intelligence while maintaining coordination with broader monitoring and response networks.

Adaptive control and feedback systems employ AI to continuously adjust system parameters and strategies based on observed performance and environmental responses rather than operating according to fixed schedules or procedures. Climate intervention systems may require continuous adaptation to changing atmospheric conditions, seasonal variations, and evolving environmental responses. AI control systems can optimize performance while maintaining stability and safety under changing conditions.

Multi-agent coordination frameworks enable large numbers of autonomous AI agents to coordinate their activities while pursuing shared objectives such as climate monitoring, environmental management, or intervention deployment. Complex climate management tasks may require coordination among many independent systems and agents operating across different scales and domains. Multi-agent approaches can provide distributed intelligence while maintaining overall system coherence and effectiveness.

Predictive adaptation capabilities use AI to anticipate future conditions and begin adaptive responses before conditions actually change, reducing response delays and improving system performance. Climate systems often exhibit predictable patterns and trends that can inform proactive adaptation strategies. AI systems can learn these patterns while implementing anticipatory responses that position systems to respond more effectively to changing conditions.

Real-time model updating and validation employ AI to continuously assess model accuracy and reliability while implementing model improvements and corrections as new information becomes available. Static models may become less accurate over time as conditions change or as understanding improves. Real-time validation approaches can maintain model quality while enabling rapid incorporation of scientific advances and operational experience.

Anomaly detection and emergency response systems use AI to identify unusual conditions or system behaviors that may require immediate attention or emergency response measures. Climate systems may exhibit anomalous behavior that indicates developing problems or opportunities for intervention. AI anomaly detection can provide early warning while triggering appropriate response procedures that account for the severity and urgency of detected anomalies.

Next-Generation Climate Models

The development of next-generation climate models represents a paradigm shift toward AI-native modeling systems that integrate artificial intelligence capabilities from the ground up rather than adding AI components to existing traditional models. These advanced modeling systems promise unprecedented accuracy, resolution, and computational efficiency while enabling new types of analysis and applications that are impossible with current modeling approaches. The integration of AI throughout the modeling pipeline creates opportunities for revolutionary advances in climate prediction and understanding.

Foundation model architectures adapted for climate applications employ large-scale pre-trained AI models that can be fine-tuned for specific climate prediction tasks while leveraging general climate system knowledge learned from comprehensive training datasets. Foundation models can provide common base capabilities that serve multiple climate applications while reducing the computational and data requirements for developing specialized models. Climate foundation models must account for the physical constraints and multi-scale interactions that characterize Earth system processes.

Multi-modal integration capabilities enable next-generation models to simultaneously process diverse data types, including satellite observations, ground-based measurements, reanalysis products, and auxiliary datasets such as topography and land use information. Traditional climate models often struggle to integrate diverse data sources effectively while maintaining physical consistency and computational efficiency. AI-native models can learn optimal data fusion strategies while providing seamless integration of heterogeneous information sources.

Physics-informed neural architectures embed physical laws and constraints directly into AI model structures, ensuring that learned relationships respect fundamental physical principles such as conservation laws, thermodynamic relationships, and causality constraints. Pure data-driven models may learn spurious relationships that violate physical principles, while physics-informed approaches can maintain physical consistency while benefiting from AI flexibility and learning capabilities.

Hybrid symbolic-neural approaches combine the interpretability and physical consistency of symbolic models with the pattern recognition and nonlinear modeling capabilities of neural networks. These hybrid approaches can provide the best of both worlds by maintaining physical interpretability while enabling sophisticated pattern recognition and relationship learning that enhances traditional modeling capabilities.

Uncertainty-native modeling architectures integrate uncertainty quantification throughout the modeling process rather than treating uncertainty as a post-processing step, enabling more accurate and reliable uncertainty estimates for climate predictions. Traditional uncertainty quantification approaches often provide limited information about model confidence and may miss important uncertainty sources. Uncertainty-native approaches can provide comprehensive uncertainty characterization while maintaining computational efficiency.

Hierarchical multi-scale integration employs AI to seamlessly connect processes operating at different spatial and temporal scales within unified modeling frameworks that avoid the scale separation assumptions of traditional approaches. Traditional climate models often struggle to represent cross-scale interactions effectively while maintaining computational tractability. AI approaches can learn scale interaction relationships while providing unified multi-scale modeling capabilities.

Interpretable AI modeling approaches ensure that next-generation models maintain the scientific interpretability that is essential for climate science applications while benefiting from advanced AI capabilities. Black-box AI models may provide accurate predictions while lacking the interpretability required for scientific validation and understanding. Interpretable approaches can provide both accuracy and understanding while supporting scientific discovery and validation processes.

Climate Monitoring Networks

The evolution of global climate monitoring networks toward AI-enhanced, interconnected systems represents a transformation that promises unprecedented observational capabilities for understanding and tracking climate system behavior. These advanced monitoring networks integrate diverse observational platforms with AI processing capabilities to provide comprehensive, real-time situational awareness of Earth system conditions. The integration of AI throughout monitoring networks enables automated quality control, intelligent data fusion, and adaptive sampling strategies that optimize information content while managing cost and resource constraints.

Intelligent sensor networks employ AI-enhanced sensors and measurement systems that can adapt their sampling strategies, perform quality control, and coordinate with other sensors to optimize overall network performance. Smart sensors can adjust their measurement parameters based on local conditions and information requirements while providing automated quality assurance and anomaly detection capabilities. AI-enhanced sensors can also coordinate with other network components to optimize spatial and temporal sampling patterns.

Satellite constellation optimization uses AI to coordinate multiple satellite missions and optimize their observational strategies to maximize global coverage and information content while managing cost and resource constraints. Large satellite constellations can provide unprecedented observational capabilities if coordinated effectively, while poor coordination may result in redundant measurements and information gaps. AI optimization can provide dynamic coordination strategies that adapt to changing observational requirements and mission constraints.

Autonomous platform networks employ AI-controlled autonomous vehicles, including drones, underwater vehicles, and surface platforms, to provide adaptive sampling capabilities that can respond to changing conditions and emerging phenomena. Autonomous platforms can provide observational capabilities in remote or dangerous locations while adapting their sampling strategies based on observed conditions and information requirements. AI control systems can coordinate autonomous platforms while ensuring safe and effective operation.

Data fusion and integration systems employ AI to combine observations from multiple sources and platforms into comprehensive, consistent datasets that provide complete situational awareness of climate system conditions. Data fusion must account for different measurement characteristics, spatial and temporal resolution, and data quality while providing seamless integration that maximizes information content. AI approaches can learn optimal fusion strategies while maintaining data quality and uncertainty characterization.

Real-time processing and dissemination capabilities use AI to process observational data in real-time while providing rapid dissemination to users who require timely access to climate information. Real-time processing must balance speed against accuracy while providing appropriate quality control and uncertainty quantification. AI systems can optimize processing workflows while maintaining quality standards appropriate for different user requirements and applications.

Adaptive sampling and targeted observation strategies employ AI to optimize observational resource allocation based on information requirements, prediction uncertainty, and observational effectiveness. Limited observational resources must be allocated efficiently to maximize information content and minimize prediction uncertainty. AI optimization can identify optimal observational strategies while adapting to changing information requirements and resource availability.

Quality assurance and validation systems use AI to provide comprehensive quality control for observational networks while identifying and correcting measurement errors, instrument problems, and data transmission issues. Large observational networks generate enormous data volumes that require automated quality control capabilities that can identify problems rapidly and accurately. AI systems can provide sophisticated quality assurance while learning from patterns in data quality and instrument performance.

The emerging field of quantum computing applications in climate science represents a potentially revolutionary development that could transform computational capabilities for climate modeling, optimization, and machine learning applications. Quantum computing approaches leverage quantum mechanical phenomena to perform certain types of computations exponentially faster than classical computers, potentially solving previously intractable climate science problems. While current quantum computers face significant limitations in terms of scale, error rates, and coherence times, rapidly advancing quantum technologies suggest that practical quantum advantages for climate applications may emerge within the next decade.

Quantum simulation capabilities for climate systems could enable unprecedented accuracy in modeling molecular-scale processes that affect atmospheric chemistry, cloud formation, and biogeochemical cycles. Quantum computers can naturally simulate quantum mechanical systems that govern chemical reactions, molecular interactions, and phase transitions that are important for climate processes. Quantum simulations could provide a detailed understanding of processes that are computationally intractable for classical computers while informing improved parameterizations for larger-scale models.

Quantum optimization algorithms could revolutionize approaches to parameter estimation, model calibration, and decision optimization for climate applications that involve large parameter spaces and complex constraint sets. Many climate science optimization problems are NP-hard and scale exponentially with problem size, making them computationally challenging for classical algorithms. Quantum optimization approaches such as the Quantum Approximate Optimization Algorithm (QAOA) could provide significant speedups for certain classes of optimization problems relevant to climate science.

Quantum machine learning approaches could enhance pattern recognition, classification, and regression capabilities for climate data analysis while providing new approaches to uncertainty quantification and model training. Quantum algorithms for machine learning may offer advantages for certain types of pattern recognition tasks while enabling new approaches to handling high-dimensional data and complex feature spaces. Quantum machine learning could be particularly valuable for processing large climate datasets and identifying subtle patterns that are difficult to detect with classical approaches.

Quantum sensing networks could provide unprecedented precision for climate observations while enabling the detection of previously unmeasurable climate phenomena. Quantum sensors can achieve sensitivity levels that exceed classical sensors through quantum entanglement and superposition effects that enhance measurement precision. Quantum sensing applications for climate science could include gravimetry for ice sheet monitoring, magnetometry for atmospheric electrical phenomena, and atomic clocks for the precise timing of climate observations.

Hybrid classical-quantum algorithms that combine classical and quantum computation capabilities could provide near-term advantages for climate applications while quantum technology continues to mature. Hybrid approaches can leverage quantum capabilities for specific computational subtasks while using classical computation for other components of climate applications. These hybrid algorithms may provide practical quantum advantages before fully quantum algorithms become feasible.

Quantum error correction and noise mitigation techniques will be essential for practical quantum computing applications in climate science, given the high accuracy requirements for climate predictions and the sensitivity of current quantum computers to environmental noise. Climate applications may require error rates that are lower than those achievable with current quantum computers, making quantum error correction essential for practical applications. Advanced error correction approaches could enable practical quantum advantage for climate applications.

Quantum algorithm development specifically for climate science problems could identify new quantum approaches that provide significant advantages over classical methods while addressing the specific characteristics and requirements of climate applications. General-purpose quantum algorithms may not be optimal for climate science problems that have a specific structure and constraints. Domain-specific quantum algorithm development could maximize quantum advantages while ensuring that quantum approaches address real climate science needs.

Reasoning Integration

The integration of multiple reasoning approaches within AI systems for climate science applications represents an advanced frontier that combines symbolic reasoning, neural learning, probabilistic inference, and causal reasoning within unified frameworks. Multiple reasoning integration enables AI systems to leverage different reasoning strengths while addressing the diverse types of problems and uncertainty that characterize climate science applications. This integration promises more robust, interpretable, and effective AI systems that can handle the full spectrum of climate science challenges while maintaining transparency and reliability.

Neuro-symbolic integration combines the pattern recognition capabilities of neural networks with the logical reasoning and interpretability of symbolic systems. Climate science applications often require both pattern recognition capabilities for analyzing complex data and logical reasoning for ensuring physical consistency and causal relationships. Neuro-symbolic approaches can provide these complementary capabilities while maintaining interpretability and physical consistency that are essential for climate applications.

Probabilistic and causal reasoning integration enables AI systems to handle uncertainty while identifying genuine causal relationships rather than merely correlational associations. Climate science requires understanding causal mechanisms that govern system behavior while accounting for significant uncertainty in observations and models. Integrated probabilistic-causal approaches can provide robust reasoning capabilities that support both prediction and intervention planning under uncertainty.

Multi-scale reasoning architectures coordinate reasoning processes operating at different spatial and temporal scales while maintaining consistency across scale interactions. Climate systems involve processes operating across multiple scales that interact through complex feedback mechanisms. Multi-scale reasoning approaches can handle these scale interactions while providing unified reasoning capabilities that span from molecular-scale processes to planetary-scale phenomena.

Analogical and case-based reasoning systems leverage historical climate patterns and events to inform understanding of current conditions and future possibilities. Climate systems exhibit patterns and relationships that may be similar across different time periods and regions, enabling analogical reasoning that provides insights based on historical experience. Case-based reasoning can complement other reasoning approaches while providing interpretable insights based on historical precedents.

Temporal reasoning capabilities enable AI systems to reason about complex temporal relationships, including causality, precedence, and temporal dependencies that are essential for climate prediction and intervention planning. Climate systems exhibit complex temporal behavior, including memory effects, lag relationships, and periodic patterns that require sophisticated temporal reasoning capabilities. Integrated temporal reasoning can handle these complexities while maintaining consistency and interpretability.

Counterfactual and hypothetical reasoning frameworks enable AI systems to explore alternative scenarios and intervention effects while maintaining grounding in observed reality. Climate science applications often require reasoning about hypothetical interventions and alternative scenarios that have not been observed historically.

Counterfactual reasoning capabilities can support scenario analysis and intervention planning while maintaining appropriate uncertainty characterization.

Meta-reasoning and reasoning coordination capabilities enable AI systems to select appropriate reasoning approaches for different types of problems while coordinating multiple reasoning processes to achieve overall objectives. Different climate science problems may require different reasoning approaches, and integrated systems must be able to select and coordinate appropriate reasoning methods. Meta-reasoning capabilities can optimize reasoning strategies while ensuring that different reasoning approaches work together effectively.

Validation Processes

The development of comprehensive success metrics and validation processes for AI-enhanced climate science applications represents a critical requirement for ensuring the reliability, effectiveness, and societal benefit of these advanced technologies. Success metrics must capture multiple dimensions of system performance, including accuracy, reliability, interpretability, efficiency, and societal impact, while accounting for the diverse stakeholder perspectives and values that influence evaluation criteria. Validation processes must provide rigorous assessment of AI system performance while maintaining scientific standards and enabling continuous improvement based on operational experience.

Multi-dimensional performance metrics capture diverse aspects of AI system performance, including predictive accuracy, computational efficiency, interpretability, robustness, and fairness across different stakeholder groups and application contexts. Traditional accuracy metrics may be inadequate for climate applications that involve multiple performance dimensions and diverse stakeholder requirements. Comprehensive metrics frameworks can provide a balanced assessment while highlighting trade-offs between different performance objectives.

Scientific validation frameworks ensure that AI systems meet rigorous scientific standards for reproducibility, falsifiability, and peer review while contributing to rather than competing with scientific understanding. Climate science applications require validation approaches that maintain scientific integrity while accommodating the unique characteristics of AI systems. Scientific validation must assess whether AI systems produce scientifically valid insights and whether they can be effectively integrated with traditional scientific methods.

Operational validation processes assess AI system performance under real-world conditions while accounting for operational constraints, user requirements, and deployment contexts that may differ significantly from research and development environments. Laboratory performance may not predict operational effectiveness due to differences in data quality, user expertise, and operational pressures. Operational validation provides essential feedback for improving AI systems while ensuring that they meet real-world performance requirements.

Long-term validation approaches evaluate AI system performance over extended time periods while assessing whether systems maintain their effectiveness as conditions change and as understanding improves. Climate applications often involve long-term deployment scenarios where system performance may degrade over time due to changing conditions or outdated training data. Long-term validation ensures sustained performance while identifying needs for system updates and maintenance.

Comparative validation methods assess AI system performance relative to alternative approaches, including traditional methods, other AI systems, and expert judgment, to provide context for performance evaluation and identify areas for improvement. Absolute performance metrics may not provide sufficient information for decision-making without comparison to alternatives. Comparative validation helps identify the relative advantages and limitations of AI approaches while supporting informed decision-making about technology adoption.

Stakeholder-centered validation frameworks incorporate diverse stakeholder perspectives and values into validation processes while ensuring that AI systems serve stakeholder needs and preferences effectively. Different stakeholder groups may have different success criteria and validation requirements based on their specific applications and values. Stakeholder-centered approaches can ensure that validation processes address relevant concerns while supporting inclusive evaluation of AI system performance.

Continuous validation and improvement processes enable ongoing assessment and refinement of AI systems based on operational experience while maintaining performance standards and adapting to changing requirements. Static validation approaches may become outdated as conditions change and as experience accumulates with AI system operation. Continuous validation approaches can provide ongoing quality assurance while supporting continuous improvement and adaptation to changing needs and conditions.

As we stand at the intersection of unprecedented technological capability and urgent planetary need, the developments explored in this final chapter illuminate both the transformative potential and profound responsibilities that define the future of AI-enhanced climate science. The convergence of artificial intelligence with climate intervention technologies, advanced computing paradigms, and comprehensive monitoring systems presents opportunities to address climate challenges with unprecedented precision and scope. However, these same capabilities introduce complexities and risks that demand equally unprecedented levels of care, transparency, and democratic oversight.

The exploration of climate intervention technologies, particularly geoengineering approaches such as Stratospheric Aerosol Injection, reveals the critical importance of explainable AI frameworks for planetary-scale decision-making. When AI systems inform decisions that could affect the climate experienced by billions of people and all natural ecosystems, the ability to understand, validate, and communicate AI reasoning becomes not merely a technical requirement but a fundamental prerequisite for democratic governance and ethical responsibility. The development of transparency standards, stakeholder communication strategies, and accountability mechanisms represents essential infrastructure for any future deployment of AI-enhanced climate interventions.

The comprehensive risk assessment frameworks discussed throughout this chapter underscore the need for sophisticated approaches to uncertainty quantification and decision-making under deep uncertainty. Climate intervention decisions must be made despite incomplete knowledge, disputed probabilities, and fundamental disagreements about values and acceptable risk levels. AI-enhanced risk assessment can provide structured approaches to these challenges while maintaining transparency about the limitations of prediction and the value judgments inherent in risk evaluation processes.

The future research directions examined in this chapter point toward transformative advances in real-time adaptive systems, next-generation climate models, global monitoring networks, and quantum computing applications that could revolutionize our understanding and management of Earth's climate system. These advances promise unprecedented capabilities for observation, prediction, and response that could dramatically enhance our ability to understand climate system behavior and respond effectively to climate challenges. However, these same advances introduce new requirements for validation, quality assurance, and governance that must evolve in tandem with technological capabilities.

The integration of multiple reasoning approaches within AI systems represents a crucial development for addressing the diverse types of problems and reasoning requirements that characterize climate science applications. The combination of neural learning, symbolic reasoning, probabilistic inference, and causal analysis within unified frameworks promises more robust, interpretable, and effective AI systems that can handle the full spectrum of climate science challenges while maintaining the transparency and interpretability essential for scientific credibility.

The development of comprehensive success metrics and validation processes emerges as a critical requirement for ensuring that these advanced AI capabilities serve societal needs effectively while maintaining scientific integrity and democratic accountability. The complexity and importance of climate applications demand validation approaches that go beyond traditional performance metrics to encompass scientific validity, operational effectiveness, long-term reliability, and stakeholder value creation.

Looking toward the future, several key themes emerge as essential for realizing the beneficial potential of these emerging technologies while managing their risks and challenges. First, integrating ethical considerations and democratic governance mechanisms throughout technology development and deployment processes will be crucial for ensuring that powerful AI capabilities serve public interests rather than narrow technical or commercial objectives. Second, the development of international cooperation frameworks will be essential for coordinating global-scale applications while respecting sovereignty and diverse governance approaches. Third, continued investment in education, capacity building, and public engagement will be necessary for ensuring that these technologies are developed and deployed through inclusive processes that reflect diverse perspectives and values.

The path forward requires unprecedented collaboration across disciplinary boundaries, institutional domains, and national borders. Climate scientists, AI researchers, ethicists, policymakers, and affected communities must work together to ensure that emerging AI capabilities are developed and deployed responsibly while addressing the urgent need for effective climate action. This collaboration must balance the urgency of climate challenges against the need for careful, inclusive, and transparent development of powerful new technologies.

The technological capabilities explored in this chapter are not distant possibilities but emerging realities that will likely shape climate science and climate action within the next decade. The choices made today about research priorities, governance frameworks, ethical standards, and development pathways will determine whether these capabilities contribute to effective climate solutions or create new problems that compound existing challenges.

The integration of artificial intelligence with climate science has already demonstrated remarkable progress in enhancing our understanding of Earth system processes and improving prediction capabilities. The future developments explored in this chapter suggest that this integration will deepen and expand in ways that could fundamentally transform both climate science and climate action. However, realizing the beneficial potential of these developments while avoiding their risks will require sustained commitment to responsible innovation, democratic governance, and ethical leadership.

As we conclude this comprehensive examination of AI applications in climate science, it is clear that we are entering a period of unprecedented technological capability coinciding with unprecedented planetary need. The artificial intelligence approaches explored throughout this book—from machine learning applications in climate modeling to explainable AI frameworks for intervention decisions—represent powerful tools for addressing climate challenges. However, tools alone do not determine outcomes; the wisdom, values, and choices of the humans who develop and deploy these tools will ultimately determine whether they contribute to human flourishing and planetary well-being.

The future of AI in climate science will be shaped not only by technological possibilities but by the ethical frameworks, governance mechanisms, and social processes through which these technologies are developed and deployed. Success will require not only technical excellence but also institutional wisdom, democratic legitimacy, and moral clarity about the purposes these technologies should serve. The stakes could not be higher, and the opportunities for positive impact could not be greater. The path forward demands both technological ambition and ethical humility, both scientific rigor and democratic engagement, both global perspective and local wisdom.

The journey toward AI-enhanced climate solutions is just beginning, and its ultimate destination will be determined by the choices we make today and in the years ahead. May those choices be guided by the best of human wisdom, the highest of human values, and an unwavering commitment to the flourishing of all life on Earth.

The development of comprehensive risk modeling frameworks for AI-enhanced climate interventions represents one of the most critical challenges in responsible geoengineering research and deployment. Unlike conventional risk assessment applications, climate intervention risks span multiple interconnected systems with complex feedback mechanisms, operate across unprecedented spatial and temporal scales, and involve deep uncertainty about system behavior under intervention scenarios. AI-based risk modeling frameworks must integrate diverse risk sources while maintaining transparency about uncertainty and enabling democratic participation in risk evaluation and management processes.

Systemic risk integration approaches employ AI to model complex interactions between climate intervention technologies, natural Earth system processes, and human social systems that could produce cascading failures or unintended consequences. Climate interventions may trigger chains of effects that propagate through interconnected systems in ways that are difficult to predict using traditional risk assessment methods. AI systems can model these systemic interactions while identifying potential cascade pathways and their associated probabilities and consequences.

Multi-scale risk analysis uses AI to assess risks that operate across different spatial and temporal scales simultaneously, from local environmental impacts to global climate system perturbations and from immediate technological failures to century-scale environmental changes. Traditional risk assessment methods often struggle to integrate risks operating at different scales, potentially missing important cross-scale interactions and feedback mechanisms. AI approaches can provide unified multi-scale risk assessment while maintaining appropriate resolution for different risk types.

Deep uncertainty quantification employs AI to characterize and communicate risks in situations where probability distributions are unknown or disputed, model structures are uncertain, and stakeholder values about acceptable risk levels vary significantly. Climate intervention risks often involve deep uncertainty where traditional probabilistic risk assessment may be inappropriate or misleading. AI systems can employ alternative uncertainty representation methods while supporting decision-making under deep uncertainty conditions.

Dynamic risk assessment approaches use AI to continuously update risk evaluations based on new scientific understanding, operational experience, and changing environmental conditions rather than relying on static risk assessments developed at the time of initial deployment. Climate intervention risks may evolve as systems operate and as understanding improves through research and experience. AI systems can provide adaptive risk assessment that responds to new information while maintaining consistency in evaluation frameworks.

Compound risk evaluation employs AI to assess situations where multiple risk sources interact simultaneously, potentially producing consequences that exceed the sum of individual risks. Climate interventions may create new risks while interacting with existing climate risks, technological risks, and social risks in complex ways. AI systems can model these compound risk scenarios while identifying interaction effects that may not be apparent when considering individual risks separately.

Tail risk identification uses AI to identify low-probability, high-consequence risk scenarios that may not receive adequate attention in conventional risk assessment but could have catastrophic consequences if they occur. Climate intervention systems operating at planetary scales could potentially produce severe consequences despite careful design and operation. AI systems can systematically explore tail risk scenarios while assessing their plausibility and potential consequences.

Risk communication and visualization frameworks employ AI to translate complex risk assessments into accessible formats that enable meaningful stakeholder engagement and democratic decision-making about risk acceptance and management strategies. Technical risk assessments may be incomprehensible to non-expert stakeholders who nonetheless have legitimate interests in risk management decisions. AI systems can provide adaptive risk communication that matches stakeholder information needs while maintaining accuracy and completeness.

The analysis of uncertainty across multiple spatial and temporal scales represents a fundamental challenge for climate intervention risk assessment due to the complex propagation of uncertainties through interconnected Earth system processes and technological systems. AI-enhanced uncertainty analysis provides capabilities for tracking uncertainty propagation while maintaining computational tractability for global-scale applications. The integration of uncertainty analysis across scales enables a more comprehensive understanding of intervention risks while supporting appropriate humility about the limits of prediction and control in complex systems.

Parameter uncertainty propagation employs AI to track how uncertainties in model parameters, physical constants, and system characteristics affect intervention predictions and risk assessments across different scales. Climate intervention models involve numerous uncertain parameters whose impacts may compound across scale interactions and feedback loops. AI systems can efficiently propagate parameter uncertainties while identifying which parameter uncertainties contribute most significantly to overall prediction uncertainty.

Structural uncertainty analysis uses AI to assess how uncertainties in model structure, process representations, and causal assumptions affect risk assessment outcomes. Different modeling approaches may produce significantly different risk estimates due to structural differences rather than parameter uncertainties. AI systems can compare multiple modeling approaches while assessing the impact of structural uncertainties on risk evaluation outcomes.

Scale interaction uncertainty focuses on uncertainties in how processes operating at different scales interact and influence each other within climate intervention systems. Cross-scale interactions may be poorly understood or represented in models, creating significant uncertainties about system behavior. AI approaches can characterize scale interaction uncertainties while assessing their implications for intervention planning and risk management.

Temporal uncertainty evolution employs AI to understand how uncertainties change over time as intervention systems operate and as natural and human systems respond to interventions. Early intervention phases may have different uncertainty characteristics than mature operational phases. AI systems can model uncertainty evolution while supporting adaptive management approaches that account for changing uncertainty levels.

Spatial uncertainty propagation uses AI to track how local uncertainties propagate across spatial scales and geographical regions through atmospheric and oceanic transport processes and ecological interactions. Local intervention effects may have regional or global consequences through complex transport and interaction mechanisms. AI systems can model spatial uncertainty propagation while identifying regions where uncertainty levels may be particularly high or consequential.

Scenario uncertainty analysis employs AI to assess how different assumptions about future conditions, policy choices, and technological development affect intervention risks and uncertainty levels. Future scenarios involve fundamental uncertainties about emissions pathways, technological development, and social responses that significantly affect intervention planning. AI systems can analyze scenario uncertainty while identifying robust intervention strategies that perform well across multiple scenarios.

Observational uncertainty integration uses AI to incorporate uncertainties in observational data, measurement systems, and monitoring capabilities into risk assessment frameworks. Intervention monitoring and evaluation depend on observational systems that have their own uncertainties and limitations. AI systems can account for observational uncertainties while assessing their implications for intervention evaluation and adaptive management.

Climate intervention decisions must be made in contexts of deep uncertainty where traditional decision-making frameworks based on probabilistic risk assessment may be inappropriate or insufficient. Deep uncertainty characterizes situations where stakeholders disagree about model structures, probability distributions are unknown or disputed, and value systems differ significantly regarding acceptable risk levels and appropriate precautionary measures. AI-enhanced decision-making frameworks for deep uncertainty provide structured approaches for making robust decisions while maintaining transparency about value judgments and uncertainty that influence decision outcomes.

Robust decision-making approaches employ AI to identify intervention strategies that perform acceptably well across a wide range of possible future scenarios rather than optimizing for single best-guess scenarios. Robust approaches explicitly acknowledge that predictions may be wrong while seeking strategies that minimize regret across multiple possible futures. AI systems can evaluate strategy robustness while identifying trade-offs between robustness and performance optimization.

Adaptive management frameworks use AI to support iterative decision-making processes that can modify intervention strategies based on new information and changing conditions while maintaining progress toward overall objectives. Adaptive management acknowledges that initial decisions may need to be revised as understanding improves and conditions change. AI systems can support adaptive management by providing decision triggers, performance monitoring, and strategy modification recommendations.

Multi-stakeholder decision integration employs AI to facilitate decision-making processes that involve multiple stakeholders with different values, preferences, and risk tolerances while seeking solutions that can achieve broad support or consensus. Climate intervention decisions affect diverse stakeholder communities who may have conflicting interests and values. AI systems can support multi-stakeholder processes by identifying areas of agreement, clarifying trade-offs, and exploring compromise solutions.

Precautionary decision frameworks use AI to implement precautionary approaches that err on the side of caution when facing potentially catastrophic risks with high uncertainty. Precautionary principles suggest that the lack of complete scientific certainty should not be used to postpone action to prevent potential environmental harm. AI systems can implement precautionary approaches while balancing caution against other decision criteria and objectives.

Real options analysis employs AI to evaluate intervention strategies that maintain flexibility and preserve options for future decisions rather than committing irrevocably to specific intervention pathways. Real options approaches recognize that uncertainty may decrease over time and that preserving flexibility may be valuable even if it requires accepting lower expected performance. AI systems can evaluate option values while optimizing portfolios of intervention investments.

Participatory decision modeling uses AI to support inclusive decision-making processes that enable meaningful participation by affected communities and stakeholders in intervention planning and evaluation. Participatory approaches recognize that those affected by intervention decisions have legitimate rights to participate in decision-making processes. AI systems can facilitate participation by providing accessible information, supporting dialogue, and integrating diverse perspectives.

Value-focused thinking frameworks employ AI to structure decision-making processes around stakeholder values and objectives rather than available alternatives, ensuring that intervention decisions serve stakeholder values rather than being constrained by existing options. Value-focused approaches can identify creative alternatives and highlight value trade-offs that may not be apparent in alternative-focused decision processes. AI systems can support value elicitation and alternative generation while maintaining transparency about value implications.

Safeguards

The development of comprehensive safeguards and fail-safe mechanisms for AI-enhanced climate intervention systems represents a critical requirement for responsible deployment that must account for the unprecedented scale and potential irreversibility of planetary-scale interventions. Safeguard systems must operate reliably across extended time periods while maintaining effectiveness despite changing conditions, institutional failures, and adversarial actions. AI technologies can enhance safeguard capabilities while creating new safeguard requirements that address the risks associated with AI system failures or misuse.

Automated monitoring and early warning systems employ AI to continuously assess intervention system performance and environmental conditions while providing timely warnings of potential problems or adverse consequences. Early warning systems must detect subtle changes in system behavior or environmental responses that may indicate developing problems before they produce serious harm. AI systems can process diverse monitoring data while providing reliable early warning capabilities that account for natural variability and measurement uncertainties.

Multi-layered safety systems use AI to coordinate multiple independent safety mechanisms that provide backup protection if primary safety systems fail or prove inadequate. Single-point-of-failure vulnerabilities are unacceptable for planetary-scale intervention systems that could produce catastrophic consequences if they fail. AI systems can coordinate multi-layered safety approaches while ensuring that safety layers remain truly independent and do not share common failure modes.

Human oversight and intervention capabilities ensure that AI systems remain subject to meaningful human control and that human operators can override AI systems when necessary to prevent harm or respond to emergencies. Autonomous AI systems operating at planetary scales could potentially cause significant harm if they malfunction or are used inappropriately. Human oversight systems must maintain effective control while accounting for the speed and complexity of AI system operations.

Reversibility and termination mechanisms employ AI to maintain capabilities for intervention termination or reversal even if original operators are no longer available or if conditions change dramatically. Long-term intervention programs may outlast the institutions and personnel who initiated them while facing changing political priorities and technical capabilities. AI systems can maintain termination capabilities while ensuring that they remain accessible to appropriate authorities under diverse future scenarios.

International coordination and enforcement systems use AI to support multilateral safeguard mechanisms that can operate effectively across national boundaries while respecting sovereignty and diverse governance approaches. Climate intervention safeguards may require international coordination that can be maintained despite changing political relationships and competing national interests. AI systems can support coordination by facilitating information sharing, monitoring compliance, and identifying cooperative enforcement mechanisms.

Adversarial resilience and security frameworks employ AI to protect intervention systems against deliberate attacks, sabotage, or misuse by hostile actors while maintaining operational effectiveness and democratic accountability. Climate intervention systems may be attractive targets for various actors who wish to cause harm, gain political advantage, or prevent intervention activities. AI systems can provide security capabilities while balancing security against transparency and accessibility requirements.

Institutional continuity and succession planning use AI to ensure that safeguard systems remain effective even if governing institutions change, fail, or lose legitimacy over time. Long-term intervention programs require institutional continuity that political changes, institutional failures, or social disruption may threaten. AI systems can support contingency planning while identifying institutional arrangements that can maintain safeguard effectiveness under diverse future scenarios.

Monitoring and Control Systems

The development of AI-enhanced monitoring and control systems for geoengineering operations represents a critical requirement for safe and effective climate intervention deployment. These systems must provide continuous assessment of intervention performance, environmental impacts, and system health while maintaining the capability for rapid response to unexpected events or changing conditions. The planetary scale and potential irreversibility of some geoengineering approaches demand monitoring and control capabilities that exceed those of any existing technological systems.

Integrated observation networks employ AI to coordinate and optimize data collection from satellite platforms, ground-based sensors, airborne measurements, and ocean monitoring systems. Comprehensive monitoring of geoengineering effects requires observations across multiple spatial and temporal scales that must be integrated to provide complete situational awareness. AI systems can optimize observation strategies to maximize information content while managing cost and resource constraints.

Real-time data fusion and analysis systems employ machine learning approaches to process diverse observation streams and extract actionable information about geoengineering performance and impacts. The volume and complexity of monitoring data generated by comprehensive observation networks require sophisticated AI approaches for quality control, pattern recognition, and anomaly detection. These systems must operate continuously to provide timely warnings of potential problems or unintended effects.

Performance assessment algorithms employ AI to evaluate whether geoengineering interventions are achieving their intended climate objectives while remaining within acceptable bounds for environmental and social impacts. Performance assessment requires comparison of observed outcomes against expected results while accounting for natural climate variability and measurement uncertainties. Machine learning approaches can identify performance trends and deviations that may not be apparent through traditional statistical analysis.

Predictive control systems employ AI to anticipate future system behavior and adjust intervention strategies proactively rather than reactively. Climate system lag times and intervention effectiveness delays mean that purely reactive control strategies may be inadequate for maintaining desired system performance. AI systems can use predictive models to anticipate future conditions and adjust interventions accordingly.

Emergency response and intervention termination systems employ AI to detect conditions requiring rapid intervention modification or cessation. Some geoengineering approaches, particularly solar radiation management technologies, may produce severe consequences if they are terminated abruptly or malfunction. AI systems must continuously assess termination risks and maintain capabilities for managed intervention phase-out or emergency cessation.

Quality assurance and validation systems employ AI to ensure the reliability and accuracy of monitoring and control systems themselves. The critical importance of geoengineering monitoring demands rigorous quality assurance procedures that can detect sensor failures, model biases, or other problems that could compromise system reliability. AI approaches can provide continuous validation and quality control for monitoring systems while identifying potential improvements or necessary maintenance.

XAI Frameworks for Intervention

The deployment of artificial intelligence systems for global-scale climate interventions demands unprecedented levels of transparency and explainability due to the planetary scope of potential impacts and the profound implications for human societies and natural ecosystems. Unlike conventional AI applications, where errors may have limited consequences, AI systems supporting geoengineering decisions could influence the climate experienced by billions of people and all natural ecosystems. This reality necessitates transparency standards that exceed those of any existing AI applications while addressing the technical challenges of explaining complex system behavior across multiple scales and stakeholder communities.

Comprehensive decision audit trails must document every aspect of AI system reasoning that contributes to geoengineering recommendations, from data inputs and preprocessing procedures through model computations and final outputs. These audit trails must be sufficiently detailed to enable independent reconstruction and verification of AI reasoning while remaining accessible to diverse stakeholder communities, including scientists, policymakers, and affected populations. Blockchain technologies may provide secure and immutable frameworks for maintaining decision audit trails that can withstand scrutiny over extended time periods.

Multi-stakeholder explanation requirements recognize that geoengineering decisions affect diverse communities with different technical expertise levels, cultural contexts, and information needs. AI explanation systems must provide technically detailed analyses for scientific experts while simultaneously offering accessible explanations for policymakers, affected communities, and the general public. Hierarchical explanation frameworks can provide appropriate detail levels for different audiences while maintaining consistency across explanation types.

Real-time explanation capabilities enable continuous understanding of AI system reasoning as conditions evolve and intervention strategies adapt. Static explanations developed during system design may become outdated as AI systems learn and adapt to changing conditions. Real-time explanation systems must provide up-to-date insights into AI reasoning while maintaining explanation quality and accessibility standards appropriate for high-stakes decision-making contexts.

Cross-cultural and multilingual explanation frameworks ensure that transparency benefits extend globally rather than being limited to specific linguistic or cultural communities. Geoengineering interventions affect global populations who may have different ways of understanding and interpreting technical information. Explanation systems must account for cultural differences in risk perception, uncertainty interpretation, and decision-making processes while maintaining scientific accuracy.

Independent verification and validation procedures provide external oversight of AI explanation quality and accuracy. The high stakes involved in geoengineering applications require independent assessment of AI explanations by qualified experts who can evaluate technical accuracy, completeness, and potential biases. Peer review processes adapted for AI explanations can provide quality assurance while building confidence in explanation reliability.

Legal and regulatory compliance frameworks ensure that AI explanation systems meet emerging legal requirements for algorithmic accountability and transparency. Geoengineering governance frameworks will likely include specific requirements for AI transparency and explainability that AI systems must satisfy to operate legally. Compliance frameworks must evolve alongside regulatory development while maintaining flexibility for technological innovation.

Effective communication of AI reasoning and geoengineering recommendations to diverse stakeholder communities represents one of the most challenging aspects of deploying AI systems for climate intervention applications. Stakeholder communities span from technical experts who require detailed scientific explanations to indigenous communities whose traditional knowledge and cultural values may be affected by intervention decisions. Communication strategies must bridge these diverse information needs while maintaining accuracy, cultural sensitivity, and democratic accessibility.

Adaptive communication systems employ AI to personalize explanations based on stakeholder characteristics, expertise levels, and information preferences. Different stakeholders require different types and levels of explanation detail, and effective communication systems must adapt their presentations accordingly. Machine learning approaches can identify optimal communication strategies for different stakeholder groups while continuously improving based on feedback and engagement metrics.

Interactive explanation platforms enable stakeholders to explore AI reasoning through guided inquiry and dynamic visualization rather than passive consumption of pre-generated explanations. Interactive systems allow stakeholders to ask specific questions, explore alternative scenarios, and understand how different assumptions or values might affect AI recommendations. These platforms can support democratic engagement by enabling meaningful participation in technical discussions.

Visual and narrative explanation approaches translate complex AI reasoning into accessible formats that non-technical stakeholders can understand without sacrificing accuracy or important nuances. Visualization techniques can reveal spatial and temporal patterns in AI reasoning, while narrative approaches can explain causal relationships and decision logic in intuitive terms. These approaches must balance simplification against the risk of oversimplification that could mislead stakeholders.

Cultural competency and indigenous knowledge integration ensure that AI explanation systems respect diverse ways of knowing and understanding climate systems while incorporating traditional ecological knowledge that may be relevant for intervention decisions. Indigenous communities possess valuable knowledge about local environmental conditions and ecosystem responses that AI systems should take into consideration. Explanation frameworks must accommodate different knowledge systems while maintaining scientific rigor.

Participatory explanation development involves stakeholder communities in the design and validation of explanation systems rather than treating them as passive recipients of AI-generated insights.

Participatory approaches can ensure that explanation systems address stakeholder concerns and information needs while building trust and ownership in AI-supported decision-making processes. Community engagement can improve explanation quality while supporting democratic governance of geoengineering decisions.

Conflict resolution and consensus-building support systems employ AI to identify areas of stakeholder agreement and disagreement while facilitating constructive dialogue about intervention options. Geoengineering decisions may involve conflicts between different stakeholder groups with competing values and interests. AI systems can support conflict resolution by identifying shared values, clarifying technical uncertainties, and exploring compromise solutions that address multiple stakeholder concerns.

The integration of ethical considerations into AI decision-making frameworks for geoengineering applications represents a fundamental requirement for responsible climate intervention development. Unlike conventional engineering applications, where ethical considerations may be externalized to human decision-makers, the scale and complexity of geoengineering systems may require AI systems to directly incorporate ethical reasoning into their recommendations and operations. This integration presents unprecedented challenges for AI ethics while raising fundamental questions about the appropriate role of AI systems in decisions affecting global environmental and human welfare.

Value alignment approaches ensure that AI systems incorporate appropriate ethical values and principles into their decision-making processes while accounting for value pluralism and cultural differences in ethical frameworks. Geoengineering decisions involve fundamental questions about intergenerational justice, environmental stewardship, and the appropriate relationship between humans and nature that different stakeholder communities may answer differently. AI systems must be capable of reasoning about these value differences while maintaining consistency with democratically determined ethical frameworks.

Multi-criteria ethical evaluation systems employ AI to systematically assess intervention options against multiple ethical criteria, including justice, sustainability, precaution, and respect for human rights. Traditional cost-benefit analysis may be inadequate for geoengineering decisions that involve incommensurable values and uncertain consequences for future generations. Multi-criteria approaches can provide structured frameworks for ethical evaluation while maintaining transparency about value trade-offs and uncertainties.

Rights-based constraint systems ensure that AI recommendations respect fundamental human rights, including rights to environmental quality, cultural integrity, and self-determination. Geoengineering interventions may disproportionately affect vulnerable populations or indigenous communities who have the right to maintain their traditional ways of life. AI systems must incorporate rights-based constraints that prevent recommendations that would violate these fundamental protections.

Precautionary principle implementation employs AI to incorporate precautionary approaches that err on the side of caution when facing potentially catastrophic risks with high uncertainty. Traditional decision theory may inadequately address situations where probability estimates are highly uncertain but potential consequences are severe. AI systems must be capable of reasoning about deep uncertainty while maintaining appropriate precautionary stances toward potentially irreversible interventions.

Democratic legitimacy frameworks ensure that AI systems support rather than undermine democratic decision-making processes about geoengineering deployment and governance. AI recommendations must be developed through processes that enable meaningful democratic participation and oversight rather than technocratic decision-making that excludes affected communities. Democratic frameworks must balance technical expertise against participatory governance principles.

Intergenerational justice considerations require AI systems to account for the long-term consequences of intervention decisions for future generations who cannot participate in current decision-making processes. Climate interventions may create benefits and risks that persist for centuries while current decision-makers bear none of the long-term consequences. AI systems must incorporate sophisticated temporal discounting and intergenerational equity principles that protect future interests.

Adaptive ethical frameworks enable continuous refinement of ethical principles and value integration based on experience, stakeholder feedback, and evolving understanding of intervention consequences. Fixed ethical frameworks may prove inadequate for managing evolving intervention programs that produce new ethical challenges as they develop. Adaptive approaches must balance consistency against responsiveness to new ethical insights and changing circumstances.

The development of robust accountability and governance mechanisms for AI systems supporting geoengineering applications represents a critical requirement for responsible climate intervention deployment.

These mechanisms must ensure that AI systems remain subject to appropriate human oversight and democratic control while providing a clear assignment of responsibility for system decisions and outcomes. The global scale and potential irreversibility of climate interventions demand governance approaches that can coordinate across national boundaries while maintaining democratic legitimacy and technical effectiveness.

Distributed governance architectures employ AI to coordinate decision-making across multiple jurisdictions and governance levels while respecting sovereignty and subsidiarity principles. Geoengineering interventions may require coordination between international organizations, national governments, subnational entities, and local communities that have different authorities and responsibilities. AI systems can support distributed governance by facilitating information sharing, coordinating policies, and identifying areas requiring interstate cooperation.

Algorithmic accountability frameworks ensure that AI system decisions can be traced, evaluated, and challenged through appropriate governance processes. Accountability requires clear assignment of responsibility for AI system design, training, deployment, and operation while providing mechanisms for redress when systems produce harmful outcomes. Legal and institutional frameworks must evolve to address the unique challenges of governing AI systems that operate across national boundaries and affect the global commons.

Oversight and audit systems employ independent institutions to continuously monitor AI system performance and governance compliance while providing public reporting on system behavior and impacts. Independent oversight can provide quality assurance and public confidence in AI systems while identifying potential problems before they produce significant harm. Audit systems must have appropriate technical expertise and authority to evaluate complex AI systems effectively.

Democratic participation mechanisms ensure that affected populations have meaningful opportunities to influence AI system design and operation through representative governance processes. Democratic participation may require new institutions and processes specifically designed for governing AI systems that affect global populations. Participation mechanisms must balance technical complexity against democratic accessibility while ensuring that participation opportunities are equitably distributed.

Liability and compensation frameworks address questions of responsibility and redress when AI systems produce harmful outcomes despite appropriate governance and oversight procedures. Traditional liability concepts may be inadequate for AI systems that operate autonomously and produce outcomes that may not be foreseeable at the time of system deployment. Compensation frameworks must provide adequate redress for AI-related harms while maintaining appropriate incentives for responsible AI development.

International coordination mechanisms employ AI to support multilateral governance processes while respecting national sovereignty and diverse governance approaches. Climate intervention governance will likely require new international institutions and agreements that can coordinate AI system governance across national boundaries. AI systems can support international coordination by facilitating information sharing, modeling policy interactions, and identifying mutually beneficial cooperation opportunities.

Termination and succession planning ensure that governance mechanisms remain effective even if AI systems are discontinued, transferred between operators, or evolve significantly over time. Long-term governance sustainability requires planning for various scenarios, including technology obsolescence, operator failures, or changes in political priorities. Succession planning must ensure continuity of governance oversight while adapting to changing technological and institutional circumstances.

Stratospheric Aerosol Injection (SAI)

Stratospheric Aerosol Injection represents one of the most studied and potentially deployable solar radiation management technologies, involving the deliberate injection of aerosol particles into the stratosphere to reflect incoming solar radiation and reduce global temperatures. The complexity of SAI systems, spanning atmospheric chemistry, aerosol physics, climate dynamics, and engineering systems, creates unprecedented challenges for modeling and optimization that require sophisticated AI approaches. The integration of artificial intelligence into SAI research and development enables comprehensive system optimization while managing the enormous parameter spaces and multi-scale interactions that characterize stratospheric intervention systems.

Aerosol microphysics modeling employs AI to predict the behavior of injected particles, including nucleation, growth, coagulation, and sedimentation processes that determine the optical properties and lifetime of stratospheric aerosols. Machine learning approaches can learn complex relationships between injection parameters, atmospheric conditions, and aerosol evolution from detailed process models and observations. These learned relationships enable rapid exploration of injection strategies while maintaining accuracy comparable to detailed microphysical simulations.

Atmospheric transport and mixing optimization uses AI to determine optimal injection locations, altitudes, and timing that maximize global cooling effectiveness while minimizing regional climate disruptions. Stratospheric circulation patterns create complex relationships between injection locations and global aerosol distribution that traditional optimization approaches struggle to navigate effectively. AI systems can learn these relationships from climate model simulations while identifying injection strategies that achieve desired global temperature reductions with minimal regional climate impacts.

Chemical interaction modeling employs AI to predict interactions between injected aerosols and stratospheric chemistry, including ozone depletion, heterogeneous chemical processes, and impacts on atmospheric composition. Stratospheric chemistry involves complex reaction networks that are sensitive to aerosol surface area, composition, and temperature conditions created by SAI operations. Machine learning approaches can predict chemical impacts while enabling optimization of aerosol composition and injection strategies to minimize adverse chemical effects.

Multi-scale coupling approaches use AI to integrate detailed process models with global climate simulations, enabling a comprehensive assessment of SAI effects across spatial scales from aerosol microphysics to global climate response. Traditional modeling approaches often require simplified representations of small-scale processes that may miss important interactions and feedbacks. AI systems can learn upscaling relationships that capture essential physics while maintaining computational efficiency for global-scale analysis.

Uncertainty quantification and robust design employ AI to identify SAI strategies that perform reliably across the range of possible atmospheric conditions and climate uncertainties. Stratospheric conditions vary seasonally and interannually, while climate change may alter atmospheric circulation patterns that affect SAI effectiveness. AI optimization approaches can identify robust injection strategies that maintain performance despite these uncertainties while quantifying confidence intervals for predicted outcomes.

Real-time adaptive control systems employ AI to continuously adjust SAI operations based on observed atmospheric conditions and climate responses. Fixed injection strategies may prove inadequate as atmospheric conditions change or as understanding of SAI effects improves through operational experience. Machine learning approaches can enable continuous optimization of injection parameters while learning from operational data to improve system performance.

Failure mode analysis and risk assessment employ AI to identify potential failure modes in SAI systems while assessing their likelihood and consequences. SAI systems involve complex technological and natural system interactions that could fail in unexpected ways with potentially severe consequences. AI systems can systematically explore failure scenarios while identifying design modifications and operational procedures that minimize failure risks.

The comprehensive assessment of environmental impacts associated with Stratospheric Aerosol Injection requires sophisticated analytical frameworks capable of evaluating effects across multiple Earth system components and scales. AI-enhanced impact assessment approaches provide capabilities for processing vast amounts of environmental data while identifying subtle but significant environmental changes that traditional analysis methods might miss. The global scale and potential longevity of SAI programs demand environmental impact assessment capabilities that exceed those of conventional environmental assessment procedures.

Ecosystem impact modeling employs AI to predict how SAI-induced changes in temperature, precipitation, and radiation patterns affect terrestrial and marine ecosystems across different biomes and regions. Climate modifications from SAI may have complex effects on ecosystem productivity, species composition, and ecosystem services that are difficult to predict using traditional modeling approaches. Machine learning systems can learn relationships between climate variables and ecosystem responses while accounting for complex interactions and feedback mechanisms.

Agricultural impact prediction uses AI to assess how SAI deployment affects crop yields, agricultural productivity, and food security across different regions and farming systems. SAI effects on temperature, precipitation, and solar radiation could significantly affect agricultural production with important implications for global food security. AI systems can integrate climate projections with crop models and socioeconomic data to predict agricultural impacts while identifying regions and crops that may be most vulnerable to SAI deployment.

Hydrological system analysis employs AI to understand how SAI affects precipitation patterns, water resources, and hydrological extremes, including droughts and floods. Changes in precipitation patterns represent one of the most significant potential impacts of SAI deployment, with important implications for water security and ecosystem health. AI approaches can analyze complex relationships between atmospheric circulation changes and regional precipitation patterns while assessing implications for water resource management.

Biodiversity and conservation impact assessment uses AI to evaluate how SAI deployment affects species distributions, habitat suitability, and conservation priorities across different taxonomic groups and regions. Climate modifications from SAI could trigger species range shifts, alter habitat conditions, and affect conservation strategies developed for current climate conditions. Machine learning approaches can predict species responses to SAI-induced climate changes while identifying conservation priorities and adaptation strategies.

Air quality and human health impact analysis employs AI to assess how SAI deployment affects air quality, human health, and environmental justice considerations. Stratospheric aerosol injection may affect air quality through changes in atmospheric chemistry, circulation patterns, and precipitation that could have important implications for human health, particularly in vulnerable populations. AI systems can integrate atmospheric chemistry models with epidemiological data to predict health impacts while identifying potentially disproportionate effects on vulnerable communities.

Marine ecosystem impact evaluation uses AI to understand how SAI affects ocean ecosystems, marine productivity, and fisheries resources through changes in ocean temperature, chemistry, and circulation patterns. Ocean systems may respond to SAI deployment through complex pathways, including changes in surface temperature, ocean circulation, and marine biogeochemistry that could significantly affect marine ecosystems and fisheries. AI approaches can model these complex interactions while assessing implications for marine conservation and fisheries management.

Cumulative and synergistic impact analysis employs AI to identify interactions between SAI effects and other environmental stressors, including continued greenhouse gas emissions, ocean acidification, and ecosystem degradation. Environmental impacts of SAI deployment will occur in the context of continued environmental change from other sources that may interact with SAI effects in complex ways. AI systems can model these interactions while identifying potential synergistic effects that may not be apparent when considering individual stressors separately.

Risk-Benefit

The systematic evaluation of risks and benefits associated with Stratospheric Aerosol Injection deployment requires comprehensive analytical frameworks capable of handling deep uncertainty, comparing incommensurable outcomes, and integrating diverse value systems and stakeholder perspectives. AI-enhanced risk-benefit analysis provides capabilities for processing complex trade-offs while maintaining transparency about value judgments and uncertainty that influence evaluation outcomes. The global scale and potential irreversibility of SAI deployment demand rigorous risk-benefit assessment that can inform democratic decision-making processes while accounting for diverse stakeholder values and interests.

Multi-criteria decision analysis employs AI to systematically evaluate SAI deployment options against multiple criteria, including climate effectiveness, environmental impacts, costs, and social considerations. Traditional cost-benefit analysis may be inadequate for SAI decisions that involve incommensurable values and deep uncertainty about consequences. AI systems can support multi-criteria analysis by processing complex trade-offs while maintaining transparency about how different criteria are weighted and combined.

Probabilistic risk assessment uses AI to quantify the likelihood and magnitude of potential adverse consequences from SAI deployment while accounting for uncertainty in scientific understanding and model predictions. Risk assessment must account for low-probability, high-impact events that could have severe consequences despite their apparent rarity. AI approaches can integrate multiple sources of uncertainty while providing probabilistic estimates of various risk scenarios.

Comparative risk analysis employs AI to compare risks from SAI deployment against risks from unmitigated climate change and other climate response options, including mitigation and adaptation strategies. SAI risks must be evaluated in the context of alternative approaches to addressing climate change that have their own risk profiles and limitations. AI systems can support comparative analysis while accounting for differences in risk types, timescales, and stakeholder impacts.

Dynamic risk assessment approaches use AI to continuously update risk evaluations based on new scientific understanding, operational experience, and changing environmental conditions. Fixed risk assessments developed at the time of initial deployment may become outdated as understanding improves and conditions change. AI systems can provide dynamic risk assessment that adapts to new information while maintaining consistent evaluation frameworks.

Distributional impact analysis employs AI to understand how SAI risks and benefits are distributed across different populations, regions, and generations while identifying potential winners and losers from deployment decisions. SAI effects are unlikely to be uniformly distributed globally, creating potential for conflicts between regions that benefit and those that experience adverse effects. AI analysis can identify these distributional patterns while supporting equity-focused decision-making processes.

Irreversibility and lock-in risk assessment uses AI to evaluate the potential for SAI deployment to create irreversible changes or technological lock-in effects that constrain future options. Some SAI effects may be irreversible or create dependencies that make termination difficult or impossible. AI systems can assess these lock-in risks while identifying deployment strategies that maintain future flexibility and options.

Value-sensitive risk evaluation employs AI to incorporate diverse stakeholder values and risk preferences into risk-benefit analysis while maintaining transparency about how different values affect evaluation outcomes. Different stakeholder groups may have different risk tolerances and value priorities that significantly affect how they evaluate SAI deployment options. AI systems can model these value differences while supporting inclusive decision-making processes that account for value pluralism.

The development of real-time adaptive systems represents a transformative frontier in climate science and AI integration, promising unprecedented capabilities for continuous learning, adaptation, and response to evolving climate conditions. These systems move beyond static models and fixed intervention strategies toward dynamic, intelligent systems that can adjust their behavior based on continuous observation and learning.

Continuous learning architectures employ AI systems that can incorporate new observational data, scientific understanding, and operational experience without requiring complete system retraining or replacement. Edge computing and distributed intelligence frameworks deploy AI capabilities across distributed sensor networks and monitoring systems, enabling rapid local processing and decision-making.

Adaptive control and feedback systems employ AI to continuously adjust system parameters and strategies based on observed performance and environmental responses rather than operating according to fixed schedules or procedures. Multi-agent coordination frameworks enable large numbers of autonomous AI agents to coordinate their activities while pursuing shared objectives.

The development of next-generation climate models represents a paradigm shift toward AI-native modeling systems that integrate artificial intelligence capabilities from the ground up rather than adding AI components to existing traditional models. These advanced modeling systems promise unprecedented accuracy, resolution, and computational efficiency.

Foundation model architectures adapted for climate applications employ large-scale pre-trained AI models that can be fine-tuned for specific climate prediction tasks while leveraging general climate system knowledge learned from comprehensive training datasets. Physics-informed neural architectures embed physical laws and constraints directly into AI model structures, ensuring that learned relationships respect fundamental physical principles.

Hybrid symbolic-neural approaches combine the interpretability and physical consistency of symbolic models with the pattern recognition and nonlinear modeling capabilities of neural networks. Uncertainty-native modeling architectures integrate uncertainty quantification throughout the modeling process rather than treating uncertainty as a post-processing step.

The evolution of global climate monitoring networks toward AI-enhanced, interconnected systems represents a transformation that promises unprecedented observational capabilities for understanding and tracking climate system behavior. These advanced monitoring networks integrate diverse observational platforms with AI processing capabilities to provide comprehensive, real-time situational awareness.

Intelligent sensor networks employ AI-enhanced sensors and measurement systems that can adapt their sampling strategies, perform quality control, and coordinate with other sensors to optimize overall network performance. Satellite constellation optimization uses AI to coordinate multiple satellite missions and optimize their observational strategies to maximize global coverage and information content.

Autonomous platform networks employ AI-controlled autonomous vehicles, including drones, underwater vehicles, and surface platforms, to provide adaptive sampling capabilities that can respond to changing conditions and emerging phenomena. Data fusion and integration systems employ AI to combine observations from multiple sources and platforms into comprehensive, consistent datasets.

The emerging field of quantum computing applications in climate science represents a potentially revolutionary development that could transform computational capabilities for climate modeling, optimization, and machine learning applications. Quantum computing approaches leverage quantum mechanical phenomena to perform certain types of computations exponentially faster than classical computers.

Quantum simulation capabilities for climate systems could enable unprecedented accuracy in modeling molecular-scale processes that affect atmospheric chemistry, cloud formation, and biogeochemical cycles. Quantum optimization algorithms could revolutionize approaches to parameter estimation, model calibration, and decision optimization for climate applications that involve large parameter spaces and complex constraint sets.

Quantum machine learning approaches could enhance pattern recognition, classification, and regression capabilities for climate data analysis while providing new approaches to uncertainty quantification and model training. Hybrid classical-quantum algorithms that combine classical and quantum computation capabilities could provide near-term advantages for climate applications while quantum technology continues to mature.

The integration of multiple reasoning approaches within AI systems for climate science applications represents an advanced frontier that combines symbolic reasoning, neural learning, probabilistic inference, and causal reasoning within unified frameworks. Multiple reasoning integration enables AI systems to leverage different reasoning strengths while addressing the diverse types of problems and uncertainty that characterize climate science applications.

Neuro-symbolic integration combines the pattern recognition capabilities of neural networks with the logical reasoning and interpretability of symbolic systems. Probabilistic and causal reasoning integration enables AI systems to handle uncertainty while identifying genuine causal relationships rather than merely correlational associations.

Multi-scale reasoning architectures coordinate reasoning processes operating at different spatial and temporal scales while maintaining consistency across scale interactions. Temporal reasoning capabilities enable AI systems to reason about complex temporal relationships, including causality, precedence, and temporal dependencies that are essential for climate prediction and intervention planning.

Validation Processes

The development of comprehensive success metrics and validation processes for AI-enhanced climate science applications represents a critical requirement for ensuring the reliability, effectiveness, and societal benefit of these advanced technologies. Success metrics must capture multiple dimensions of system performance, including accuracy, reliability, interpretability, efficiency, and societal impact.

Multi-dimensional performance metrics capture diverse aspects of AI system performance, including predictive accuracy, computational efficiency, interpretability, robustness, and fairness across different stakeholder groups and application contexts. Scientific validation frameworks ensure that AI systems meet rigorous scientific standards for reproducibility, falsifiability, and peer review while contributing to rather than competing with scientific understanding.

Operational validation processes assess AI system performance under real-world conditions while accounting for operational constraints, user requirements, and deployment contexts that may differ significantly from research and development environments. Long-term validation approaches evaluate AI system performance over extended time periods while assessing whether systems maintain their effectiveness as conditions change.

Stakeholder-centered validation frameworks incorporate diverse stakeholder perspectives and values into validation processes while ensuring that AI systems serve stakeholder needs and preferences effectively. Continuous validation and improvement processes enable ongoing assessment and refinement of AI systems based on operational experience while maintaining performance standards and adapting to changing requirements.

As we stand at the intersection of unprecedented technological capability and urgent planetary need, the developments explored in this final chapter illuminate both the transformative potential and profound responsibilities that define the future of AI-enhanced climate science. The convergence of artificial intelligence with climate intervention technologies, advanced computing paradigms, and comprehensive monitoring systems presents opportunities to address climate challenges with unprecedented precision and scope.

The exploration of climate intervention technologies, particularly geoengineering approaches such as Stratospheric Aerosol Injection, reveals the critical importance of explainable AI frameworks for planetary-scale decision-making. When AI systems inform decisions that could affect the climate experienced by billions of people and all natural ecosystems, the ability to understand, validate, and communicate AI reasoning becomes not merely a technical requirement but a fundamental prerequisite for democratic governance and ethical responsibility.

The comprehensive risk assessment frameworks discussed throughout this chapter underscore the need for sophisticated approaches to uncertainty quantification and decision-making under deep uncertainty. Climate intervention decisions must be made despite incomplete knowledge, disputed probabilities, and fundamental disagreements about values and acceptable risk levels. AI-enhanced risk assessment can provide structured approaches to these challenges while maintaining transparency about the limitations of prediction and the value judgments inherent in risk evaluation processes.

The future research directions examined in this chapter point toward transformative advances in real-time adaptive systems, next-generation climate models, global monitoring networks, and quantum computing applications that could revolutionize our understanding and management of Earth's climate system. These advances promise unprecedented capabilities for observation, prediction, and response that could dramatically enhance our ability to understand climate system behavior and respond effectively to climate challenges.

The integration of multiple reasoning approaches within AI systems represents a crucial development for addressing the diverse types of problems and reasoning requirements that characterize climate science applications. The combination of neural learning, symbolic reasoning, probabilistic inference, and causal analysis within unified frameworks promises more robust, interpretable, and effective AI systems that can handle the full spectrum of climate science challenges while maintaining the transparency and interpretability essential for scientific credibility.

Looking toward the future, several key themes emerge as essential for realizing the beneficial potential of these emerging technologies while managing their risks and challenges. First, integrating ethical considerations and democratic governance mechanisms throughout technology development and deployment processes will be crucial for ensuring that powerful AI capabilities serve public interests rather than narrow technical or commercial objectives. Second, the development of international cooperation frameworks will be essential for coordinating global-scale applications while respecting sovereignty and diverse governance approaches. Third, continued investment in education, capacity building, and public engagement will be necessary for ensuring that these technologies are developed and deployed through inclusive processes that reflect diverse perspectives and values.

The path forward requires unprecedented collaboration across disciplinary boundaries, institutional domains, and national borders. Climate scientists, AI researchers, ethicists, policymakers, and affected communities must work together to ensure that emerging AI capabilities are developed and deployed responsibly while addressing the urgent need for effective climate action. This collaboration must balance the urgency of climate challenges against the need for careful, inclusive, and transparent development of powerful new technologies.

The technological capabilities explored in this chapter are not distant possibilities but emerging realities that will likely shape climate science and climate action within the next decade. The choices made today about research priorities, governance frameworks, ethical standards, and development pathways will determine whether these capabilities contribute to effective climate solutions or create new problems that compound existing challenges.

As we conclude this comprehensive examination of AI applications in climate science, it is clear that we are entering a period of unprecedented technological capability coinciding with unprecedented planetary need. The artificial intelligence approaches explored throughout this book— from machine learning applications in climate modeling to explainable AI frameworks for intervention decisions—represent powerful tools for addressing climate challenges. However, tools alone do not determine outcomes; the wisdom, values, and choices of the humans who develop and deploy these tools will ultimately determine whether they contribute to human flourishing and planetary well-being.

The future of AI in climate science will be shaped not only by technological possibilities but by the ethical frameworks, governance mechanisms, and social processes through which these technologies are developed and deployed. Success will require not only technical excellence but also institutional wisdom, democratic legitimacy, and moral clarity about the purposes these technologies should serve. The stakes could not be higher, and the opportunities for positive impact could not be greater.

The journey toward AI-enhanced climate solutions is just beginning, and its ultimate destination will be determined by the choices we make today and in the years ahead. May those choices be guided by the best of human wisdom, the highest of human values, and an unwavering commitment to the flourishing of all life on Earth.

References

Pearl, J. (2009). Causality: Models, Reasoning, and Inference. Cambridge University Press.

Spirtes, P., Glymour, C., & Scheines, R. (2000). Causation, Prediction, and Search. MIT Press.

Woodward, J. (2003). Making Things Happen: A Theory of Causal Explanation. Oxford University Press.

Hannart, A., Pearl, J., Otto, F. E., Naveau, P., & Ghil, M. (2016). Causal counterfactual theory for the attribution of weather and climate-related events. Bulletin of the American Meteorological Society, 97(1), 99-110.

McGraw, M. C., & Barnes, E. A. (2018). Memory matters: A case for Granger causality in climate variability studies. Journal of Climate, 31(8), 3289-3300.

Runge, J., Petoukhov, V., Donges, J. F., Hlinka, J., Jajcay, N., Vejmelka, M.,... & Kurths, J. (2015). Identifying causal gateways and mediators in complex spatio-temporal systems. Nature Communications, 6(1), 8502.

Ebert-Uphoff, I., & Deng, Y. (2012). Causal discovery for climate research using graphical models. Journal of Climate, 25(17), 5648-5665.

Kretschmer, M., Coumou, D., Donges, J. F., & Runge, J. (2016). Using causal effect networks to analyze different Arctic drivers of midlatitude winter circulation. Journal of Climate, 29(11), 4069-4081.

Nowack, P., Runge, J., Eyring, V., & Haigh, J. D. (2020). Causal networks for climate model evaluation and constrained projections. Nature Communications, 11(1), 1415.

Barnes, E. A., Hurrell, J. W., Ebert-Uphoff, I., Anderson, C., & Anderson, D. (2019). Viewing forced climate patterns through an AI lens. Geophysical Research Letters, 46(22), 13389-13398.

Labe, Z., & Barnes, E. A. (2021). Detecting climate signals using explainable AI with single-forcing large ensembles. Journal of Advances in Modeling Earth Systems, 13(8), e2021MS002464.

Stuart, A. M., & Teckentrup, A. L. (2018). Posterior consistency for Gaussian process approximations of Bayesian posterior distributions. Mathematics of Computation, 87(310), 721-753.

Runge, J. (2020). Discovering contemporaneous and lagged causal relations in autocorrelated nonlinear time series datasets. Proceedings of the 36th Conference on Uncertainty in Artificial Intelligence, 1388-1397.

Tibau, X. A., Reimers, C., Eyring, V., Camps-Valls, G., Mahecha, M. D., Reichstein, M.,... & Runge, J. (2022). Spatiotemporal causal discovery for climate model evaluation. Journal of Advances in Modeling Earth Systems, 14(9), e2021MS002856.

Weigel, K., Bock, L., Gier, B. K., Lauer, A., Righi, M., Schlund, M.,... & Eyring, V. (2021). ESMValTool v2.0–diagnostics for extreme events, regional and impact evaluation, and analysis of Earth system models in CMIP. Geoscientific Model Development, 14(6), 3159-3184.

Index

atmosphere, 6, 8, 10, 11, 12, 13, 14, 15, 29, 31, 32, 33, 34, 69, 91, 122, 123, 127, 198, 220, 349
atmosphere-chemistry, 30
atmospheric circulation, 13, 48, 52, 55, 56, 83, 91, 120, 123, 148, 150, 155, 276, 335, 409, 411
atomic, 375
attribute, 48, 308
audit, 177, 270, 344, 398, 405
backpropagation, 238
backup, 180, 394
Bacon, Francis, 40
bagging, 54
Bayesian, 23, 88, 89, 99, 105, 110, 125, 135, 157, 160, 161, 183, 195, 201, 234, 235, 250, 251, 424
Bayesian methods, 160
Beer-Lambert law, 28
benchmark, 29, 68, 69, 174, 275
bias, 14, 22, 47, 49, 55, 61, 65, 68, 86, 103, 112, 125, 154, 157, 166, 182, 185, 192, 203, 225, 226, 229, 236, 247, 248, 249, 253, 254, 264, 269, 270, 271, 280, 284, 290, 312, 315, 321, 325, 327, 334, 335, 343, 344, 397, 400
big data, 71, 75, 106
biogeochemical cycles, 13, 15, 257, 258, 374, 417
biosphere, 6
blending, 218
blockchain, 398
boosting, 55, 281
carbon, 6, 7, 34, 37, 83, 129, 130, 170, 171, 172, 173, 174, 175, 176, 177, 178, 179, 180, 182, 186, 187, 188, 198, 258, 284, 293, 349, 350, 354
causal graphical model, 71

causal relationship, 20, 64, 71, 79, 81, 82, 84, 87, 88, 91, 92, 93, 94, 95, 96, 97, 98, 99, 100, 101, 102, 103, 105, 134, 151, 162, 256, 277, 278, 279, 285, 303, 310, 313, 329, 331, 345, 377, 401, 418
Central Processing Unit (CPU), 245
centralization, 126
centralized, 367
change management, 270
classification, 16, 20, 52, 53, 54, 60, 112, 145, 163, 259, 335, 375, 417
climate causation, 81, 84
climate change, 8, 15, 25, 29, 34, 38, 45, 46, 48, 49, 50, 51, 69, 72, 75, 76, 83, 100, 101, 102, 105, 112, 123, 128, 150, 151, 186, 190, 234, 265, 269, 276, 283, 285, 292, 313, 335, 349, 409, 413
climate model, 7, 10, 11, 14, 17, 19, 20, 21, 22, 27, 29, 30, 32, 33, 34, 37, 38, 49, 51, 68, 69, 70, 71, 101, 109, 116, 122, 125, 191, 193, 211, 213, 217, 220, 221, 225, 230, 232, 246, 248, 254, 263, 264, 281, 310, 312, 336, 342, 343, 344, 348, 352, 369, 370, 371, 383, 415, 420
Climate Model Intercomparison Project (CMIP), 98
climate science, 5, 8, 15, 16, 20, 21, 22, 23, 25, 26, 27, 28, 39, 40, 41, 42, 43, 51, 52, 53, 54, 55, 56, 57, 58, 59, 60, 61, 62, 63, 64, 67, 68, 70, 71, 72, 73, 74, 75, 76, 77, 78, 79, 81, 94, 104, 105, 106, 107, 108, 111, 116, 118, 119, 121, 122, 124, 125, 127, 128, 129, 131, 166, 186, 190, 191, 193, 196, 197, 255, 259, 260, 262, 263, 264, 265, 271, 274, 276, 279, 280, 281, 283, 285,

www.ingramcontent.com/pod-product-compliance
Lightning Source LLC
Chambersburg PA
CBHW071537210326
41597CB00019B/3027